Counting Girls Out
(new edition)

Studies in Mathematics Education Series

Studies in Mathematics Education Series: 8

Counting Girls Out:
Girls and Mathematics
(new edition)

Valerie Walkerdine

UK   Falmer Press, 1 Gunpowder Square, London, EC4A 3DE
USA   Falmer Press, Taylor & Francis Inc., 1900 Frost Road, Suite 101,
           Bristol, PA 19007

First published in 1998

A catalogue record for this book is available from the British Library

ISBN 0 7507 0816 6 cased
ISBN 0 7507 0815 8 paper

Library of Congress Cataloging-in-Publication Data are available on request

Jacket design by Caroline Archer

Typeset in 10/12 pt Times by
Graphicraft Typesetters Ltd., Hong Kong.

Printed in Great Britain by Biddles Ltd., Guildford and King's Lynn on paper which has a specified pH value on final paper manufacture of not less than 7.5 and is therefore 'acid free'.

Every effort has been made to contact copyright holders for their permission to reprint material in this book. The publishers would be grateful to hear from any copyright holder who is not here acknowledged and will undertake to rectify any errors or omissions in future editions of this book.

Contents

Acknowledgments

This book reports the outcomes of the collaborative research of the Girls and Mathematics Unit, whose members were: Lorraine Cullen, Marilyn Hayward, Helen Lucey, Gilly Shiress, Rosie Walden, Eileen Ward and Diana Watson, as well as Valerie Walkerdine. Although Valerie compiled the final book, this would not have been possible without the contributions of all of these other members of the Unit.

We are very grateful to the funding bodies that made this research possible. The empirical studies were funded by grants from the ESRC, the Leverhulme Trust and the Equal Opportunities Commission. We are also extremely grateful to the Nuffield Foundation for a Social Sciences Fellowship to Valerie Walkerdine in the academic year 1987/8 to write this volume.

In addition we wish to thank the many teachers, children and parents who took part in these studies.

Series Editor's Preface

Mathematics education is established world-wide as a major area of study, with numerous dedicated journals and conferences serving ever-growing national and international communities of scholars. As it develops, research in mathematics education is becoming more theoretically orientated. Although originally rooted in mathematics and psychology, vigorous new perspectives are pervading it from disciplines and fields as diverse as philosophy, logic, sociology, anthropology, history, women's studies, cognitive science, semiotics, hermeneutics, post-structuralism and post-modernism. These new research perspectives are providing fresh lenses through which teachers and researchers can view the theory and practice of mathematics teaching and learning.

The series *Studies in Mathematics Education* aims to encourage the development and dissemination of theoretical perspectives in mathematics education as well as their critical scrutiny. It is a series of research contributions to the field based on disciplined perspectives that link theory with practice. This series is founded on the philosophy that theory is the practitioner's most powerful tool in understanding and changing practice. Whether the practice concerns the teaching and learning of mathematics, teacher education, or educational research, the series offers new perspectives to help clarify issues, pose and solve problems and stimulate debate. It aims to have a major impact on the development of mathematics education as a field of study in the twenty-first century.

Paul Ernest
1998

Changing Views of 'The Gender Problem' in Mathematics

Paul Ernest

It is a unique privilege to be able to introduce this new edition of *Counting Girls Out*. This book, together with the other related publications of Valerie Walkerdine and her collaborators at the Girls and Mathematics Unit, has done more to change the perceptions of 'the gender problem' in the educational research community than any other publication in Britain, and probably throughout the rest of the world. Furthermore, this shift in perception has been accomplished through a deep and important re-theorization of 'the problem', by bringing in a powerful post-structuralist analysis of girls, women and femininity, and of the construction of their identities through social, educational and mathematical discourses. Valerie Walkerdine was an important contributor to the critical re-theorization of psychology in the seminal work *Changing the Subject* (Henriques et al., 1984), and it is no accident that a chair in critical psychology has been created for her at the University of Western Sydney to further develop her groundbreaking work. The re-theorization of the subject, including the learner, the school curriculum subject, and the academic discipline of psychology, was necessary in order to reconceptualize 'the gender problem' in mathematics and science.

Counting Girls Out still reads as fresh as it did in 1989, and readers of the first edition will be fascinated to see Valerie Walkerdine's *Afterword* with its continuation of the stories of the girl subjects as they grow into women. The *Afterword* also documents Valerie Walkerdine's continued thought in the area, and her problematization of the social construction of masculinity as an important aspect of gender in society. Although some of the contemporary literature on gender and mathematics has become technicized and apolitical, Valerie Walkerdine never loses sight of the deep interaction between gender, race and class, and through it, the essentially political nature of her critique. In particular, class is the central element of social structure on which inequality hinges, and which Valerie Walkerdine finds to be implicated in many of the educational injustices suffered by women.

In this introduction I hope to accomplish two things. First of all, to show how Valerie Walkerdine's analysis and work has been validated and confirmed by subsequent developments and results in the area of gender and mathematics. The mainstream analyses of 'the gender and mathematics problem' which located one or other 'lack' in girls and women as the root of the problem, have simply been refuted by recent results concerning girls' and women's attainments in mathematics. Secondly, I hope to show how profoundly influential Valerie Walkerdine's work has been in the areas of theoretical thought and research concerning gender and mathematics. I offer my own brief treatment of 'the gender and mathematics problem', but even in the places where I do not explicitly cite her publications it is clear how firmly this treatment rests on her work.

Researching Gender and Mathematics

In the research literature it is often taken for granted that there is a problem concerning gender and mathematics. Using the 'lenses' supplied by the work of Valerie Walkerdine I want to question this starting point and the assumptions underpinning it. But it is important to distinguish two different aspects of the so-called gender and mathematics problem. First of all, there is the claim that there are significant sex differences in participation rates in mathematics (and science) education studies, and in related careers. Second, there is the claim that girls and women perform significantly worse, on average, than boys and men do on mathematical tasks, activities and examinations. I consider each of these separately.

Female Participation in Mathematics Post-16

Since the Education Reform Act of 1988, and the National Curriculum it introduced, mathematics has been compulsory in maintained schools in Britain, up to the age of 16. Even before this statutory compulsion the study of mathematics by both sexes was near universal, although cases of girls being allowed to opt out of mathematics were known to occur in some all-girl schools. After the age of 16 all education is voluntary, and here differences in participation rates in mathematics (and other science-related subjects) emerge. It is undeniable that there are major sex differences in participation rates in mathematics and science post 16, certainly in most English-speaking countries.

The Cockcroft report (Cockcroft, 1982) included data on the number of British men and women completing mathematical degrees in the late 1970s and showed that out of an annual total of around 2500 graduates women made up less than 30 per cent of the total. By 1989–90 this increased to around 58,000 annual graduates in mathematical sciences (admittedly this is based on a broader definition including operational research, computer science, etc.) but women still made up less than 35 per cent of the total, constituting a marginal, proportional improvement (DES, 1992).

Similar but not so marked differences are found in the school or college leavers (typically aged 18) who have gained 2 or more General Certificate of Education Advanced level examinations (or 3 more Scottish Certificate of Education Higher grades) by subject combinations. For example, in 1989–90, mathematics/science combinations were achieved by 7 per cent of females but by 15 per cent of males, and mixed results including mathematics were obtained by 21 per cent of females but by 30 per cent of males (DES, 1992).

Such imbalances are widespread in the English-speaking world and in some other developed countries. However a recent development in Latin and Latin-American countries and the Caribbean is that a higher proportion of women participate in mathematics and science studies and occupations, and in some such countries the women now outnumber the men in such occupations. A similar trend, or at least parity, may be noted in Scandinavia. Thus care must be exercised in generalizing from the British and anglophone experience, and attention must be paid to the shifting nature of demographic data. However it can be said that in a number of countries including those in the United Kingdom and North America there is currently a significant gender imbalance in adult participation in mathematics and other science-related studies and occupations.

Sex Differences in Mathematical Performance

The second area of possible sex differences mentioned above concerns the relative under-performance in mathematics by girls during schooling up to the age of 16 years. The widespread public and received view is that girls are significantly poorer performers in school mathematics. What does this view actually entail? The claim is not that all or most girls perform worse than all or most boys in school mathematics. Rather the claim is statistical, namely that there are significant statistical differences between the mean scores of boys and girls in mathematics in favour of boys. Even where such data has been noted, it should be remarked immediately that there are much greater similarities in the attainment levels of the genders than differences. But to what extent is the perception that males score better than females in mathematics justified?

First of all, consider the data concerning the United Kingdom. The level of mathematical performance of 11-year-olds as measured in the 1980s did not differ that greatly between sexes in the large-scale Assessment of Performance Unit primary surveys (APU, 1985 and 1991). However, there were several significant differences in performance. For example, in two categories concerning measures the success rate favours the boys. This might be significant given the claim reported in Walden and Walkerdine (1982) that boys are perceived to be better at mathematics where spatial ability is required. The only area in which girls had a higher success rate was that of algebra. However, as Walkerdine demonstrates in the present volume, there was much more similarity than difference between the genders in mathematical attainment, and the differences are often much exaggerated. The trends in gender differences identified by the APU in the late 1970s remained relatively unchanged until the end of the 1980s. The trend still favoured boys in measurement topics by up to 10 per cent of the marks scored, which was statistically significant.

Gender differences in the 1987 APU (1991) survey for pupils at the age of 15 were more pronounced. One might expect that the difference in performance levels would be greater at that age than at 11, given the differences in public examination results at the time, with males outperforming females (41 per cent of boys obtained a pass in the national mathematics examinations at age 16 in 1987, whereas only 34 per cent of girls passed[1]). Although there was a significant difference in performance between boys and girls in mathematics at the age of 15, it must be remarked that these are differences of mean scores, and that once again the within-gender differences are many times more significant than the across-gender differences. Furthermore, the APU data showed that differences are not necessarily significant in England, Wales and Northern Ireland simultaneously. Regional variations in the UK account for almost as much difference as gender. Gender differences were most pronounced in Wales and least pronounced in Northern Ireland, suggesting the differential impact of extraneous cultural factors in the different regions.

However, since then, UK differences between the genders in test results have been diminishing. Margaret Brown noted that girls did slightly better than boys in the national mathematics tests for 14-year-olds trialed in 1991 (Hackett, 1993, p. 4). This phenomenon has become more widespread, as the results of the GCSE examinations in mathematics for 16-year-olds demonstrated. In the period 1979–96 the percentage of the school population obtaining grades A–C or equivalent in the CSE/GCE/GCSE mathematics exam rose from under 40 to nearly 50 per cent for boys, and from under 30 to nearly 50 per cent for girls (sources: Cockcroft, 1982; Department for Education and Science; annual reports of Statistics of Education Public Examinations). Not only did the girls improve their rate of examination success by double the amount the boys did, but by the mid-to-late 1990s they had equaled and slightly surpassed boys in their overall exam success in the national GCSE examinations in mathematics at age 16.[2] Since the examinations at age 16 are the most important indicator of mathematical achievement during the period of compulsory schooling it can no longer be claimed that there is a gender problem of girls' underachievement in mathematics in the UK. Valerie Walkerdine's claim that this was a spurious difference has been vindicated.

Thus an examination of the data on the gender differences in mathematical achievement up to the present in the UK and internationally indicates that females are not consistently under-performing relative to males, and in many places (including the UK at age 16) the situation is reversed. However there are still areas of relative poorer achievement, such as at GCE 'A' level mathematics in the UK for 18-year-olds. In 1993, a greater proportion of girls achieved grades A–C, by 0.4 per cent. However a greater proportion of boys achieved grades A and B, by 1.8 per cent (Dean, 1994).[3] Given that twice as many boys as girls take the examination, this is not as equitable as it looks.

From 1994 onwards, girls have equalled and then overtaken boys at age 16 in the GCSE mathematics examination, so it has been argued that the gender problem in mathematics has been solved, and indeed one segment of it can be said to have been surmounted. However female participation rates in the post-compulsory years (i.e. at GCE 'A' level and in higher education) remain very largely overshadowed by those of males by factors of two or more to one. The exception is in mathematics teacher education, where females often outnumber males, especially on primary courses. So in overall terms, the British problem might be said to have shifted from one of female under-achievement to one of female under-participation.

Table 1   *Stanford achievement scores in mathematics in Hawaii 1991, by ethnic group*

Ethnic Group	Girls' Mean	Boys' Mean	Difference	Significance
Hawaiian	705.74	694.92	10.82	Significant
Filipino	720.12	709.39	9.73	Significant
Caucasian	731.99	726.74	5.25	Not significant
Japanese	759.53	749.88	9.65	Almost significant

The sex differences in mathematical attainment that have been examined, equivocal as they are, could only be taken as evidence for an intrinsically lower level of mathematical aptitude amongst females if patterns of poorer attainment persist over differing locations and times. The data have already shown that the pattern does not persist over time. Furthermore, international findings on gender and mathematics show that in a number of different cities, states and countries, males have not outperformed females in mathematics and science, as the following brief survey indicates.

Hanna (1989) analysed the data from the Second International Mathematics Survey (SIMS) taken from 20 countries in the 1980s and found that there were no gender differences in achievement in arithmetic, algebra and statistics. In five countries, no gender-related differences at all were noted. Ethington (1990), in a study of the results in eight of the countries involved in SIMS, found no substantial gender differences in any of the content areas, and when any slight effects were noted they favoured girls more often than boys.

Smith and Walker (1988) in a study of over 15,000 students taking the 9th, 10th and 11th year New York state mathematics examinations found that the 9th and 11th year examinations favoured the females but were not statistically significant. For the 10th year examinations the difference favoured the males. Stockard and Wood (1984) studied 570 7th to 12th graders representing all of the high schools in one USA city. Except for 7th graders, where there were no gender differences, females' grades in mathematics were significantly higher than males' for all mathematical topics and grade levels. Brandon and Jordan (1994) compared achievement levels of 10th graders in Hawaii taking the Stanford achievement test in mathematics in 1991. They analysed their data by ethnic group as is shown in Table 1. In each ethnic group the girls' mean score exceeded that of the boys', and for two of the groups this was statistically significant. Brandon and Jordan remark that Hawaii is the only state in the USA to exhibit such dramatic differences, and they go on to offer hypotheses about cultural and other factors which might be responsible for the poor performance of Hawaiian males.

Cheung (1989) studied over 5600 pupils drawn from schools in Hong Kong and found that while the boys attained better scores in geometry and the girls in mathematical manipulation problems, there were no significant gender differences in overall mathematical achievement. In a study of the 1992 Barbados Secondary School Entrance Examination, Cumberbatch (1993) found that there was a significant gender difference in achievement in favour of the girls. The boys' mean raw score was 51.35, whereas the girls' score was 58.43, which is almost 14 per cent higher. At each point of comparison the girls scored higher, except for the top 10 per cent in achievement, where there was no difference. Other gender differences in mathematics achievement favouring girls have been noted internationally, such as in Bermuda, the Caribbean and Latin American countries. Furthermore, according to Greer 'there are five times as many female scientists in Latin American countries as there are in Anglo-Saxon' (Pile, 1993, p. 19). So the problem seems to be more severe in Anglo-Saxon countries than in some others.

Changing Perceptions of the Gender Problem in Mathematics

Examining the literature reveals that the so-called gender and mathematics problem varies with time and with country. No unambiguous differences in achievement levels can be identified and participation rates in mathematics are lower for women only in some countries. The issue is made more complicated by the fact that there are widely differing perceptions of what constitutes the so-called gender and mathematics problem. What is problematized in the relation between gender and mathematics varies greatly according to the underlying conceptualization and the theoretical outlook adopted.

In Ernest (1991), building on Raymond Williams' (1961) seminal historical analysis, I distinguish five perspectives or educational ideologies identified with socially located interest groups in the UK. The proposed model suggests that each interest group has distinct aims for mathematics education and different views of the nature of mathematics, and related views of the nature and cause of the 'gender and mathematics' problem. These groups, their relations to Williams' analysis, and some of their views, are summarized in Table 2. Thus, according to this analysis, the different social groups have different historical origins and political orientations, differing views of the nature of mathematics, and in a special relationship with these, partly consisting of consequence, partly of coherence, different aims for the teaching of mathematics and views of the so-called gender and mathematics problem. This last element links with the theory of social diversity in the original model and depends to a large extent on the values, theory of the child, and theory of society of the social groups (Ernest, 1991).

The different views of gender and mathematics of the five groups in the model are as follows.

1　The Industrial Trainers subscribe to fixed views of knowledge and society, and analogously believe that fixed biological differences are the sources of differences in mathematical ability, and in particular, make males better at maths. Thus, from this perspective, feminism and attempts at equal opportunities and equity in mathematics are undesirable political interventions in the natural state of affairs. 'Sex equality is an impossible dream' (Campaign for Real Education, 1989, p. 2).

2　The Technological Pragmatists are pragmatic and utilitarian in their thought. Consequently they see the gender and mathematics problem as a utilitarian

Table 2   Five interest groups and their views of the 'gender and mathematics problem'

Interest Group	Industrial Trainers	Technological Pragmatists	Old Humanist Mathematicians	Progressive Educators	Public Educators
Relation to Williams (1961)	Reactionary part of Williams' (1961) group of 'industrial trainers'.	Progressive part of Williams' group of 'industrial trainers'.	Mathematical cultural-restorationist version of Williams' group of 'old humanists'.	Liberal progressive part of Williams' group of 'public educators'.	Radical activist part of Williams' group of 'public educators'.
Social location	Radical 'New Right' conservative politicians and petty bourgeois.	Meritocratic industry-centred industrialists, bureaucrats, industrial mathematicians.	Conservative mathematicians preserving rigour of proof and purity of mathematics.	Professionals, liberal educators, welfare state supporters.	Democratic socialists and radical reformers concerned with social justice and inequality.
Mathematical aims	Back-to-basics numeracy and social training in obedience (authoritarian).	Useful mathematics to appropriate level and certification (industry-centred).	Transmit body of pure mathematical knowledge (maths-centred).	Creativity, self-realization through mathematics (child-centred).	Critical awareness and democratic citizenship via mathematics.
View of mathematics	Absolutist set of decontextualized but utilitarian truths and rules.	Unquestioned absolutist body of applicable knowledge.	Absolutist body of structured pure knowledge.	Absolutist body of pure knowledge to be engaged with personally.	Fallible knowledge socially constructed in diverse practices.
View of gender and maths problem	Fixed biological differences make males better at maths.	Utilitarian problem to be ameliorated for benefit of society even if females inferior.	Maths ability inherited and primarily male but ablest women to be encouraged as mathematicians.	Girls/women lack confidence and hold themselves back, i.e. an individual problem.	Gender inequity due to underlying sexism and stereotyping in society in maths.

problem to be ameliorated for the benefit of society, since a well-educated workforce of both men and women is needed, even if, as many in this grouping believe, females are inferior at mathematics.

3   The Old Humanists are conservative mathematicians committed to preserving the purity of mathematics. This group are committed to hierarchical and structural views of various kinds and thus see mathematical ability as inherited, and primarily concentrated among males. However this group, in the interest of mathematics, also want the ablest women to be encouraged to be mathematicians, and to progress as far as their 'nature' will allow them.

4   The Progressive Educators are traditional liberal progressive supporters of education, subscribing to a primarily individualistic ideology. Thus mathematics and education problems are located within individuals, and in particular the gender and mathematics problem is understood to be due to the

lack of confidence and poor mathematical attitudes of girls and women, who thus hold themselves back. The solution is thus to encourage and support girls and women more in mathematics.

5   The Public Educators are radical reformers concerned with social justice and equity. They view knowledge and social structures as socially constructed. Gender inequity is thus seen to be due to underlying sexism in society and schooling, as well as the stereotyping of mathematics as male, and femininity as non-mathematical. This results in the construction of gendered identities which embrace and admit mathematics (mainly masculine identities) or exclude it. But since gendered identities are socially constructed there is variation according to local contextual differences, and the possibility of rectification and improvement remains open.

Before exploring this last perspective further, two points are worth making. First of all, the model indicated in Table 2 illustrates the central point I am making, namely the range of different readings, perceptions and interpretations of the gender and mathematics problem. That is, there is no unique 'gender and mathematics problem', for it is 'read' differently from different perspectives. Secondly, the model shown in Table 2 is, of course, a gross simplification. Although researchers in a number of countries have found it valuable and illuminating, if taken too literally it can be problematic. Thus it is not claimed that there is a *logical* link between the interest group, the aims for teaching mathematics, the view of the nature of mathematics, and the view of the gender and mathematics problem. What is claimed is that these can be found to occur together to a greater or lesser degree, historically, among a subset comprising core members of the social group specified. However, attempts to apply this model more widely by identifying the educational beliefs and ideologies of teachers and others have revealed a complex and shifting picture with mixed combinations of beliefs for individuals which by no means correspond with single columns in Table 2, and which may differ according to whether the views are espoused or enacted (Ernest and Greenland, 1990). Thus no claim is made for the predictive power of the model. Rather it is meant to be an illuminating conceptual tool. The issue of the complexity of the links between the elements of such models is discussed further in Ernest (1995).

The Public Educator View of the Gender and Mathematics Problem

The Public Educator view is that the gender and mathematics problem is a product of the distorted social construction of gender roles and differences and of mathematics itself (Ernest, 1991 and 1997). Thus dominant discourses impose a 'regime of truth' (Foucault, 1980) in which views such as *maths = male*, *maths ≠ feminine* and *female = inferior* are confirmed and sustained. Walkerdine argues that the powers of rationality and mathematical thinking are so bound up with the cultural definition of masculinity, and 'that the discursive production of femininity [is] antithetical to masculine rationality to such an extent that femininity is *equated* to poor performance, even when the girl or woman is performing well' (Walkerdine,

1989, p. 268). In other words, the dominant ideology of patriarchal societies imposes a view that makes many of its members see this difference, even where none exists.

The outcome is a lack of equal opportunities in school mathematics and lowered expectations for girls, with some girls' successes at mathematics being discounted (see the present volume). All members of society internalize these distorted stereotypes and myths, but they are particularly important in affecting many girls' and women's perception of mathematics as a male domain, and their mathematical confidence and self-concept, which have been correlated with lower attainment and participation in mathematics (Tartre and Fennema, 1995). This is illustrated in Figure 1, which suggests a vicious cycle sustaining the gender and mathematics problem as perceived from this perspective.

Figure 1 shows that girls' and women's lower examination attainments, where they are in fact lower, and their lower participation rate and take-up in mathematics leads to women getting reduced (unequal) opportunities for entry to study and work, the 'critical filter' effect of mathematics. Mathematics serves as a 'critical filter' controlling access to many areas of advanced study and better-paid and more fulfilling professional occupations (Sells, 1973). This concerns those occupations involving scientific and technological skills, but also extends far beyond this domain to many other occupations, including commerce, financial services, education, and the caring professions.

The 'critical filter' effect leads to many women getting lower paid work, which thus constitutes the reproduction of gender inequity in society (in the UK and many anglophone countries). This fact of gender inequity in turn helps to reinforce gender stereotyping, confirming it as a 'lived truth', and sustaining stereotyped cultural views such as *maths = male* and *maths = rational ≠ irrational = female.*[4] Such a climate of opinion permeates education leading to a lack of equal opportunities in mathematics learning in school, in a variety of documented ways (Burton, 1986; Open University, 1986). Even where this is resisted by anti-sexist schooling other socializing influences such as social gender stereotyping negatively influences many girls' perceptions of mathematics and their own abilities in mathematics. The outcome of this is once again girls' and women's lower participation rates in mathematics and possibly lower examination attainments, completing the vicious cycle. Only if every link in the cycle is attacked can the reproductive cycle of gender inequality in mathematics education be broken. Thus women's underachievement and underparticipation in mathematics, where they exist, play an important part in reproducing of gender inequity and stereotyping in society.

Much of the research on girls and women and mathematics documents the problems caused by the stereotypical perceptions of mathematics as a male domain (Burton, 1986; Walkerdine 1988; Walkerdine et al., 1989; Weiner, 1980). A number of researchers have offered models of how these values impact differentially on women, including Burton, (1986), Fennema (1985), Walkerdine (1988), Walkerdine et al. (1989), Ernest (1991 and 1995). One of the most powerful models is due to Isaacson (1989) who coordinates a number of different factors including both in-school and out-of-school experiences which are mediated by their influence on girls' or women's belief systems. Central to her account are the concepts of 'double

Figure 1   *The reproductive cycle of gender inequality in mathematics education*

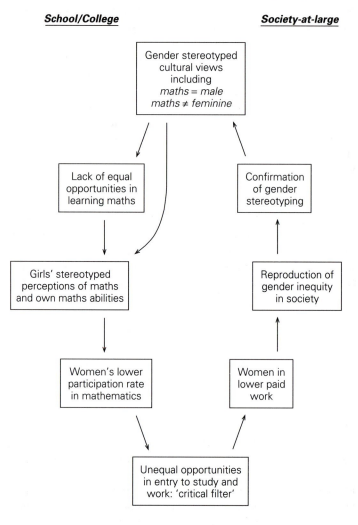

School/College   **Society-at-large**

Gender stereotyped cultural views including *maths = male maths ≠ feminine*

Lack of equal opportunities in learning maths

Confirmation of gender stereotyping

Girls' stereotyped perceptions of maths and own maths abilities

Reproduction of gender inequity in society

Women's lower participation rate in mathematics

Women in lower paid work

Unequal opportunities in entry to study and work: 'critical filter'

conformity' and 'coercive inducement'. Double conformity is a term due to Delamont (1978). It describes the dilemma of a situation where there are two mutually conflicting sets of standards or expectations to which persons have to conform. If mathematics is understood to be stereotypically male and unfeminine, conforming to mathematical standards conflicts with standards of femininity. This, at its simplest, means that women must choose to be feminine or choose to be successful at mathematics. If they opt for both, they have to live with the contradiction *mathematics ≠ femininity*. For some women this is possible, especially those who have been encouraged to develop their mathematical talents by significant male others (like their fathers) during the formative adolescent years, but for many others it is a strong disincentive and repulsive force.

Coercive inducement is a way of describing the social pressures for women to conform with the stereotype of femininity. Women are rewarded for choosing the path of conventional femininity by social approval on all sides (from fathers, mothers, peers, boys, teachers, society, etc.). To reject this path is to give up very considerable rewards and inducements. Since approval is something widely craved, the inducements are coercive. Girls are 'forced' by their needs to succumb to the overwhelming pressures and inducements to accept the conventional feminine role.

Isaacson argues that both double conformity and coercive inducement impact strongly on the girl or woman's internalized belief system, which includes the nature of femininity and 'a woman's role', and their relation with her identity as a gendered person (a woman). This belief system plays a key role in how the woman/girl views herself with regard to mathematics and performs as a learner of mathematics.

Additional explanations such as Labelling Theory due to Becker and others (Ruthven, 1987) account for the self-fulfilling elements of the gender and mathematics problem. Dweck and Respucci (1975) put forward the idea of learned helplessness in mathematics. Girls attribute their failures in mathematics to lack of ability despite perceiving mathematical tasks as not very demanding, and learn to give up. Walkerdine (this volume and 1988) goes on to offer deeper analyses of the relations of gender, reason, mathematics and context drawing on semiotics, Lacanian psychology and post-structuralism, and I direct the interested reader to her work.

Thus from the public educator perspective, the problem of women's underparticipation in mathematics is seen to be due to deeply entrenched cultural discourses which identify mathematics with masculinity and power, which by the means described work to exclude women, and the consequence of these forces is to 'count girls out' of mathematics (Walkerdine et al., 1989).

Finally, it should be pointed out that the Public Educator position could not have been formulated as it has been above without the seminal feminist analysis of the gendered character of reason and mathematics due to Walkerdine and her collaborators, reported in Walden and Walkerdine (1982 and 1985), Walkerdine (1988 and 1989), Walkerdine et al. (1988 and 1989), Walkerdine and Lucey (1989) and elsewhere.

Walkerdine continues to develop her ideas concerning mathematics, reason, gender, race and class in numerous further publications including Walkerdine (1990a, 1990b and 1994). Evidence is emerging in a number of countries that middle-class girls (and boys) face differentially lesser problems than working-class boys and girls do. The present volume illustrates how many working-class girls are underachieving in mathematics, irrespective of their talents and abilities. Recent data from Australia suggests that students in the last two years of compulsory schooling are twice as likely to opt to study mathematics and science if they are from the higher socio-economic status bands, compared with the lower bands (Maslen, 1995). Another study indicates major gender differences, again on the basis of class (Atweh and Cooper, 1995).

Valerie Walkerdine has also been at the forefront in identifying another emerging gender-related problem in the United Kingdom with the increasing resistance of working-class boys to schooling, and their associated declining academic attainment. While their posture of resistance is understandable, given the recent loss of blue collar work and the growth of unemployment in Britain, it indicates the shifting problems of gender-identity construction in modern society, as Valerie Walkerdine indicates in her *Afterword* to this volume. Sexism and stereotyped gender-role expectations damage all in modern society, including boys and men, even if traditionally their main effect was to deny women equality.

Finally, it is worth remarking that the significance of Valerie Walkerdine's analysis in this volume and elsewhere is not solely restricted to illuminating the gender problem in mathematics education. In addition to the issues of race and class mentioned above, her analysis suggests deeper semiotic, post-structuralist and contextual analyses of mathematics education and the mathematics classroom, and I predict that we shall see a significant growth of research building on these novel perspectives in the new millennium, foreshadowed in two previous volumes in this series (Ernest, 1994a and 1994b).

Notes

1 Throughout the UK, excluding Scotland, a 'pass' is understood to mean obtaining grades A–C in the General Certificate of Education (GCE) examination or obtaining grade 1 in the Certificate of Secondary Education (CSE) examination; from 1988 onwards a pass is understood to mean obtaining grades A–C in the General Certificate of Secondary Education (GCSE) examination.
2 They were already significantly ahead of boys in most other school subjects, with the exception of some of the physical science such as physics and chemistry.
3 General Certificate of Education 'A' (Advanced) level examinations have five levels of pass: grades A–E.
4 If this seems a bit far-fetched it is interesting to recall that hysteria, the ultimate expression of irrationality (and hence the opposite of rationality and mathematics), comes from the Greek word *hystera* meaning the womb, i.e. the biological essence of the female, with which hysteria was formerly thought to be connected in medicine. Indeed an eminent Victorian physician claimed that if women devoted too much time to studying mathematics and science, their wombs would wither away. Although ill-founded medically, this claim confirms the cultural definition expressed in the inequality *femininity* = *irrational* ≠ *mathematics*.

References

ASSESSMENT OF PERFORMANCE UNIT (1985) *A Review of Monitoring in Mathematics 1978 to 1982* (2 volumes), London: Department of Education and Science.

ASSESSMENT OF PERFORMANCE UNIT (1991) *APU Mathematics Monitoring (Phase 2)*, Windsor: National Foundation for Educational Research.

ATWEH, B. and COOPER, T. (1995) 'The construction of gender, social class and mathematics in the classroom', *Educational Studies in Mathematics*, **23**, 3, pp. 293–310.

BRANDON, P.R. and JORDAN, C. (1994) 'Gender differences favoring Hawaii girls in mathematics achievement: Recent findings and hypotheses', *Zentralblatt fur Didaktik der Mathematik*, **94**, 1, pp. 18–21.

BURTON, L. (ed.) (1986) *Girls into Maths Can Go*, London: Holt, Rinehart and Winston.

CAMPAIGN FOR REAL EDUCATION (1989) *Campaign for Real Education Newsletter*, **3**, 3.

CHEUNG, K. (1989) 'Gender differences in the junior secondary (grade 7) mathematics curriculum in Hong Kong', *Educational Studies in Mathematics*, **20**, 1, pp. 97–103.

COCKCROFT, W.H. (Chair) (1982) *Mathematics Counts: Report of the Committee of Enquiry into the Teaching of Mathematics in Schools*, London: Her Majesty's Stationery Office.

CORRAN, G. and WALKERDINE, V. (1981) *The Practice of Reason. Volume 1: Reading the Signs of Mathematics*; mimeo, London: University of London, Institute of Education.

CUMBERBATCH, G. (1993) 'An investigation into the effects of gender and teacher perception on pupils' performance in mathematics in the secondary schools entrance examination in Barbados', Unpublished MA Thesis, University of the West Indies, Cave Hill, Barbados.

DEAN, C. (1994) '"Friendly" boards help girls at A-level', *The Times Educational Supplement*, 28 October 1994, pp. 1–2.

DELAMONT, S. (1978) 'The contradictions in ladies' education', in DELAMONT, S. and DUFFIN, L. (eds) *The Nineteenth Century Woman: Her Cultural and Physical World*, Beckenham: Croom Helm.

DEPARTMENT OF EDUCATION AND SCIENCE (1992) *Education Statistics*, London: Her Majesty's Stationery Office.

DWECK, C. and RESPUCCI, C. (1975) 'Learned helplessness and reinforcement responsibility in children', *Journal of Personality and Social Psychology*, **25**.

ERNEST, P. (1991) *The Philosophy of Mathematics Education*, London: Falmer Press.

ERNEST, P. (ed.) (1994a) *Mathematics, Education and Philosophy: An International Perspective*, London: Falmer Press.

ERNEST, P. (ed.) (1994b) *Constructing Mathematical Knowledge: Epistemology and Mathematics Education*, London: Falmer Press.

ERNEST, P. (1995) 'Values, gender and images of mathematics: A philosophical perspective', *International Journal for Mathematical Education in Science and Technology*, **26**, 3, pp. 449–62.

ERNEST, P. and GREENLAND, P. (1990) 'Teacher belief systems: Theory and observations', in PIRIE, S. and SHIRE, B. (eds) *BSRLM 1990 Annual Conference Proceedings*, Oxford: BSRLM, pp. 23–6.

ETHINGTON, C. (1990) 'Gender differences in mathematics: An international perspective', *Journal for Research in Mathematics Education*, **21**, No. 1, pp. 74–80.

FENNEMA, E. (1985) 'Explaining sex-related differences in mathematics: Theoretical models', *Educational Studies in Mathematics*, **16**, pp. 303–20.

FOUCAULT, M. (1980) *Power/Knowledge* (edited by C. Gordon), New York: Pantheon Books.

HACKETT, G. (1993) 'Case against co-eds still not proven', *The Times Educational Supplement*, 8 October 1993, p. 4.

HANNA, G. (1989) 'Mathematics achievement of girls and boys in grade eight: Results from twenty countries', *Educational Studies in Mathematics*, **20**, 2, pp. 225–32.

HENRIQUES, J., HOLLOWAY, W., URWIN, C., VENN, C. and WALKERDINE, V. (1984) *Changing the Subject: Psychology, Social Regulation and Subjectivity*, London: Methuen.

ISAACSON, Z. (1989) 'Of course you *could* be an engineer, dear, but wouldn't you *rather* be a nurse or teacher or secretary?' in ERNEST, P. (ed.) (1989) *Mathematics Teaching: The State of the Art*, London: Falmer Press.

MASLEN, G. (1995) 'Posh boys and girls choose physics', *The Times Educational Supplement*, 27 January, p. 15.

OPEN UNIVERSITY (1986) *Girls into Mathematics*, Cambridge: Cambridge University Press.

PILE, S. (1993) 'King's College: What went wrong with the bluestocking revolution?' *The Daily Telegraph*, 15 March, p. 19.

RUTHVEN, K. (1987) 'Ability stereotyping in mathematics', *Educational Studies in Mathematics*, **18**, pp. 243–53.

SELLS, L. (1973) 'High school mathematics as the critical filter in the job market', *Proceedings of the Conference on Minority Graduate Education*, Berkeley: University of California, pp. 37–49.

SMITH, S. and WALKER, W. (1988) 'Sex differences on New York state regents examinations: Support for the differential course taking hypothesis', *Journal for Research in Mathematics Education*, **19**, 1, pp. 81–5.

STOCKARD, J. and WOOD, J. (1984) 'The myth of female underachievement: A re-examination of sex differences in academic underachievement, *American Educational Research Journal*, **21**, 4, pp. 825–38.

TARTRE, L.A. and FENNEMA, E. (1995) 'Mathematics achievement and gender: A longitudinal study of selected cognitive and affective variables', *Educational Studies in Mathematics*, **23**, 3, pp. 199–217.

WALDEN, R. and WALKERDINE, V. (1982) *Girls and Mathematics: The Early Years* (Bedford Way Papers 8), London: Institute of Education, University of London.

WALDEN, R. and WALKERDINE, V. (1985) *Girls and Mathematics: From Primary To Secondary Schooling* (Bedford Way Papers 24), London: Heinemann.

WALKERDINE, V. (1988) *The Mastery of Reason*, London: Routledge.

WALKERDINE, V. (1989) 'Femininity as performance', *Oxford Review of Education*, **15**, 3, pp. 267–79.

WALKERDINE, V. (1990a) 'Difference, cognition and mathematics education', *For the Learning of Mathematics*, **10**, 3, pp. 51–6.

WALKERDINE, V. (1990b) 'Post-structuralism and mathematics education', in NOSS, R., BROWN, A., DRAKE, P., DOWLING, P., HARRIS, M., HOYLES, C. and MELLIN-OLSEN, S. (eds) (1990) *Political Dimensions of Mathematics Education: Action and Critique*, Proceedings of the First International Conference, April 1–4, London: University of London Institute of Education.

WALKERDINE, V. (1994) 'Reasoning in a post-modern age', in ERNEST, P. *Mathematics, Education and Philosophy: An International Perspective*, London: Falmer Press, pp. 61–75.

WALKERDINE, V. and LUCEY, H. (1989) *Democracy in the Kitchen*, London: Virago.

WALKERDINE, V. and THE GIRLS AND MATHEMATICS UNIT (1988) *Girls and Mathematics: Some Lessons for the Classroom*, London: ESRC.

WALKERDINE, V. and THE GIRLS AND MATHEMATICS UNIT (1989) *Counting Girls Out*, London: Virago.

WILLIAMS, R. (1961) *The Long Revolution*, London: Penguin Books.

1   Subtracting the Feminine

> The chief distinction in the intellectual powers of the two sexes is shewn by man's attaining to a higher eminence, in whatever he takes up, than can woman . . . if men are capable of a decided pre-eminence over women in many subjects, the average mental power in man must be above that of woman. (Darwin, 1896, p. 564)

Of course it is not a new trick to subtract the feminine, to render it worthless and in so doing to count girls out. Charles Darwin demonstrates for us how easily the slippage is achieved from the idea of men's superior attainment to their greater mental capacities. But the slippage is most simplistic in understanding women's and girls' participation and attainment in Mathematics. The connection made by Darwin — between eminence and mental powers — is commonly asserted when discussing why women are under-represented in higher-level careers requiring Mathematics. From there one progresses easily to the idea that such under-representation is produced by the mass psychopathology of the female mind.

Women, after all, are clearly irrational, illogical and too close to their emotions to be good at Mathematics. Or so the story goes. Endlessly repeated variations on the theme are still being reworked, in one empirical investigation after another. Girls and women are said to be different, lacking, while boys' and men's 'mastery' of Mathematics, their claim to superior rationality and scientific truth, is unchallenged, as though their 'attaining higher eminence' were proof enough. When examining these issues one can fall into the trap of attempting either to prove exactly what girls lack so that it can be put right, or to demonstrate that there is no lack at all. We think that such approaches trap us, and the girls and women we shall meet in these pages, like flies in a web, into playing the game by patriarchal rules. We believe that it is necessary to avoid stepping into this trap and to ask afresh why the questions were posed in this way.

It is facile, however, to assert that these facts and ideas are mere rhetoric and that we can easily uncover 'what really happens' or girls' 'real' performance. We will demonstrate that there is no simple 'real' on the basis of which interventions can be made. How we carry out the research, what questions we ask, what counts as data, what is judged to be true are all entangled in the pursuit of 'the truth', and we get caught up in this too. Our research becomes a process of disentangling, of pulling ourselves free of the web. It is like unpicking knitting, the wool still bearing the imprint of the knots which formed it into a garment. This garment often seemed to fit us well and even to keep us warm on winter nights. Taking it apart can be painful and does not reveal the easy certainty of *answers*. Of course, one can hide behind complexity, use it as a way of failing to address the possibility of real interventions and struggles. But there have been so many 'easy' answers which told us what was wrong with girls and how to put it right. Such answers do more harm than good, because they insist that there is something wrong with girls that has to be corrected.

We want to tell a different story, full of fact and fiction and fantasy. It is a story of women doing research from which we cannot and will not extricate ourselves as the narrative unfolds. The story in this book is also in many ways our own story. That is, the issues we will raise reflect our own histories not only as women but also as women who went on to higher education and academic work in a university. Our careers were channelled through those routes usually open to women; secretarial work and the so-called 'caring professions'. Although we were all well qualified — in psychology, sociology, and education — none of us had had straightforward academic careers. We all had to struggle for a sense both of the importance of the work we wanted to do and of our own worth. It was often difficult to remember that research such as this, challenging existing assumptions, methods and theories, produced hostility and resentment, which were difficult for us to deal with, especially when combined with power. The Unit was not, however, composed of mathematicians. Some of us had been good at Mathematics at school, while others had not. While some might think that this sort of work should be carried out by mathematicians, it was precisely our different approaches and experiences which allowed us to address these questions in new ways.

Our approach is developed from work done in Britain, and builds upon Post-Structuralism (see Derrida, 1972; Squire, 1989; Parker, 1989; Henriques et al., 1984). This work has been very influential in challenging some of the ideas about mind based on Structuralist universals, which are common in Mathematics education today. It puts into historical perspective the construction of scientific ideas (or truths) about girls and boys, men and women, minds and Mathematics. It allows us to take apart these truths and their forming and informing of practices in which girls and women are taken to be poor at Mathematics. We shall explore existing explanations of girls' performance and suggest that there is more behind them than meets the eye, then go on to document the theoretical and empirical evidence underlying our account. This will lead us to test scores and classrooms. We shall meet teachers, children and parents in homes, nursery, primary and secondary schools to examine how the relation between theory and practice is actually lived. Our research represents six funded studies, each concentrating on a different age group, between 1978 and 1987.

Our first project was a pilot study, part of a larger piece of work on cognitive development in nursery and infant schools. In this we formulated the basis of our work on power and concluded that girls were not failing in the early years of schooling. On the basis of this work, we obtained another grant to examine the transition of a group of children from the top classes of two junior schools into the first year of a comprehensive. We proposed that if there was no falling-off in performance in junior school, we should examine what happened in secondary school: the period of the reputed falling-off. We backed this up with a further study in the same comprehensive of children in fourth-year Maths and English classes. In both studies we found no falling-off — indeed, in general terms the girls were outperforming the boys. We decided that an entirely different account of the issues was needed.

We then went on to research the early socialization arguments by following a group of girls who had been the object of a previous study at four; we set out to discover what had happened to them at ten. Because we had data on their inter-action with their mothers we were able to add an investigation into the transition from home to school and to examine the effects of early socialization on later per-formance. Since this sample consisted of all white girls stratified by social class, we could examine aspects of class-based division. This work led us to be very crit-ical of socialization accounts, especially those which laid stress on the mother's role. We argued that mothering was the object of certain scientific truths which constantly naturalized some practices and pathologized others, laying educational success and failure at the door of all mothers. We also carried out a more detailed study of 6-year-olds at home and at 1 infant school, and further confirmed the ana-lysis of the 4- and 10-year-olds. We were then fortunate enough to obtain 2 grants to reassess and reanalyse all the data, from 4 to 15, and to present our analysis in a coherent manner. Here is that accumulated analysis, theoretical and empirical.

While we established that girls were felt to lack something, even when they were successful, it seemed equally and positively that boys were felt to possess the very thing that girls were taken to lack. It would seem easy to prove or disprove this by recourse to empirical evidence. However, we shall argue that things are not so straightforward. Girls are still considered lacking when they perform well and boys are still taken to possess something even when they perform poorly. In other words, we need carefully to examine the relationship between evidence and explanation.

There have been so many accounts of 'the problem' and many attempts to inter-vene with forms of anti-sexist practice. We are critical of many of the taken-for-granted assumptions of such practice — not because we are critical of it in general but because we think that some of it has perpetuated the problem it was intended to cure. Blame has fallen on girls themselves, or on their mothers or female teachers. In addition, approaches on the basis of getting girls to 'choose' non-stereotyped sub-jects also tend at the very least to be confounded when they continue to opt for the more traditionally 'feminine' subjects. We shall argue that both the theoretically tra-ditional approaches and the kind of anti-sexist interventions sometimes attempted make things worse. Although our central project was to examine theoretical and em-pirical evidence relating to Mathematics, we argue that Mathematics becomes a foil or filter for examining more general issues of gender and education.

First we situate our work within the existing empirical approaches, then we start to outline some of the historical and theoretical background. We decided to begin with the youngest children and end with our study of 15-year-olds. However, this method presents problems, since some of the work on older children was under-taken before that on younger children. Our ideas developed as we went along. This means that we shall present work informed by a more complex theoretical analysis before some of that on older children. We hope that readers will understand and bear with us, because when presenting research of this quantity and complexity some organizational method must be found. We decided on this one because it allows examination of the issues as they relate to girls progressing through their school careers. First of all, however, we shall return to the question of truth in order to examine the basis on which the issue of girls and Mathematics has been understood.

2   The Truth about Girls

What Is the Truth?

This may seem a strange way to begin, but we do not think that finding the truth about girls and Mathematics is possible. There are scientific 'facts', of course, but we shall demonstrate that these are open to serious question. We should, however, state straight away that we do not want to argue that current work on girls and Mathematics is a false or pseudoscience and that what is needed is a feminist science, which will unproblematically tell the unbiased and undistorted truth. The issues of truth, scientificity and method are more complex, and in the next three chapters we shall outline our approach to these issues.

As we stated in Chapter 1, we saw, throughout our work, the need to rethink the entire debate about girls and Mathematics, based as it is on the assumption of female failure. In this chapter, however, we examine existing approaches, particularly work on statistical significance upon which many of the claims about girls' failure rest.

When James Callaghan, then prime minister, launched the 'Great Debate' in a speech at Ruskin College, Oxford, in 1976, he referred to the needs of industry and to the production of a curriculum that would get 'talented young people into science and engineering subjects'. As part of this he asked: 'Why is it that such a high proportion of girls abandon science before leaving school?'

While questions have been raised about women's minds for many centuries, Callaghan's question matches the recent interest in, and explanations of, girls' performance in Mathematics. Let us first examine these, for different concerns at different historical moments have themselves helped to produce different definitions of — and solutions to — the 'problem'. In other words, no single and unbiased research question will locate the absolute truth about girls and women. Rather, it is important to show how different kinds of question lead to different interventions.

Our starting point is that there is no simple category 'woman' which can be revealed by feminist research, but that as feminists we can examine how facts, fictions and fantasies have been constituted and how these have affected the ways in which we have been positioned, understood and led to understand ourselves. Hence, while much feminist counter-research has attempted empirically to disprove the facts about girls' and women's performance, we felt that a fundamental problem remained. Accepting the categories and terms within which the issues were framed left feminist work always on the defensive and trapped within empiricism. This chapter should explain some of the details of our method, but first we examine the terms of recent debate.

Although explanations of girls' performance tend to treat girls as a unitary category and to consider girls versus boys, this deflects from the specificity of the issues and the debate. To understand these we must examine two aspects concerned with the context of education within the developmental framework of the modern state.

Current approaches may be understood in relation to general theories of Mathematics education, especially to the notion of reason and reasoning. The important context is the concern expressed by James Callaghan. While British education since the war had shown considerable concern for inequality, this was always within a meritocratic system aimed at selecting children of aptitude and ability to join the ranks of professionals. In the post-war period the focus was on working-class boys. By the 1970s it was on girls in general, partly due to the impact of the women's movement. But for our purposes, the important aspect of this debate was the link that was made between wastage, talent and finding talent. The debate was understood and acted upon according to theories and practices within the psychological literature of ability. This literature sought to find high-achieving girls by a set of testing procedures which already designated ability as a product of a certain sort of mental equipment. Debates therefore keyed right into the contested areas of success, failure and mind, especially tenaciously held ideas about differences between male and female minds, brains and modes of thinking.

So the wastage-of-talent argument was couched in terms of the generic category 'girls', within which we could not possibly encompass girls in general: a point which is glossed over. The expressed concern was about the numbers of girls and women entering high-level careers requiring Mathematics and science; such careers require at least A levels and usually a university degree. Only 10 per cent of 18-year-olds in this country take A levels, however, and an even smaller proportion go to university. We are talking then about a very specific and extremely small proportion of girls, though you would not think so from the literature. The purpose of this examination is to outline some of the problems in existing approaches and explain how we developed our own approach and methodology.

There are several traditions of work in the field, most of which emanate from the United States and reflect the concerns of American psychology, especially social psychology, in supporting the way nation is 'produced'; while British work stems from post-war developments in social democracy, with the consequent concerns about ability and aptitude, testing, finding bright pupils.

Let us briefly review the way in which different traditions of work have viewed 'the problem'. These divide roughly into 'nature' and 'nurture' arguments. While some researchers claim differences in spatial ability and brain lateralization, others suggest that 'personality' factors and socialization experiences are to blame. Most studies work from the premiss that girls *are* worse at Mathematics and then attempt to explain this by global generalizations about females. But since we have already established that the issues which gave rise to concern in the first place were fairly specific, there seems to be a problem about these assumptions and starting points.

The most hotly disputed approach deals with alleged sex differences in spatial ability, supported either by a genetic or an environmental reading. The genetic lobby would link the work to differences in verbal and non-verbal intelligence and with research on brain lateralization. The environmentalists use ideas of sex-role stere-otyping to suggest that girls and boys have different play and developmental experiences. There is scant definition, however, of the precise link between performance on visuo–spatial tests and school Mathematics. It has generally been considered more progressive to locate girls' supposed 'lack' within the environment, although this may be just as oppressive, for it ignores women's biology altogether. This is not to argue for a return to genetic approaches, but to locate our examination and understanding within a critique of that dichotomy.

The spatial-ability issue has gained widespread acceptance at a common-sense level and has featured widely in anti-sexist interventions in early education. It has often, for example, been suggested that girls do badly because they do not play enough with construction toys. They are then encouraged to play with Lego, but teachers are still dismayed that they tend to construct not vehicles but houses (see Chapter 5).

Environmental approaches, especially in the American literature, concentrate on factors which may produce female drop-out from high-school Mathematics. The literature on fear of success (Leder, 1980) uses classic research to examine higher Mathematics as a 'masculine' field of study. 'Bright' girls tend to display 'fear-of-success' responses in relation to Mathematics in far greater numbers than boys. This led Leder to conclude not only that such girls were less likely to take Mathematics in the first place, but that those who did were more likely than boys to leave the field early. It was, moreover, girls who appeared to be particularly vulnerable to social pressures towards traditional femininity who were least likely to choose Maths.

Maths anxiety became another concern, and women particularly were said to have a phobia about Maths and numbers. Again, the dominant theme was the take-up of higher-grade courses. However, studies of Maths anxiety do not report consistent findings: there are few differences between boys and girls. Nevertheless, a few studies have examined 'extreme' anxiety and their results support the hypothesis that more women than men are 'Math anxious' (Brush, 1978). Fennema and Sherman (1976) have noted several deficiencies in this approach, suggesting that it does not allow for the face that men may be more socialized into not openly *displaying* their anxiety. Such anxiety may also arise from being tested and from a lack of confidence in one's ability to learn the subject. In our view, however, anxiety cannot be separated from complex social processes nor from the involvement in Mathematics of fantasies about masculinity and femininity. Dweck and her associates (Dweck and Repucci, 1973; Diener and Dweck, 1978) have attempted to demonstrate that helplessness in the face of failure is a factor which particularly affects girls and may, therefore, affect their mathematical performance. They argue that there are important differences between children who display either 'learned helplessness' or 'mastery orientation' when faced with mathematical and other academic tasks.

This construct, 'learned helplessness', has been applied in an effort to explain sex differences in Mathematics performance. The evidence suggests that girls may be more prone to a learned-helplessness response, especially in tasks involving Maths. Careful review of this literature suggests that the sex differences are neither as consistent nor as strong as has been postulated (Parsons, 1983). Dweck also suggests, however, that teachers help to create this situation by responding to boys and girls in different ways, seeing girls' poor performance as due to lack of ability and boys' to lack of effort. This idea of helplessness implies that so-called female passivity is a learned response.

There is also a literature based on attribution theory (Weiner, 1971), where it is generally argued that boys tend to attribute their success to internal, stable causes (ability) and their failures to external, unstable causes (lack of effort), whereas girls tend to reverse this pattern, taking personal responsibility for their failures, but not for their successes (Bar-Tai, 1978). Studies focusing on Maths have shown that girls rate lack of ability and/or skill as a *slightly* more important cause of their mathematical failure than boys. It is also argued that people with positive perceptions of their ability approach tasks with confidence and high expectations of success, and, consequently, perform well (Eccles et al., 1983). Females have lower estimates of their abilities, performance and expectations of success in some situations, even when their performance is equal to — or better than — males' (Parsons et al., 1976). Several researchers, however (McHugh et al., 1982), argue that it is the male sex-typing of experimental tasks which may account for the apparent consistency of these sex differences. Underlying this argument is the assumption that when this sex-typing is altered or manipulated, girls will expect to do less well than boys on male-typed tasks but at least as well on 'feminine' or neutral tasks. Although we consider teachers' attributions extremely important, we do not consider attribution theory adequate as an explanatory device.

Although this tradition of work contributes significantly to the study of girls and Mathematics, there are several problems with these approaches in British research. Our work suggests that an orientation towards traditional femininity, for example, does not necessarily impede *performance*. Girls' mean scores are roughly equivalent to those of boys, even in secondary school. The major surveys carried out by the Assessment of Performance Unit (1980a, 1980b, 1981a, 1981b, 1982a, 1982b) demonstrate that there are no sex differences of practical significance (Walkderdine, Walden and Owen, 1982; Walden and Walkerdine, 1985), except in the top 25 and 15 per cent of children in secondary school. It is these children who, roughly speaking, until recently entered for O and A levels. In this sense the issue of performance and take-up of Mathematics is related, but *only* for those who have the opportunity to enter professional careers. It is also important to note, as we shall demonstrate, that social class is a major feature of difference between boys and girls.

There is certainly evidence in Britain (Holland, 1981) to suggest that working-class girls experience stronger pressures towards traditional feminine occupations than middle-class girls. Moreover, the top-performing 25 per cent of school pupils are predominantly middle-class. There seems to be an important and interesting phenomenon relating to the differential performance, attitudes and experience of middle- and working-class adolescent girls.

The few American studies which have examined classroom contexts (Becker, 1976) demonstrate that the quantity and type of teaching varies according to the sex of the students and the subject taught. In general, teachers tend to interact more with boys than with girls, especially in Maths and science classes. 'High-potential' boys also receive more praise for their achievement and more total interactions than 'high-potential' girls. There is some evidence to suggest that teachers direct more negative comments at boys for their conduct, rather than for the academic content of their work. In contrast, girls are more likely to be criticized for the quality of their work (Dweck, Davidson, Nelson and Enna, 1978). Similar observations have been made on the British *Girls into Science and Technology Project* (Kelly, Whyte and Smail, 1984; Kelly, 1981; French, 1982).

Several researchers propose that sex differences in Maths achievement and course selection can be explained by different socialization experiences. These studies refer mainly to the attitudes of socializing agents: teachers, parents and counsellors, who may reflect cultural stereotypes regarding boys' and girls' mathematical ability. Male and female socializers are said to adopt different attitudes and behaviour towards Mathematics and therefore create differences through their power as role models (Maccoby and Jacklin, 1974). Aiken (1970) cites data indicating that female student teachers have lower estimates of their mathematical competence, and openly admit they are less comfortable teaching Maths than are their male peers. Many studies suggest that parents and teachers have higher educational expectations for boys than girls (Cooper, 1979), although this bias emerges *only* at high-school level.

The majority of British work on Mathematics has concentrated on interpretations of major sex-difference surveys. There have been some attempts (Shuard, 1981 and 1982) to argue that girls' performance is better on those items requiring only low-level or rote skills (such as computation) while boys do better on more complex Mathematics. The few British studies conclude that there are few performance differences and that attitude differences may be very important (Sheffield City Polytechnic, 1983; Joffe, 1983). However, because the British work has concentrated so much on large-scale surveys, it has tended to rely on the idea that statistically significant differences in quantitative data are 'real' and that other methods are 'soft', thus not generating 'hard fact'. We refute such claims by demonstrating that the idea of basing truth in statistical significance is somewhat ill-founded positivism, and that researchers have made unwarranted claims about girls' performance (or lack of it) on the basis of statistical significance.

Most of the data used to explain sex differences in mathematical performance derive from tests. Briefly, explanations have centred on a particular set of assumptions:

1 Boys are significantly better on test items requiring 'spatial ability';
2 Boys are better at more complex items requiring abstract thought, problem-solving, breaking set, conceptualization;
3 Girls are better at simple, repetitive tasks requiring low-level skills such as rule-following (Shuard, 1981; APU Primary and Secondary Surveys, 1980a and 1980b).

The reification of the categories 'girl' and 'boy' produces explanations which favour sex-specific characteristics, so that more complex analyses of masculinity and femininity are impossible. In addition, certain important implications of current work using test and survey data have been poorly treated in the literature. These relate to the — often hidden — problems of interpretation and, therefore, of determining the validity of findings using statistical criteria. Such findings are often treated as 'hard' evidence, as compared to the 'soft' data of the more interpretative traditions in psychology and the social sciences. As questions of truth and validity are central to our argument, we shall review some problems with the interpretation of existing test data relating to sex differences in mathematical performance (Walkerdine, Walden and Owen, 1982).

The issue of the interpretation of performance data relating to girls is important for several reasons. The search for difference in performance has had a long and infamous history, in which claims about 'reality' have been produced in support of arguments about the position and status of women. In other words, the political consequences of such statements are profound. Research on sex and gender overwhelmingly uses methods which search for *differences*, usually differences which can be quantified, reified by the use of statistical techniques. Similarities are usually treated in terms of their failure to show significant differences: in other words, similarities become non-results. Then there is the way questions are posed and techniques used to produce certain kinds of data on which only certain kinds of claims can be made, while other issues are ignored.

This brings us to the point at issue: the interpretation of statistical data. We quoted elsewhere (Walden and Walkerdine, 1982) from the Assessment of Performance Unit surveys, pointing out that they emphasize the trivial nature of any differences in mathematical performance at age 11. However, various commentators, remarking on our statements, have argued that we have misinterpreted the survey data by claiming that these differences are trivial, when in fact they are statistically significant. We therefore feel that it is crucial to explore the issue of statistical significance with respect to performance data. If significance is used as a basis for claiming that girls are performing poorly relative to boys in primary school Mathematics, this has to be investigated.

An advantage of large-scale sample surveys is that they allow a fairly precise description of the population in question. Unfortunately, routine application of the significance-testing procedures developed for small-scale experiments can be misleading. There is a close link between sample size and statistical power: the ability of a statistical test to detect a difference. Consequently, in large surveys trivially small differences may be highly significant statistically, and this significance may be deceptive. Discussions of some recent surveys of primary school Mathematics attainment over-evaluate small differences.

We shall concentrate on the first two Assessment of Performance Unit primary Mathematics surveys for 1978 (APU, 1980a; Ward, 1979) and the Schools Council study (Ward, 1979). The first APU study involved about 13,000 11-year-old pupils, each question being answered by about 1,500. The second involved about 14,500 pupils, with each question answered by 1,000. Ward (1979) tested 2,300 10-year-olds; each question was answered by about a quarter of the pupils. All three studies are circumspect in their conclusions on sex differences. The APU study states: 'The data on sex differences show a slight, and generally non significant, advantage to the boys in most sub-categories, but girls perform significantly better statistically in computation (whole numbers and decimals)' (p. 72); and 'The boys' mean score is significantly higher statistically in three sub-categories: length, area, volume and capacity, applications of number, and rate and ratio' (p. 68). (Note the emphasis on *statistically* significant differences.) Earlier the report states: 'Throughout this report references are made to statistically significant results but the educational implications of these are usually left to the reader' (p. 11), but it goes on to caution: 'If very large samples have been used even small differences can become statistically significant' (ibid.).

The second APU study is equally unemphatic, saying only that 'the boys' mean score is significantly higher in five of the sub-categories in 1979: the two measure ones, concepts (fractions and decimals), applications of number, and rate and ratio' (p. 60); and 'the boys generally obtained higher mean scores than the girls although the sex difference is only statistically significant in five of the sub-categories' (p. 64). This report includes an appendix on statistical significance which fails to mention the importance of sample size.

Ward says, about sex differences: 'The girls in the sample did slightly better at the straightforward computation questions than the boys. The boys made up for this by performing slightly better on problems put in words and those involving an understanding of the structure of number' (p. 39). He does not use the term 'significance', nor does he discuss significance testing.

So all three give little emphasis to sex difference, and where statistical significance is mentioned, caution is stressed in its interpretation. Yet this caution is not always observed, so that Howson (1982) points out that between the first and second APU studies 'the boys had notched up significantly better performance in two further sub-categories', with no indication of the magnitude of these differences. In fact, the standard deviations for these sub-categories are 7.2 and 8.3 respectively, so that even the larger difference is equivalent to only about $1\frac{3}{4}$ IQ points — a trivially small difference by any reckoning. The largest sex difference in the second survey was of 1.4 units in the sub-category 'applications of number'; with a standard deviation of 7.5 this is approximately equivalent to 3 IQ points.

How could such small differences be considered so important? Part of the problem is the seductive word 'significant': surely something that is significant (with or without the adjective 'statistically') must be important. This concept of 'significance' is part of the pidgin statistics of social science. Yet its meaning is not sufficiently appreciated. Conventional significance tests invoke a null hypothesis that in some ideal population there is exactly zero in the mean or some variable in some chosen groups. In practice no one believes in this strict null hypothesis, and the question is whether the differences which do exist are big enough to take into consideration. Typically, researchers do an experiment or make observations, then carry out a significance test. Rarely, if ever, is any consideration given to the power of such a test.

The power of a statistical test is the probability that it will yield statistically significant results at a given level of significance when a difference of a certain size does exist. To achieve a power of three-quarters would require samples of about 60. As the sample size increases, the probability of detecting a given difference (the power) also increases; alternatively, increasingly small differences will have an increasingly high probability of being statistically significant. So samples of the size used by the APU mean that small differences between the scores of girls and boys are highly likely to be *statistically* significant, even though they may have no *educational* significance.

Shuard (1981 and 1982) draws on data from all three studies in two discussions of sex differences in primary school Mathematics attainment. In an article in *The Times Educational Supplement* (1981) she focuses mainly on Ward's work, but also draws on the APU studies. She says that Ward 'gives a picture of the 1974 crop of 10-year-old girls and boys setting out towards secondary school mathematics with some of their strengths and weaknesses already fixed', but does not mention that the APU studies show that regional differences are generally far greater than sex differences.

In her 1982 paper, Shuard again draws on the Schools Council and APU studies, but also includes much of her other work. Discussing non-mathematical tests, she rightly points out that 'on all tests, however, the overlap between the sexes is very large, and it would be a gross distortion to expect that most boys would be better than most girls' (p. 279) on any particular task. Yet when it comes to Mathematics she is quite willing to talk about the differences between girls and boys as if they were two quite distinct groups. Also, in her *TES* article Shuard clearly has in mind a view of the issues of girls' performance in Mathematics which is the driving force behind her analysis of the Schools Council data: that girls perform better than boys at computation and those aspects of Mathematics considered low-level, while boys do better on the more complex aspects, particularly 'spatial' questions.

There are several points of contention here. First, Shuard misinterprets the data to suggest that girls were good only at computation, whereas the results reveal that on the majority of items there are no sex differences. This is, however, necessary if it is to be argued that girls' performance is not up to standard. Shuard blames primary schools which, she claims, stress low-level computation because it is easy to teach, thus hindering the development of 'real' Mathematics. So, girls are not 'only' good at computation, but this argument actually negates their performance by implying that even where they are successful, their success is only low-level and can therefore be discounted.

This brings us to the second point of contention: the distinction between computation as low-level and spatial tasks as 'real' Mathematics. There are good reasons for Shuard to make this judgment, backed by the data on sex differences in certain spatial tasks. Even here, though, the issue is far from clear-cut (Walden and Walkerdine, 1982). What is particularly contentious, however, is the downgrading of certain aspects of Mathematics as not 'real', or as only 'rule-following', and upgrading others. It so happens, of course, that since girls do well at 'low-level' aspects, there is a failure to point out that they also perform well on others considered 'real'! It is a moot point whether rule-following should be considered low-level at all or whether 'real understanding' plays the part in school Mathematics which some Mathematics educators would have us believe.

If we now look at the APU secondary surveys (1980b, 1981b and 1982b) similar points may be stressed. Although there are larger sex differences than in the primary surveys, the results must be treated with the same caution. The sex differences in Mathematics attainment in the primary surveys were very small. In the three secondary surveys the differences are both larger and more often statistically significant. They are also consistently in favour of boys. None of the three secondary surveys gives standard deviations for the sub-category scores, so one cannot make simple direct comparisons with the primary surveys, nor represent the size of the sex differences as notional 'IQ point differences'. However, one can compare the size of the sex differences with the sizes of differences on the other 'background' variables.

The differences between boys and girls ranged from 1 or 2 per cent to about 8 per cent. They were considerably smaller than the differences between pupils living in metropolitan areas and those in non-metropolitan areas, and were totally swamped by differences between the regions of the United Kingdom or between schools having high or low percentages of free school meals.

Two of the surveys (APU, 1980b and 1982b) discuss not just the means for girls and boys, but also the distributions. For both surveys, 'the higher mean scores of boys over girls are largely due to the greater preponderance of boys among the high scorers rather than of girls among the lower scorers' (1982b, p. 73). The third survey looked for consistencies between three secondary surveys and for continuities between the primary and secondary surveys. For consistency they looked at the pattern of sex differences in the sub-categories, and found an average correlation of over 0.6 between the three surveys. It is suggested that the areas where boys' mean scores are highest relative to girls' are those of Mathematics, which 'are important in several secondary curriculum options, such as physical sciences, technical drawing and woodwork, which are taken by more boys than girls' (p. 143).

There is no suggestion that the mean differences between boys and girls found in the primary surveys were consolidated or amplified in the secondary years. It is, however, suggested that the 'profiles of relative strengths and weaknesses across the different areas of mathematics' (APU, 1982b, p. 145) are consistent. Girls stay relatively better at things they were better at in the primary years (computation, for example), but 'the boys' profile of attainment moves up about two percentage points relative to the girls' (ibid.). Consequently, 'whatever factors are causing the differences in the profiles of attainment are already operating by the time the pupils are in their primary schools.'

It is important, then, to recognize that we are talking of sex differences which, were they established, are no greater than 4 IQ points (for example, scores of 112 and 116). The significance of such an example is in no sense a truth or validity outside the practices in which such differences have real and practical effects. For example, in so far as such scores will be used as cut-off points for educational provision, and to determine the opportunity, experience and curricula for girls and boys, we can say that they have 'real' effects whose materiality and power stand outside any 'basic' guarantees of truth or interpretation. We might well conclude that nothing can be usefully said about differences between scores of 112 and 116. What matters are their crucial consequences for practice. Such an analysis of the power of these 'truths' is vital, because it allows us to examine the complexity of the production of the 'truth' about girls' performance and the effects on their schooling.

The question, then, is whether girls and women are lacking or different. Most of the arguments about their performance relative to men take difference as indicative of something real: high performance indicating that something is present, low that something is missing. The idea that girls lack spatial ability or mastery orientation or autonomy or holistic thinking, or whatever the next incapacity turns out to be, is not best served by trying to prove *either* that they really have it *or* by trying to find the cause of their deficit. Deficit theories tend to blame the victim. Such approaches fall into the trap of treating these differences as caused by something real and true. We want here to explore quite a different way of approaching the issue, one which treats truth not as something easily empirically verifiable but as slippery stuff created out of fantasies and fictions which have been made to operate as fact. The basis of this approach comes from a body of work known as Post-Structuralism, which underlies our theoretical and empirical work. We shall try to draw out these ideas as we work through the various pieces of our research, but let us begin by examining how we might approach some of the arguments about the truth of the differences between boys and girls.

3　Science, Reason and the Female Mind

To investigate the production of modern truths about girls and Mathematics we must understand something of the history of both modern Mathematics teaching and ideas about the female body and mind. We must uncover the way in which certain scientific ideas are developed and gain currency within practices such as schooling and then serve as devices which claim to tell the truth about and to regulate those practices. Thus, we are aiming to understand how the modern 'common sense' that there is something wrong with girls in relation to Mathematics, and conversely that boys possess something which makes them successful — assumptions which explicitly or implicitly underpin most of the research reviewed in the last chapter — come to have such a stranglehold today. It is necessary both to deconstruct the terms, the sets of oppositions between male and female which are set up, and to conduct what is called a *history of the present* — Foucault's term for an examination of the conditions which produced our taken-for-granted practices so that they come to seem obvious and unchallenged facts. This requires an examination of the evolution of certain practices and discourses concerning Mathematics, gender and sexuality. This would occupy a book in itself and cannot therefore be undertaken here; instead, we shall outline some of the issues and methods involved (see Walkerdine, 1984; Weeks, 1981; Bland, 1981; Rose, 1985).

The central focus of this examination is the way in which certain observations made about girls in relation to their classroom performance and to results of mathematical tests are presented as 'hard evidence'. For example, when confronted with the evidence that girls are indeed well-behaved, diligent, and so forth, it is difficult to discount such data, especially when they accord so nicely, so to speak, with the 'evidence of our own eyes'. The principles used to explain performance in primary school Mathematics derive from theories of cognitive development: successful Mathematics performance is the attainment of concepts, particular stages of logical thought. In this view of learning, *real understanding* (based on concepts) is to be contrasted with *rule-following* or *rote-memorization* (which were stressed by the old principles and practices of Maths teaching), which yields success without the solid foundation of real understanding. An easy example is the contrast between understanding multiplication as cumulative addition and only being able to chant one's tables.

There is no space here to discuss in detail the rise of child-centredness upon which modern Mathematics education depended (see Walkerdine, 1984 and 1988). However, certain key issues are important. Child-centredness emerged as a movement in the private sector from the 1920s onwards. Although it has been widely associated with progressivism and hailed as freeing and liberating children from the

authoritarianism of 'chalk-and-talk' methods, it can, in fact, be viewed quite differently. It can be argued that the shift has been not from authoritarianism to liberation, nor from power to no power, but from overt disciplining to covert disciplining,
in which 'scientific pedagogy' plays a major role. It is science, particularly the science
of psychology, which is to provide a description of the nature of the learner and of
learning, and later of the idea of a natural sequence of development towards rationality. This mapping of the individual learner allowed disciplining to take a different turn. Now it was no longer a question of correct and incorrect answers, but of
the monitoring of what were considered the characteristics of the 'normal' learner.
Despite the hope that these methods would produce freedom, children were observed
and monitored as never before. Theories of evolutionary biology (particularly the
work of Darwin) were used to show that the development of a child towards adulthood mirrored the development of the species itself. By a series of sleights of hand,
the bourgeois order came to seem natural, so that children had to be disciplined by
a monitoring of their 'natural and normal development' and this was held to be the
saving grace of the new democracy (Walkerdine, 1988; Walkerdine and Lucey,
1989). As we shall see, part of this process was the idea that development must
take place within a facilitating environment, and women were corralled into the
new science of mothering and scientific pedagogy. Our purpose here is to indicate
that the things we take for granted — ideas of child development, child-centredness,
for instance — can be taken apart and placed within their historical and political
location, and so viewed in a completely new light which allows us to question the
naturalness of the categories of boy and girl as defined in performance terms.

Many commentators note how the Industrial Revolution and the rise of Capitalism depended upon developments in science. As part of this process new sciences
of the population began to be devised. Foucault calls these sciences of population
management, and they include statistics, epidemiology, psychology and developments in medicine, law and social welfare. Thus, numerical calculation of known
facts about the population became a central tool of modern government. These
modern forms of government, according to Foucault, made use of 'sciences and
technologies of the social' to produce a new form of power, based on the regulation
of the population through these knowledges. This later became Mathematics, not as
calculation but as reason and reasoning. The powers of the mind were to be mar-
shalled in order to govern a population through reason, and that population would
itself be developed enough to reason. But there were, of course, already bodies of
knowledge which situated women outside rationality. The categories of subjection
and the mode of government were intensely political and far from natural. However, by the time the primary Mathematics curriculum was changed, in the post-war
period, these issues had become hidden, and it was thought progressive for the main
target of Mathematics education to be the production of reasoning, which should
proceed according to natural laws.

Howson (1978) provides an overview of the changes in Mathematics education since the 1950s. He sees the Mathematical Association's 1956 report *The Teaching of Mathematics in Primary Schools* as a watershed in initiating far-reaching
changes in early Mathematics education:

It was a remarkably forward-looking document which expressed very clearly the point of view which was to dominate national thinking on primary education during the next twenty years.

This point of view is encapsulated in this often-quoted extract from the report:

> ... children, developing at their own individual rates, learn through their active response to the experiences that come to them through constructive play, experiment and discussion ... children become aware of relationships and develop mental structures which are mathematical in form and are in fact the only sound basis of mathematical techniques. The aim of primary teaching, it is argued, is the laying of this foundation of mathematical thinking about the numerical and spatial aspects of the objects and activities which children of this age encounter. (pp. v, vi)

As a guiding principle in Mathematics education this view was quite new. The report advocated treating children as individuals, guiding their responses to everyday experiences and constructive play, and fostering the development of appropriate mental structures. This seems to have been accepted, because, as a Schools Council report published 10 years later makes clear, Mathematics was lagging behind other areas of the curriculum:

> How can we contrive situations in which children can make their own discoveries? It is surely reasonable to apply to Mathematics the principles of learning which have already affected other aspects of the curriculum. (Schools Council, 1965, p. 3)

But if we consider the key terms of this quotation, the stage is set for a particular understanding of the nature of learning and the characteristics of both proper learning and proper pedagogy. These ideas are now almost common-sense and teachers use them unproblematically. As we shall see, they are in fact deeply gendered and problematic, because of the way they define both Mathematics and the learner.

In discussion of Mathematics itself a distinction has long been made between two qualitatively different kinds of knowledge and thinking. This distinction is a recognition of the fact that when people wish to complete some practical task successfully they may do so simply by following rules, by applying a procedure, but still have little idea of why the rules are effective, or of their range of application. On the other hand, people who apply a procedure and at the same time know its rationale may have a deeper understanding of the meaning of what they are doing and why the procedure works. In discussions of mathematical education the distinction has gone under different names. Most often 'basic skills' or 'computational techniques' are counterposed to 'understanding'. Buxton (1978) has called it 'the old distinction between "knowing how" and "knowing that"'. A group in the British Society for the Psychology of Learning Mathematics has incorporated this distinction in the contrast between 'instrumental understanding' and 'relational understanding' (Skemp, 1976; Byers and Herscovics, 1977; Backhouse, 1978).

Mathematics teaching will be approached differently depending on whether its aims stress one side of the distinction or the other. Which side is stressed may depend upon what the educator thinks Mathematics education is for: what use the pupils will make of it. Those who stress teaching children ultimately to take money and give change in shops, to count components on a production line, to measure up rooms to lay carpets, tend to stress the 'procedural'. Those, on the other hand, teaching budding computer programmers, mathematicians and physicists stress the 'propositional'. However, this distinction is not simply of theoretical value. Ever since the inception of compulsory schooling there has been a debate about what kind of Mathematics was to be taught to different pupils. The distinctions are, of course, class-, gender- and race-specific, and naturalistic arguments are brought in easily to show that some pupils are simply more naturally suited to the menial rather than the intellectual. In the 1960s and 1970s a similar debate raged in America about the education of black children.

In Mathematics education, then, the 'procedural–propositional' distinction is the basis of the view that while rule-following will do for everyday life, to understand Mathematics properly a person needs to understand its conceptual basis. The different Mathematics taught in relation to different kinds of career is, of course, most marked in secondary schools.

Another long-standing view among mathematicians is that Mathematics is important not only because it generates necessarily true propositions which are immensely powerful when applied, but because, when *individual* mathematicians have 'real' understanding, Mathematics provides aesthetic pleasure and the possibility of creative experience. Certainty and order — and the production through a trial-and-error process of theorems which look retrospectively as if they were always true and always waiting to be discovered — can apparently motivate individuals. The mathematician's dream is a seductive one (Rotman, 1979; Walkerdine, 1988).

Those who so enthusiastically participated in the post-war changes in early Mathematics education were sympathetic to the view that even very young children could develop a deeper, more 'real' propositional understanding of the subject and, indeed, that they could experience the 'intrinsic motivation' which is one of the rewards of such understanding. Of course the procedural aspect was not ignored. We have stressed the distinction which is expressed when such terms as 'techniques', 'procedures', 'skills', 'algorithms' and correspondingly 'rote-learning', 'drill' and so on are used, as opposed to 'having a concept', 'understanding', 'developing a schema', and so on. But it is obvious that the aim of good teaching would be to produce *both* kinds of knowledge. Here the notion of *foundations* is crucial, because it was used to conceptualize the ideal relationship between understanding and technique, between the propositional and procedural. As the Mathematical Association's report clearly implies, the latter should be based on the former, and the teacher's job is to try and make sure that it is. A central reason for the rejection of so-called 'traditional' Mathematics was that it did not provide a sound basis for technique in the deeper understanding of the subject. It was thought that without this basis, calculating, rote-learnt knowledge of relationships and so on could only leave children with a somewhat mystifying and possibly meaningless collection of techniques, however useful.

Important political issues are at stake here. In particular, the Mathematics educators' dream was to produce a rationally ordered democracy, free from extremes and totalitarianism. It is this hope which is fulfilled by producing children who can reason and are not swayed by darker and deeper instincts, but beneath all this lies a covert regulation of the autonomous and reasoning subject, for whom freedom has become a chimera. This is a central argument for us.

It is axiomatic for the view of Mathematics learning that became dominant in primary schools that proper success is based on mastering concepts in a mode of practice designed to promote and produce 'real understanding': propositional know-ledge, relational understanding, and so on, learning through activity, not chanting tables. Success at Mathematics is taken to be an indication of success at reason-ing. Mathematics is seen as *development* of the reasoned and logical mind. This is where the important issue of girls' success comes in. Those explanations which allow girls success at all say that it is based on low-level rule-following, rote-learning and computation, not on proper understanding. Hence they negate that success even as they announce it: girls 'just' follow rules. They are good compared with 'naughty' boys, who can 'break set' (make conceptual rules). Moreover, girls' correct perform-ance is seen not only as wrong but as pathological. Girls threaten the smooth run-ning of the child-centred classroom because they seem to learn in ways which have been outlawed for leading to authoritarianism and producing the wrong kind of development. Girls, therefore, constitute a problem for the teacher because they do not appear to function like natural children as defined in the theories. So, is there some-thing wrong with the theory or, as is usually assumed, something wrong with girls?

This explanation is totally *internal* to the theory about the production of rea-son and rationality. Girls may be able to do Mathematics, but good performance is not to be equated with proper reasoning. This is taken into account in relation to later 'failure', where abstract reasoning is required. On the other hand, boys tend to produce evidence of what is counted as 'reason', even though their attain-ment may itself be relatively poor. This differentiation between classroom perform-ance, its posited cause, and the consequent problem of 'the real', returns again and again. Throughout the age range, girls' good performance is down played, while boys' often relatively poor attainment is taken as evidence of real understanding; any counter-evidence (poor attention and so forth) is explained as peripheral to 'the real' (Walden and Walkerdine, 1985). It is interesting that (as in all judgments about attainment), girls' attainment itself is not seen as a reliable indicator. In this view, right attainment can, in principle, be produced for the wrong reasons. It becomes important, therefore, to establish as permissible only that attainment taken as premissed on 'real understanding'. Only this attainment, then, is *real*. The rest, although apparently real, is actually false.

Counting girls' performance as evidence is not distinct from the issue of what it is taken to be evidence of. We have not only to debate the data but also to engage with the reason for this decision, its meaning, and its practical consequences for girls' education. Classically, the truth of such statements has been the subject of epistemological critiques, but these treat truth as though it were timeless, separating the conditions of its production from truth itself. The question is not 'Are the arguments true?' but 'How is this truth constituted, how is it possible, and what effects does it have?' Arguments derived from Foucault can help us begin to deconstruct this truth about girls. Only if we understand its historical production and its effectiveness can we begin to go beyond it. We can chart the historical antecedents of the position that females do not possess a capacity for reason or 'mathematical minds' and so document how and why the arguments in its support have such force now, and how we might challenge them.

Our argument, in a nutshell, is that ideas about reason and reasoning cannot be understood historically outside considerations of gender. Since the Enlightenment, if not before, the Cartesian concept of reason has been deeply embroiled with attempts to control nature. Rationality was taken to be a kind of rebirth of the thinking self, without the intervention of a woman. The rational self was a profoundly masculine one from which woman was excluded, her powers not only inferior but also subservient. The 'thinking' subject was male; the female provided the biological prop both to procreation and to servicing the possibility of 'man'. Philosophical doctrine was transformed into the object of a science in which reason became a capacity invested within the body, and later mind, of man alone.

During the nineteenth century 'human nature' became the object of a scientific enquiry that, from its inception, was deeply patriarchal. The female body and mind became the objects of the scientific gaze. It began to be possible to make 'true' statements about female nature, no longer an object of debate but resolvable by resort to evidence. Yet 'female nature' does not pre-exist the development of those doctrines, bodies of knowledge and scientific practices which produced it. In this sense, the truth of scientific statements is not discovered: it is produced.

Moreover, we cannot monitor the effects of such 'facts' on the fate of particular girls and women. For example, the legitimation of their exclusion and of practices of discrimination could now be based on fact: their *proven* inferiority. It was quite common to exclude women from higher education and the professions on the grounds that they were swayed by their emotions and therefore had no capacity for rational judgment. Within arguments such as this the sexed body (the seat of 'nature') becomes the site for the production and explanation of mind. Since the very differentiation between men's and women's bodies is central to this approach, reason can never be gender-neutral.

This shows how we get today's common sense about 'women's minds' being the opposite of hard science and Mathematics. Often social psychologists are content simply to state that these are the views that women and men, girls and boys have about femininity and masculinity, perhaps as a function of socioeconomic factors. But unless we change the way in which such ideas are internal to — and productive of — the way we understand reason, we are left with only attitude or economic change as bases of transformation.

Helen Weinreich-Haste (1978) reproduces nicely for us the 'common sense' which accrues from such discourses. She asked science students and schoolchildren to rate science and scientists on the dimensions of hard/soft, masculine/feminine, and so on. These polarized constructs, of course, are already given in the 'common sense' of which we have spoken. It is not surprising, therefore, that science came out as 'hard, intellect-based, complex and masculine'. However, what is interesting is that there was no 'feminine discipline' cluster: the arts were not seen as feminine either (Parker and Pollock, 1981). Although such work gives us important information, we need to understand how these views came to be held — otherwise we are again left with a quasi-scientific judgment that such views are 'incorrect', and therefore attitude change is needed to modify them. Such a position plays down the way these sets of attitudes about women are central conceptions about science and rationality.

'Woman' as the object of nineteenth-century science was gentle, not profound, the holder of the moral order through mothering. Typical were weak and fainting middle-class Victorian women whose minds, like butterflies, were unable to concentrate, moving from a little embroidery to a little this, a little that; gentle, accomplished, but shallow. It certainly matters that individual women may not have fitted the stereotype, but it is equally important that no woman would be able to stand outside the power of that scientific truth. The fact that women's nature was located in their bodies immediately made them naturally external to a capacity for reason. It is important to see this not as a distortion or a simple mistake but as an effective productive force. Developing from this poor, frail, moral woman whose failure to reason was produced through incapacity rather than oppression, we come to the argument which sees it as dangerous for women to reason — physiologically dangerous and imperilling the future of the species by the strain of an act so unnatural for women's bodies.

What a burden, therefore, girls and women had to bear! Not only were they harming themselves, they were also endangering the species. Such moral imperatives would render opposition difficult, and it is not surprising that those who opposed them were understood as 'hard', 'masculine' women of dubious sexuality, subjected to pejorative evaluations and general scorn.

The regulation of sexuality became central to such concerns. Femininity itself became the target and the object of a variety of scientific theories and medico-legal practices (Foucault, 1979; Weeks, 1981; Bland, 1981).

Rearing children in the privacy of the home became the norm. This relates specifically to the rise of the bourgeoisie, in which the woman becomes 'mother', looking after her children, not the employed nanny of upper-class homes. Here issues of class are foregrounded, not as causal but rather in the displays of abnormal, non-nurturant, passionate and active sexuality amongst working-class women. At the same time the teaching profession, requiring 'natural capacities for nurturance' to facilitate child development, was opened to bourgeois women. The rise in bourgeois women's education and in teacher training go hand in hand (Dyehouse, 1981; Widdowson, 1983).

It is also possible to demonstrate why particular struggles by women took the form they did. If women were excluded from various public domains by confinement to the domestic sphere, clearly resistance by certain groups would be aimed at entry into the barred fields of education, academe and politics. Indeed, women's struggles in education related specifically to being allowed to enter the public domain. Changes in educational practices at the end of the nineteenth century made the written examination the arbiter of ability, success and entry into higher education. This allowed entry on the basis of merit rather than birth and was particularly important to the emergent bourgeoisie.

Bourgeois women's resistance, therefore, took the form of being allowed to enter examinations: to prove themselves equal to men. But many problems remained. Women still had to prove that they, like men, were rational. They had to fight on the same terms and could not change them. Examination failure would only confirm their 'incapacity', as it still does. Girls entering these exams had to struggle against enormous odds. Not only were they putting their 'maternal femininity' at risk, but Mathematics education was often totally inadequate. Moreover, arguments about degeneracy, common at the time, meant that middle- and upper-class women had to reproduce to save the race from the lower orders. This process began in the nineteenth century and continued until the 1950s.

Since competitive exams could only ever be open to a small percentage of girls, the focus became recruitment into higher education and the professions. Then as now, failure meant almost exclusively failure to obtain high-grade passes at O level and to enter for the university entrance A level. The biologistic explanations for this are not entirely absent, even today.

So discussions about girls' failure have focused on a minority. Of course, it is not surprising that later science 'discovered' the 'female intellect' so that women, taken also to possess the capacity to reason, were allowed to enter the competition if they had *enough* ability — if they could prove themselves equal to men. We have tried to show why we should not accept the terms of the debate but, indeed, should question their very foundation. We would argue that exposing the 'truth' about girls as a production in which there are no *simple* matters of fact is a central and strategic element of our struggle.

If those successes for which girls have struggled are refused as data it is still possible to explain as a fault within women themselves the relatively small number in the professions (except the caring professions, to which they are 'naturally' suited). 'Brilliant' women are few indeed, but women's painstaking attention to detail and their 'capacity for hard work' make them excellent material for the support of a 'brilliant academic male'. For the rational self, like the reasoning child, cognitive development, 'proper conceptualization' and rationality are attained naturally; no work is involved. In modern lower schools, work is subjugated to play. When girls work hard, therefore, there is something wrong. Women's labour (domestic and otherwise) does indeed make intellectual enquiry, as play, relatively easy. It shoulders all the work that makes such creativity possible.

'The child' (gender unspecified) is taken to develop within a 'facilitating environment'. These two terms form a couple: a *child* developing in an *environment*. Further analysis suggests that mother and teacher both become part of that environment (see Chapter 4). They are defined by the very qualities that are opposite those of 'the child', who is active and enquiring and whose activity leads to 'real understanding'. The teacher and the mother, by contrast, are necessary not to instruct but to watch, observe, monitor, and facilitate development. They are defined as 'passive' in relation to the child's 'active'. They are nurturant, facilitating, sensitive and supportive, and they know when to intervene but not to interfere.

We have argued elsewhere (Walkerdine, 1986a) that this opposition — passive teacher to active child — is necessary to support the illusion of autonomy and control upon which child-centred pedagogy is founded. In this sense, then, the 'capacity for nurturance' grounded in a naturalized femininity, the object of the scientific gaze, becomes the basis for woman's fitness to facilitate knowing and reproduce the knower: the support for — yet opposite to — the production of knowledge. The production of knowledge is thereby separated from its reproduction and split along a sexual divide which renders production and reproduction the natural capacities of the respective sexes (see Walkerdine, 1988).

The child, then, has a nature which is basic: a baseline below which nothing can enter. The child is active, enquiring, discovering. The child can, therefore, be discerned by its nature, described, detailed, classified. Mathematics becomes cognitive development. Cognitive development becomes a description of the child. In this way a regime of truth comes to exist, a system of classification, in which what counts as a properly developing child may be recognized, in which certain behaviours are required and produced.

What precisely is it that produces current truths? We have argued that certain claims rest upon a constant 'will to truth' (Foucault, 1979): they invest certainty in 'man', constantly seeking to find man's other and opposite in 'woman'. This truth is constantly reproven within classrooms, where the apparatuses themselves differentiate between success and its posited causes. This has profound material effects upon the life chances of girls.

We have suggested that within current school Mathematics, certain fantasies, fears and desires invest 'man' with omnipotent control of a calculable universe, which at the same time covers a desperate fear of desiring the other, 'woman'. 'Woman' becomes the repository of all the dangers displaced from the child, itself 'father' to the man. The need to prove girls' mathematical inferiority is not motivated by a certainty, but by a terror of loss. In this story these fantasies, fears and desires become the forces that produce the actual effectiveness of the construction of fact and of current discursive practices. We could take the signifiers *child*, *teacher*, and *girl*, or the dichotomies *active/passive*, *rote-learning/real understanding* as examples. We can ask how these contradictions are lived and how they affect the production of subjectivity: for example fears, desires and fantasies (Walkerdine, 1985).

First, and most important, there are no unitary categories *boys* and *girls*. If actual boys and girls are created at the intersection of multiple positioning, they are inscribed as masculine and feminine. It follows, therefore, that girls can display *real understanding* or boys *nurturance*. What matters is the effects of these positions. We shall explore later how some rare girls do indeed appear to display that combination of qualities that makes them both the 'ideal girl' and the 'ideal child'. We shall concentrate here on the designation *rote-learning* and its related signifiers *rule-following, hard work,* and *passivity*.

At first sight it seems curious that such qualities could be displayed within a pedagogy designed specifically to produce their opposite and to avoid their appearance at all costs. In classroom discourse itself there appears to be an overt message about activity, exploration, openness, derived from child-centred pedagogy. However, our work in primary classrooms suggests that the discourse of good behaviour, neatness, and rule-following exists *covertly* alongside overt messages. It has to be covert because it is the exact opposite of what is supposed to take place. Moreover, all those aspects — good behaviour, neatness, and rule-following — are considered harmful to psychological and moral development. Thus they act as a fear- and guilt-inducing opposite. It is not surprising that teachers cannot afford to acknowledge the presence of such qualities in the classroom or, if they do, that they pathologize their appearance in girls, while failing to recognize that they are demanding the very qualities they simultaneously disparage. This allows us to explore how girls come to desire in themselves qualities that appear to be the opposite of those that the pedagogy is set up to produce.

We shall take this analysis a little further, using the distinctions *work/play*, *rote-learning/rule-following* and *real understanding*. *Work* forms a relation in the 'old discourse'. In the new, children learn through doing, activity and *play*. For example, the whole of the scheme *Early Mathematical Experiences* is founded upon play as a device for Mathematics learning:

> It was found that there were many different methods of presenting activities and learning situations to the children, but these could be grouped loosely into four main categories:
>
> 1 Children playing freely with as many activities and materials as possible, with adult intervention.
> 2 Children playing with materials which had been deliberately provided by teachers to encourage the acquisition of certain concepts, but still without adult intervention.
> 3 Children playing with materials of their own choice with the active participation of an adult.
> 4 Children playing with materials which had been selected by a teacher who was leading and guiding them towards the acquisition of certain facts.
> (Matthews and Matthews, 1978)

Work forms an opposition to this. Work is bad, because it relates to sitting in rows, regurgitating 'facts to be stored', not 'concepts to be acquired' through active exploration of the environment. *Work*, then, forms a metaphoric relation with *rote-learning* and *rule-following*. Each describes a practice, a mode of learning, which is opposite and antithetical to the 'joy of discovery'. Play is fun. Other aspects of work could be further elaborated: it leads to resistance. Children regulated in this way do not become self-regulating (Walkerdine, 1984). But *work* is also a category to be outlawed by a system of education set up in opposition to child labour. It frees *the child* to be something distinct, playful, not an adult, outside productive labour, innocent, natural. A series of values, fantasies, fears and desires is incorporated into the discursive practices. Multiple significations connect, weaving in and out. It follows that *work*, as an opposite of *play*, can be recognized as everything which does not signify play. It is also recognized as a danger point to be avoided. It is pathologized. It is learning by the wrong means. It is not *natural to the child*. If any child is observed 'doing work' this is likely to be understood as a problem. Hence the distinction between *rote-learning* and *real understanding* discussed in the last chapter.

What happens when a child produces high attainment as well as behaviour to be read as *work*? If play is the discourse of the school, through what discourse do children read their performance? If *real understanding* is coterminous with the fantasy of possessing total power and control, how is it distinguished and what is the relation of this to 'getting the right answer', 'being certain'? How does *possession of real understanding* provide a fantasy, a chimera, which has constantly and continually to exist out of a terror that lurking around every corner is its other: *rote-learning, work*? Why is there such remorseless and unrelenting pressure to 'prove' that real understanding causes real attainment and that certain children have *it* while others just as surely do not, despite high attainment?

One feature of the apparatuses and technologies of the social, the modern production of truth through science, is that *proof* and practices for the production of evidence are central. The certainty of 'real understanding' is ceaselesly proved, though the evidence is often ambiguous. Here we want to dwell not so much on the evidence itself as on the question of the motivation to provide proof — in particular on the opposition of *work* and *play*, *rote* and *real*.

Now, if the power of control over the universe invested in mathematical discourse is a fantasy, we are not setting out to demonstrate the *reality* or *prove* that girls *really can* do Maths or boys actually *do not* have real understanding. Rather, we are interested in how those categories are produced as signs and how they 'catch up' the subjects, position them and so create a truth. For if girls bid for *understanding*, is that not the greatest threat of all to a universal power or a truth that is invested with a fantasy control of 'woman'? Teachers will often go to great lengths to demonstrate that boys have real understanding. By the metaphoric chain created, *activity* is frequently read as a sign of understanding. Understanding, then, is evidenced by the presence of some attributes and the absence of others. Activity — playing, making use of objects (Lego, for example), rule-breaking (rather than rule-following) — may encompass naughtiness, even displays of hostility and conflict towards the teacher. All these and more are taken as evidence. Conversely, good behaviour in girls, working hard, helpfulness, neat and careful work, are all read as danger signals of a lack. The counter-evidence — hard work in boys and understanding in girls — is also produced as evidence, but then other disparaging factors are brought into play (see Walkerdine, 1984).

Evidence of real understanding emerges from a set of practices in which *real understanding* is the goal of an explicit framework of 'activities' set up, as in all our examples. Then it becomes possible to read off the correct accomplishment as the result of understanding, and failure as produced by a lack of the requisite experience, readiness and concepts. Finally, the likelihood of one explanation of success being favoured rather than another depends upon the characteristics which define a real learner.

One of the central features of the logico-mathematical discourse is the production of formal logic, modes of making a case, constructing an argument: rational argument (see Walkerdine, 1988). An argument, therefore, apparently has as its component the ultimate in rationality, conducted by experts — power through the winning mode of argument: the mastery of its form. Yet, as we shall elaborate, it is replete with conflict. The destruction of the other is both feared and desired — necessary, but removed from the form and content of the discourse itself. It is a contest for control, a struggle for power. In these accounts of the production of rational argument relating to home and early education, a central component in the production of the 'capacity' for such argument is how conflict is controlled. In the home, mothers are encouraged to deflect overt conflict so that the child feels it has free will: conflict is channelled into reasoned argument, not fighting. Walkerdine and Lucey (1989) maintain that this transformation is central to the production of the reasoning and reasonable citizen. In school the old methods of rigid, hierarchical organization and overt discipline gave way to a more invisible form of power: again, conflict between teacher and pupil becomes displaced on to rational argument, in which a central trope is the illusion of 'control' (Newson and Newson, 1976).

The practices centre more and more on rendering invisible the power relation and offering the child an elaborate fantasy of omnipotence, mastery, control. The Newsons present this as engineering disciplinary conflicts so that the child believes itself to have 'chosen' the solution, rather than suffered its external imposition. Conflict becomes 'feelings'. The child is so positioned as to have not 'seen' power, and believes itself the originator, the controller of its actions, its choice. This powerful illusion of choice and control over one's destiny is therefore centrally implicated in the concept of 'rational argument'.

This displacement goes further when power is invested in 'winning' the argument. The rationally ordered child can rationally order in return. There is no 'authority' outside the mastery of the form of the discourse itself. This is vital, for it is central to the modern pedagogic practices of 'disciplining' and means that regulation can be accomplished by rational argument. The teacher's power, then, is invested only in that mastery: not in hierarchy, policing, or other methods of government. Challenging the claim to know is thereby central. However, it seems that it must be supported by certain key features. The learner must recognize, or join in, the illusion of choice and control; feel secure in making a challenge — albeit replete with conflict — to authority. S/he must not, therefore, be afraid, but rather welcome such a challenge. These criteria are central to modern discursive practices: the illusion of choice, security and safety are key features of 'correct' classroom life.

The facilitating and nurturant other is necessary, in both domestic and pedagogic practices, to a naturalized sequence of development in the child. From this it follows that *the child* as signifier within the circulation of meaning in developmental psychology, family and pedagogic practices sits uncomfortably upon actual little girls, for if *woman* is other to rationality, its support and facilitation, how is *girl* lived: as *child* or as potential *woman?* Certain contradictions in these positions are lived out in the very practices for delivering mathematical attainment.

Let us explore two aspects of this. First, girls' attainment, relative to boys', is itself not in any simple or general sense the problem. Rather, the indicated cause invests the attainment with value as reproduction (rote-learning, rule-following) and not production (real understanding). It follows, therefore, that this very attainment, the object of much agonizing about girls' poor performance, is precisely the one required for girls' entry into the 'caring professions'; in this case, specifically, the profession of teaching young children. Recruitment to elementary teacher training in Britain requires advanced qualifications, but usually at a lower standard than for university entrance.

Second, the production of reasoning requires an investment of desire in knowing, as in the phrase 'love of learning', for example. Rational argument requires the transformation of conflict into discourse so that the nurturant other facilitates an illusion of autonomy or control, rendering invisible the power of parenting and teaching. Moreover, mathematical reasoning presumes mastery of a discourse in which the universe is knowable and manipulable according to particular algorithms. This , along with the production of hard 'facts', is usually understood as the very basis of certainty. However, we might understand it as the fear, the need for proof against the terror of the other — the terror of loss of certainty, of control: an attempted control of loss. We might understand it as the impossibility of the object of desire, 'woman', and elaborate fantasies to control consequent desire and avoid dependency or powerlessness.

In modern British elementary schooling, the 'nature of the child' is the bedrock of all educational practice. Practice is devoted to the monitoring, observing and facilitating of the sequence of development. The dichotomy between rote-learning and real understanding, activity and passivity, appears also in the shift from the old 'traditional' pedagogy to modern 'child-centred' practices. Teaching and the transmission of facts were condemned as regimenting and stifling discipline; they were replaced by a classroom in which everyone was to learn at their own pace (Walkerdine, 1984). Into this new pedagogy was built the shadow of its other: the old chalk-and-talk, the fearful and dangerous spectre of authoritarianism. Thus any evidence of rote-learning was taken to be not only success for the wrong reason but a danger signal threatening the moral order, a pathology to be remedied. It is important to understand the location of this feared and frightening other within those classifications, particularly when they relate to girls' performance. Yet, as we have argued, these contradictions set girls up to achieve the very thing which is simultaneously desired and feared: passivity. It is feared in 'children', yet it is the very quality desired in nurturant care-givers, women as mothers and teachers.

4   Mothers and Daughters at Four

Many approaches to the issue of girls' performance in Mathematics imply that problems in early socialization may produce performance differences in adolescence. This link between early childhood and adolescence is not new; it is often assumed that 'problems' at this time have been caused by pathologies in the mother–child relationship. This argument is extended in two ways: to make early experiences salient in later educational success, and to suggest that children acquire roles from agents of socialization, particularly parents, and that early feminine stereotyping will later produce stereotyped performance. In this chapter we shall look at some of the arguments about mothers' preparation of girls for school and for Mathematics. Much of the literature (see, for example, Hartnett, Boden and Fuller, 1979) holds mothers responsible for the provision of the correct early socialization environment for a daughter: one which will allow her to develop the propensities necessary for success in Mathematics and at school generally. The following account is taken largely from an analysis of transcripts of conversations between 30 white mothers and their 4-year-old daughters, the sample stratified by social class. The discussion is taken from a much longer and more detailed treatment of these cases (Walkerdine and Lucey, 1989). However, our account does not provide much support for commonly held views about stereotyping, play, conditioning and so on. It suggests a far more complex process, ensnaring both mothers and daughters, which offers no simple support for the 'wrong experiences' type of approach.

We want to concentrate here on the way in which routine accounts of intellectual development emphasizing a naturally occurring development of logico-mathematical structures do so by sleight of hand. The activities which are supposed to be a part of every small child's day turn out to be produced through a transformation of women's domestic labour into playful learning. We cannot date this shift exactly, but we know that the mother became a pedagogue at about the time when mothering became a naturalized phenomenon. Her role as pedagogue is crucial, for it gives her the task of making the world safe for democracy by ensuring the correct development of her children. In the liberal order it is she who bears the burden of her child's success and failure, and we shall see that non-feminist and feminist arguments alike join forces in holding the mother responsible for her daughter's future success or failure.

If we examine the kinds of tasks which are supposed to aid the intellectual development of young children, we find that they are almost all routine domestic tasks transformed into a pedagogy in which the mother can engage while she is, for instance, making the family meal. The following example, taken from a suggested school handout to parents on early Mathematics, makes this clear:

You are probably helping your child to get ready for Mathematics in many ways, maybe without realising it! Here are some of the many activities that you can do *with your child* which will help. Laying the table — counting, getting the knives in the right place, etc.

> Going shopping — handling money, counting items in basket.
> Dressing and undressing — sorting clothes into piles.
> Helping with cooking — weighing, measuring.
> Playing with water — at bathtime, washing up.
> Tidying away toys.
> *Left* and *right* games.
> Spotting shapes (circles, squares, etc.), colours, comparing sizes, etc., whether
>   at home or on walks . . .

But don't turn it into a lesson [emphasis added]. All these things can be done incidentally as a part of day to day events. (Matthews and Matthews, 1978)

How can women's domestic labour have been naturalized so that it becomes understood not as work but as a central aspect of natural mother-love, essential to the production of educational success? We want to examine the part mothers are supposed to play in the mathematical success of their daughters and to demonstrate some of the problems in growing up which daughters have to face.

On one level you might say that finding the principles of intellectual development in the routine activities of women's domestic labour is demonstrating that such activities or experiences are everywhere. But we could ask deeper questions: Why is domestic labour transformed into the very basis of children's cognitive development, and what is the relationship between this and the idea that the sensitive mother is necessary to meet the child's intellectual and emotional needs? To answer this, we must examine how domestic work became mothering, first looking at the terms on which 'women's work' as a specific category has come to be understood in feminist literature, and then discussing the relationship between housework and mothering.

We would argue that we can no longer differentiate between the physical tasks which make up women's housework and the work of mothering. The two are the same. By using extracts from conversations between mothers and daughters while they were sitting together, eating lunch or writing out a shopping list, we can show how the work of mothering goes on, even though the event may be the result or the prelude to domestic labour in a crude sense (cooking the dinner or doing the shopping).

Housework can no longer be seen simply as physical, 'valueless' drudgery, designed for the constant maintenance and reproduction of an exploited workforce. These tasks are not just keeping the house clean, the family healthy and fed and fit for another day's work. They have another function, ignored or missed by the domestic labour debate.

This transformation of housework into playful learning was most evident in transcripts of middle-class families. Given that this idea of intellectual development has become a 'truth' routinely incorporated into educational, social welfare and medical practices alike, why has this not been uniformly taken up within the house-holds in the sample? Here we are concerned to explore why we *see*, in some working-class households, women whose day is one continual round of domestic chores, the constraints of which are painfully evident to both mother and daughter (not to mention the researcher); whereas in most middle-class homes there is no sense of drudgery, of not having enough hours in the day. We *find* and *read* a relaxed mother creating a relaxed and unharried environment, yet of course most of these women have to do cleaning, cooking, shopping, and so on.

Naomi's mother lectured in English one-and-a-half days a week, had two pre-school children and was expecting twins in a few months, yet her work remains hidden and does not intrude on the day we witness in the transcript. Was her organization so radically different from that of Jacky's mother, who also works, this time at home as a childminder, and has a young baby, but who, although she and Jacky have a friendly relationship, makes her work apparent and gets it done? When did Naomi's mother fit in all her chores? In the evening, for example?

To demonstrate how this invisibility is achieved we will listen to Sarah and her mother, who gets her to clean out the fish-tank and sets up the task of transfer-ring the goldfish back into the clean tank as a logic problem for the child.

> M: Now, how are we going to get the fish out of the big bowl and into the little one, d'you think?
> C: I know, well we get a thing and then we put some water in it and then put it into there. Catch the fish.
> M: And catch the fish?
> C: Yes.
> M: How about something like that?
> (M holds up a plastic pot.)
> C: Yes, I think that would do. Wash it out!

Notice how the mother transforms the task into an educational one from which Sarah can learn about capacity, size and even more complex mathematical concepts such as the effect of refraction through glass and water on the size of objects:

> M: They look a bit bigger through their glass, don't they?
> C: Yes.
> M: Even the small one looks pretty big, doesn't it?
> C: Through the glass.
> M: Look over the top and see if it looks different.
> C: No, that one's little now, when I look from the top. And it's bigger when I look from . . . through the glass.

We have argued that women's domestic labour has become the basis of modern ideas about how children learn, so that tasks taken to aid the accomplishment of intellectual development are nearly all domestic. But the interpretation is that cog-nitive development is everywhere and therefore anything can form the basis of an intellectual task. The mode of analysis which sees tasks as embodiments of a particular structure of action and of thought conceals the fact that they are domestic, and that women must aid their children's development by transforming their domestic labour into a pedagogy. Of course, not *all* housework is endlessly transformed in this way: obviously at times the children are not around. But from these examples we can begin to see how these women's housework may become hidden and transformed into the very basis on which they are judged to be sensitive mothers, because in responding to children's 'needs', they are aiding their development.

We can immediately see how something as pressing as domestic work could conflict with the demands of a small child, but the sensitive mother must be constantly ready to meet needs. Theories of child development stress the importance of a 'free atmosphere', in which the child can explore and discover. How sharply this notion contradicts the equally powerful idea of the 'ideal home', always clean and well ordered. We can see, then, that the sensitive mother must walk a tightrope of conflicting and impossible demands. Her work becomes the basis of the child's play. This, we found, was much more common in middle-class homes. On the other hand, in working-class homes especially, the time distinction between the mother's housework and play with her daughter is much more marked. Let us take a closer look at what we mean by the mother transforming her labour into the foundation of play. Sarah does not work at cleaning the fish-tank: it becomes a kind of game. This is just as it should be! Many developmental texts insist that 'play is the proper medium of expression for children'. Many curriculum materials for young children exemplify the idea that every task must be presented as play and not as work.

Housework appears to be a far less pressing demand in middle-class homes. It can be and frequently is abandoned in favour of the daughters' demands for help, attention or for a playmate. While a few working-class mothers certainly do no housework during the afternoons of the recordings, this is not the norm. Most make their domestic labour apparent and a priority over the child's demands, especially to play. On the other hand, middle-class mothers seem to find it even more difficult to refuse their daughters' requests to play — even when, on occasion, they make it clear that they have housework to do (see Boulton, 1983). Some do attempt to resist such demands, saying how busy they are, but the strategy we wish to explore here — which more middle-class mothers use — is to incorporate housework into play.

Penny and her mother have been playing a card game called 'Jumble Sales', but when it is finished Penny insists that they play another game:

    C: I said, what are you going to play with? Mummy?
    M: Don't want to play with anything. I . . . I should do some cooking really.
    C: No.
    M: Get the dinner ready . . .
    C: No.

Her mother complies and Penny initiates a fantasy game, into which her mother is drawn. Eventually she decides that she must get on with preparing dinner and ends the fantasy episode by saying:

M: Would you like me to make you some pastry?

C: Oh yes! (squeals)

M: Don't scream! You can make . . . you can play with the pastry while I do some cooking.

It is interesting that this task begins with Penny's nagging for play and her mother's ineffectual resistance. Now, developmental accounts would point precisely to how much Penny learned from 'helping mummy cook': the valuable mathematical concepts of shape, size and quantity in making and manipulating the pastry. There might indeed be such concepts involved in domestic work, but this description converts the practice into a logico-mathematical structure and masks precisely the transformation that is going on, insisting on proclaiming such structures without examining the content from which they are abstracted. Thus the account misses the point we are trying to make: the mother is forced to make her domestic work the basis of her daughter's play and in this way may be seen as sensitive to her needs and aiding her development.

Charlotte's mother is considered sensitive by Tizard and Hughes (1984). Charlotte constantly asks questions which her mother answers patiently and explicitly. Throughout the afternoon, she engages Charlotte in essentially domestic tasks — some commonplace, like helping mummy put the shopping away; others involving making things. Charlotte helps her mother to make muesli, and this becomes a site for number work. Unlike Penny's mother, she does not have to resist her daughter's demands because she immediately and consistently sets up what she must get done alongside strategies for amusing her. This form of mixing domestic work and play forms a particular mode of regulation, a way of disciplining the child.

A mother who resists her daughter's demands is in a difficult position, for she may be judged insensitive, not helping her development and not allowing her autonomy: making her feel powerless (Newson and Newson, 1976). So what can she do? Either she must find some way of giving in, like incorporating the demand into her work, or she must reason with the child, explain to her, which may not work.

Emily's mother tries to resist her insistence that they play another game by explaining patiently how she must 'get on' and carefully suggesting they play the game after lunch:

C: Shall we play — Mummy, I want you to play this with me.

M: All right . . . No, shall we . . . shall we start our lunch and play it afterwards? Do you think?

C: No . . . Orange, blue, yellow, green, red.
   (c has already got the game out and is pointing to different coloured clowns on the box.)

M: Shall we do our lunch and then do it afterwards?

C: No.

M: I think it's going to take us rather a long time, that game.

C: No! (screams)

Working-class women like Emily's mother tend to regulate and discipline their daughters in a completely different way which makes strong distinctions between domestic work and play and delineates clearly that domestic work has to be accomplished in a specific time, usually before father gets home or she has to go off to work. This means that it is important that the child does not interfere, can learn to play by herself, to be self-reliant. Thus if she does interfere she can be told not to be demanding. So the mother makes her power explicit, especially her power to withhold her attention. So, while working-class mothers do use domestic settings to 'teach' their daughters, they do not do it as often and they are much more likely *successfully* to resist the child's demands. They do not use such instances as regulative devices. So the daughter is also learning a very important lesson, some new concepts, but they are different lessons, different concepts, in different circumstances from her middle-class counterpart:

NICKY: I wanna do some painting.
M: I've gotta do washing first, then we'll do painting.

This is a very different scene to middle-class homes, where helping mum make muesli becomes a rich educational and social context in which the child can interact, talk and learn. Joanne wants her mother to come and look at what she is playing with. She calls for her.

M: I said I'll come and see you in a minute when I've done this. Won't be a minute, I must do some washing first or else I'll get shot.

A very different picture from the one where helping mum put old Christmas cards away becomes a counting exercise while the mother, as an incidental bonus, can at the same time complete her chores — but, much more importantly, where the pair can 'discover' mutuality.

SALLY: Are you going to sit down with me?
M: Not yet, I'm going to peel . . . finish peeling the potatoes.

In contrast there is no sense in the middle-class transcripts of the harassed housewife, the 'drudge'; middle-class women can be read as discovering both the mutual enjoyment of time spent with their daughters and that housework *can* be fun! We gain a different sense of what time means in such homes. There is *more* time — to talk, play, explain, explore and enjoy. Or is there? Later we will see just how much *hard-work* goes into this apparently effortless scene.

It is important to note here that a few working-class mothers did little or no housework during the recordings and spent almost the entire afternoon playing with their daughters. Conversely, a small minority of middle-class mothers spent little time playing compared to the rest. However, in the majority of working-class homes housework was evidently quite separate from — and had priority over — play. This apparent contradiction between work and play becomes the site for much resistance between mother and daughter. The working-class girls did make more demands than the middle-class girls, but crucially, their mothers successfully resisted them much more frequently. So while middle-class girls appeared less demanding, we would argue that this is because their mothers actually gave in to them more frequently.

The separation of work and play in working-class homes, and the incorporation of work and play through the transformation of domestic labour in middle-class homes, are crucial in examining the construction of the 'good mother'. But many questions remain to be asked. Why do middle-class mothers achieve this shift in their labour, blurring the distinction between work and play so that they *can* be sensitive mothers as well as good housewives? Why cannot working-class mothers do the same?

Mothers' facilitation of young children's play became loaded with all the investments we described in the last chapter. Throughout the 1960s and 1970s such notions were popularized, and special 'educational' toys and kinds of play were favoured. These were usually those which were supposed to aid language, cognitive development and educational success. More than anything, however, play was the opposite of work because it was pleasurable and intrinsically motivating, just as mothering was not seen as work either, but as 'love'. On this basis, it became impossible for mothers guiltlessly to extricate themselves from so monumental a role.

Play and learning, then, become inseparable. The learning environment becomes the entire home; every possible permutation of events, actions and conversations becomes a 'not-to-be-missed' opportunity for a valuable lesson. But this lesson cannot be discovered by the child alone. It must be directed carefully and sensitively taught by the good mother who must always be there. So not only the 'formal' lesson or the 'educational game' but imaginative play, mealtimes, housework, conversations, questions, demands, resistance and arguments *all* become sites of learning . It is therefore not so difficult to see why middle-class mothers especially allow their time and space to be invaded much more than working-class mothers and how, also, mothers who readily give up their own work to talk, play and rationalize with their daughters are 'read' by the researcher as *sensitive*, constantly attuned to their daughters' needs. We do not see a woman who is, in a very real sense, chained by an awareness of her child's cognitive and developmental 'needs' and of how she fits into fulfilling them, but a relaxed and nurturant facilitator. In short, we see but one facet of the fantasy mother.

Housework, by its transformation, has achieved a different value. An inadequate view of it in terms of 'reproducing' the labour force glosses over too easily the differences between women's labour and what housework means to women of different classes. Housework oppresses, of that we are sure, but not in a universal way. Both working-class and middle-class women must get their work *done*, but middle-class women must also make it *fun*. So the relationship between work and play, work and time relates both pairs to the women's different circumstances — to their work, their wealth and poverty, but also to the way in which these are cross-cut by women's understanding and familiarity with modern accounts of child development (Urwin, 1985). Housework becomes fun, and learning is accomplished through play. Now you see it, now you don't. Is the sensitive mother only a sleight of hand? A conjurer, pulling play out of work, like a rabbit out of a hat?

Given that modern psychological and developmental theories are integrated into the common sense of mothering, the bedrock of liberal training in the caring professions, it is hardly surprising that some feminists seized on an environmental approach, amenable to change. Unfortunately, that creates a series of problems for feminism, by firmly rooting the mother as both cause of and solution to women's problems. This empiricism is worrying on several grounds. First, because it presents a fantasy of mothers solving patriarchy at a stroke by getting mothering right, and second, because it entails a kind of predictive tendency which reads off the surface of socialization, assumes it to work and then charts its effects in girls' future educational success. This kind of approach is ubiquitous in the debates about girls and Mathematics and girls and education more generally. We are deeply critical of this empiricist reading and its attendant woman-blaming.

Mothers are often held responsible for preparing their daughters for school, but here we want to examine the effects for the daughter of the prospect of leaving her mother to face growing up and away from her to enter the world of the school outside. Here the idea of separation comes in. Many accounts suggest that mother and daughter must have 'bonded' sufficiently to allow the daughter to separate from the mother to grow up to independence and autonomy. However, this does not at all engage with the fact that when girls go to school they enter into another set of practices in which they are positioned as children. How, then, do the mothers and daughters in our study make sense of this transition, and how is it lived?

We frequently observed that girls resisted the notion of growing up. This resistance was expressed in various ways: by a refusal to perform practical tasks for themselves or for their mothers; by maintaining a 'helpless' position, saying things like 'I *can't* . . .' — do my buttons up, reach the cupboard, and so on. Some girls want to be carried, held all the time, they do not want to walk. This hostility to the idea of growing up often involved jealousy of a sibling — sometimes, but not always, a younger one. In general, though, we can say that some girls expressed desires to stay 'little babies'.

Our evidence suggests that it is not only *older* siblings, faced with a new born brother or sister, who 'imitate' babies (see Dunn, 1984). Some girls in our study were themselves the youngest, but displayed very 'babyish' or infantile behaviour. An account which reduces this to 'modelling' and 'imitation' loses the crucial dimensions of power and emotion; of understanding the child's *investment* in remaining a helpless baby. For there is, indeed, much to be gained from this position. Girls who avoid growing up and doing things for themselves, who are waited on by their mothers, can wield great power. Such work also neglects the possibility of the girl not *wanting* to separate from her mother: not because her needs are going unmet, but because the forfeiting of such a powerful position is too frightening. Let us look at the sorts of strategies some girls use to regulate their mothers and remain helpless.

Amanda is playing a word puzzle with her mother. It is obvious from Amanda's fidgeting that she wants to go to the toilet, but despite her mother's coaxing, she steadfastly refuses to go.

    M: Darling, if you're going to walk about like that, we must go upstairs. Now
        come on, Amanda . . .

    C: No . . . Nooo!

    M: It'll be much better. Then you can enjoy it, because you're just . . . I know
        you . . . come on.

    C: Nooo . . .

    M: Come on!

    C: No, no, no, no, no!

    M: Otherwise . . .

    C: No, no, no, no . . . Ah, err . . . no!

    M: Come on, you've got to go upstairs. You're just being silly now.

    C: Nooo!

The power of Amanda's resistance is enormous. By steadfastly refusing her mother's reasonable coaxing, she is eventually positioned as a baby, for at this point her mother carries her upstairs, undresses her and sits her on the toilet, brings books in to her, and when she has finished, wipes her bottom. In a complex way, Amanda's powerful resistance to going to the toilet could be construed as a resistance to self-sufficiency, taking responsibility for her own body.

'Helplessness' as a strategy for regulating the mother, for getting her to 'service' the child, is not confined to middle-class girls. Kerry's mother is designated 'sensitive' and spends most of the afternoon playing with and amusing her daughter. Even though Kerry has her mother's attention almost all the time, she behaves quite helplessly on occasion, often getting her mother to perform tasks that she herself could quite easily do. For instance, Kerry is sitting at the dining table eating lunch, while her mother sits with her, drinking tea or coffee. The television is on and they discuss the puppet show and how the hand-puppets work. Casually, Kerry asks her mother to feed her.

    M: No, he puts his hand inside . . . puts his hand inside . . . and then he makes the
        puppet move . . . and then he talks . . . and it looks as though . . .

    C: Feed me. (*c* gives *m* the fork.)

    M: . . . the puppets [are] talking . . .

With only the slightest halt or faltering in the conversation, Kerry asks to be fed and her mother complies, feeding her as if she were a baby. But Kerry is *no* baby. She becomes powerful enough to tell her mother what food and how much to put on the fork:

    C: Put one more on . . .

    M: No, you can't put too much in your mouth.

    C: Yes, did you put that other . . .

    M: All right.

    C: . . . did you put some egg on?

    M: All right . . . nice?

Cathy Urwin (1984) outlines how young children can take positions in discourse which regulate the mother, on whom they are dependent. This provides a fiction of power and control for them, masking their vulnerability. Regulating the mother who regulates you *is* very powerful. Thus being helpless, attempting to remain a baby, is not simply a learned and reinforced behaviour but can be the site of enormous power and the refusal of the terror and pain of losing mother. Simultaneously, of course, daughters' growing up may be very painful for mothers. When we talk about a 'struggle', it is not only the girls' struggle to grow up which is significant. There is the struggle between mother and daughter, and in addition there is the struggle of the woman herself. For many women who long for the sensations of satisfaction, pleasure, being needed, having an important job to do, that children can provide, it is very hard to let their daughters become 'big girls'. If the modern concept of sensitive mothering sets so much store by mothers as guardians of the future social order, this makes mothering important.

The Meanings of Growing Up

What does it mean, therefore, to be a child from the viewpoint of the adult women, the mothers in our study? These mothers, interacting with their daughters, give them covert and overt meanings and rules through which they are to understand what it means to be a child and what and how a child should be. These meanings — for example, what it means to be big and to be little — are also, of course, the supposed stuff of pre-Mathematics. They are 'mathematical meanings'; so we move on to another aspect of the mother's preparation of her daughter for school: the generation and development of word meaning.

These are different for working- and middle-class girls: indeed they are more or less the converse of each other. Basically, middle-class mothers tend to sanction physical dependency, yet push their daughters hard to be intellectually independent. Conversely, working-class mothers tend to expect physical self-reliance and are much more willing to allow that their 'little' daughters 'do not know' about intellectual matters. This is perhaps most starkly expressed in Amanda's case — her mother tolerates and sanctions her failure to be able to wipe her own bottom, while this girl has a reading age way above her chronological age and is pushed by her mother to achieve more. There is therefore a stark contrast between permitted kinds of 'childishness' and what counts as adult behaviour.

It is important to note here that the working-class girls more frequently expressed desires to remain babies than the middle-class girls. This point needs some clarification, as it is also true that the middle-class girls were more often likely to display dependency and helplessness, and to insist that they couldn't achieve some task (usually practical) by themselves. While the working-class girls more often *openly* expressed their wish to be helpless babies, this wish was consistently — although not always successfully— resisted by their mothers. It is these situations that the pair big girl/baby was most frequently evoked, though not always in these exact terms:

> *M:* Nicky, you're not helpless, you're three years old, you can quite . . . all that . . . go up the stairs and put 'em in yourself.
> *C:* I can't!
> *M:* You're not a baby.
> *C:* I am, I am . . .
> *M:* If you wanna act like a baby, Mummy'll treat you like a baby.

Being 'a big girl' is closely linked with growing up and, characteristically, maturity relates to physicality and self-reliance, *not* to intellectuality. Being a baby, therefore — helpless, wanting to be carried — is not a position which these working-class girls are so easily allowed to occupy. Their mothers will not and cannot let them. Instead, they need their daughters to be self-reliant:

> *M:* I'm not touching it, I told you . . . you've got two good legs yourself, go and put it up yourself.

Middle-class girls can take a position of helplessness because their mothers stress *intellectual* self-reliance. The helpless behaviour marked in the working-class transcripts by struggle and resistance is dealt with quite differently. It is not seen as punitive, unlike a working-class mother refusing to help her daughter get dressed. For example, working-class mothers tend to resist their daughters' demands by teasingly calling them 'baby', a pejorative term. While this strategy is unsuccessful in that it does not curb the girls' demands, the mothers do not 'give in'. For middle-class mothers, however, there is not the same investment in resisting the child's desires to be a baby:

> *M:* What do you want, darling?
> *C:* Some of Ribena in the little bottle, some Ribena in the little bottle. (She is given a baby's bottle.)
> *M:* There you are, baby.

Working-class mothers stress physical independence. Big girls can keep out of mum's way when she is busy, play by themselves, go to the toilet unaided, wash their own hands. They can 'look after themselves' in the home, and learn how to survive in the dangerous world outside. There are also strong elements of nurturance, for big girls look after not only themselves but others too, often helping mum in caring for younger siblings. There is no simple helplessness for either set of girls, but the different terms do key into differences made by schools, which tend to expect intellectuality from middle-class girls and teacherly helpfulness from working-class girls.

Moreover, the 'mathematical terms' relating to size learnt here obviously have connotations quite outside those of school Mathematics, but how are the emotions and anxiety within those meanings present or absent there? In Chapter 6 we examine how school mathematical discourse produces forms devoid of referential content, how their emotional content is suppressed in the production of the mathematical string itself, and the effect for the fantasy of mastery embodied within such discourse.

Mathematical meanings — indeed, the development of language and word meanings in general — cannot be separated from the practices in which the girls grow up. The mother is positioned as regulative in these practices, in which desires, fears and fantasies are deeply involved. So 'mathematical meanings' are not simply intellectual, nor are they comprehensible outside the practices of their production. Yet in school this is precisely what happens to them. Children have to learn that there are special meanings to these terms, which are not necessarily those used at home. These meanings lead to the generation of mathematical statements of enormous power, because they can relate to anything (see Walkerdine, 1988). All the meanings at home are produced in aspects of domestic regulation. For example, taking the pair *more/less*, all instances of *more* in these transcripts come from the mother's regulation of the child's consumption of commodities and are therefore part of her regulation of the domestic economy. We analysed the transcripts of recordings of 30 mother–daughter pairs by Professor Barbara Tizard (see also Walkerdine, 1988; Walkerdine and Lucey, 1989) to draw out all occurrences of *more* and *less*. While there were many examples of *more*, *less* did not occur once. At first one might think that this is because *more* is a semantically easier term than *less* and therefore acquired first. However, this interpretation is not so easily supported when it is noted that all instances of *more* come from mother–daughter exchanges where the daughter's consumption of scarce or expensive resources and food is regulated by the mother:

> *c:* I want some more.
> *m:* No, you can't have any more, Em.
> *c:* Yes! Only one biscuit.
> *m:* No.
> *c:* Half a biscuit?
> *m:* No.
> *c:* A little of a biscuit?
> *m:* No.
> *c:* A whole biscuit?
> *m:* No.
> *c:* Who gave you that? (Cleaning fluid for sink.)
> *m:* Granny gave me that little bit 'cause I ran out.
> *c:* Has you still got some more?
> *m:* Hm?
> *c:* Have you still got some more?
> *m:* Just enough for today and get some more tomorrow.

The dimension of *less* is simply not relevant. The opposite of *more* in food regulative practices is something like *no more, not as much,* and so on. *More* and *less* form a contrastive oppositional pair only with respect to certain practices, and these practices are pedagogic.

It is striking that almost all the examples of *more* from this corpus relate to the regulation of consumption. In every case initiated by the child, she either wants more precious commodities on which the mother sees it as her duty to limit consumption, or does not want to finish food which the mother sees it as her duty to make her eat. Here these terms act as relations of signification within practices where the mother's domestic labour embodies meanings which regulate the child. Thus, for the girls they carry strong emotional and regulative content and act as signifiers in very different relations from the word pair *more/less* as used in school Mathematics. Again, though, shifts from these practices and emotions to understanding 'mathematical terms' — in this case the *more/less* pair in terms of the comparison of quantities — will have to be accomplished. This is usually thought of as an abstract aspect of children's natural development, which has nothing to do with the specificities of women's domestic labour.

Most accounts of little girls growing up *are* accounts of socialization which assume that girls are successfully stereotyped into roles. This is partly the consequence of an assumed empiricism. You read the *surface* (the manifest content) of the observations of these little girls and their families, their homes, their schools, and you see with much empirical clarity 'socialization going on'. Empirical modes within psychology and sociology, then, use socialization approaches to posit cause and effect, but as we have begun to show here, these approaches are inadequate. Socialization, if it is ever achieved at all, is a struggle. Women are consistently positioned as lacking, as abnormal, and this has painful effects on their insertion into practices which regulate them, as we shall see. Gender and class divisions cannot easily be crossed. When girls go to school, these fantasies are realized, since in the classroom something is usually found to be wrong with them. 'Failure' is lived as difference, and difference as pathology.

The mother is often held responsible for producing the correct early environment that allows her children to 'separate' from her. This separation then paves the way for independence and autonomy, which leads to educational success. We have stressed that separation, leaving home, involves entering a difficult world of difference, division, otherness, and that theories of separation hold the mother responsible without dealing with these issues. That leaving home *is* difficult, painful and different for the different groups of girls is something we wish to explore here. Their mothers are set up as guarantors of a certainty which, in practice, they cannot produce.

The working-class mother is seen as *lacking*. Primary schools hold that working-class parents 'get it wrong'. They do not 'understand children's needs' and are blamed either for *not* helping their children or for doing it in the wrong way. They teach them sums instead of letting them explore concepts; they buy the wrong books and toys. The whole discourse of parental involvement assumes that teachers must teach parents (almost always mothers) how to prepare and help their children. The target is, almost invariably, black and white working-class parents. There is no sense of listening to and learning from these parents; they are already defined as wrong and reactionary (see Craft, 1980; Becher, 1981; Clift, 1981).

But the working-class mothers who 'lack' also know a lot, as we have seen. They prepare their daughters for the world as they know it; but this is a frightening lesson, not a cosy reassurance. Often, then, working-class girls at school acquire knowledge which their mothers do not have. They read books, sing songs, do work that is unfamiliar to them. Middle-class mothers 'know'. They often have the books at home and therefore give their daughters a sense of safety and similarity between home and school. Most of them seemed much more familiar with the discourse on learning in the nursery school, 'knowing' the methods used to teach the alphabet, for example. Working-class women, in contrast, seemed puzzled by — even resistant to — the 'new ways of learning'. Sally's mother attempts to get Sally to do a 'real' lesson where she actually 'teaches' her the 'correct' art of writing — exactly what she is not supposed to do. She writes SALLY at the top of a page and asks her child to copy the letters.

> M: You try and copy that.
> C: No!
> M: Underneath, you do it underneath.
> C: I want to do see . . .

Sally's mother is very clear about how the nursery school approaches writing. Children are taught to trace over the letters, rather than copy them. But she does not want Sally to do it like that, so she pushes her to do it *her* way:

> M: Not over the top of it. Not like you do at school, you do it by yourself, underneath. You try and copy it.
> C: Can't. (Makes a scribble.)

The episode is punctuated by the child's resistance to her mother's way of teaching. She often says she 'can't do it', thereby resisting attempts to introduce a 'different' practice. There is strong tension between school *practice* and what the mother considers to be *real* pedagogic practice. Eventually and grudgingly, Sally complies with the lesson, but then only to *reject* her mother's help:

> M: Put a little bump.
> C: *I'm* doing it.

We could understand this as the child's struggle to be intellectually independent through 'confident challenge', but her rejection must also be bound up with what she perceives as her mother's *lack* of knowledge. Sally must gain control of the lesson, because as far as she is concerned her mother has made it clear that she does not know what is right.

The working-class women are therefore rendered powerless. This gives considerable power to their daughters — like Nicky, who has to teach her mother the songs she learned at nursery school:

> C: I will tell you mine.
> M: You help me. You gotta help me.
> C: Come on, then.
> M: 'Cos I never learnt that one at school.

This might be a powerful lesson for Nicky. She, like many working-class girls, is picked out as 'clever' and 'knowing' at 10. This gives her considerable status, which will be important to her. But to see it only in this way suppresses another aspect: the pain of the gap, the widening chasm of difference between the girl and her mother: a difference which the mother seems powerless to rectify. The mother 'lacks', she does not have the knowledge, and this must be painful to many little girls. Her knowledge is stupid, wrong, pathological, and is therefore no knowledge at all. We suggest that the problems of 'separation', of going to school, leaving home and growing up are, in the literature, totally conflated with insensitivity. This mother is not hopeless, but powerless. This suggests power, difference and the pain of splitting, as opposed to the safe and cosy transition so beloved of the developmental literature.

However, we should not give the impression that everything in the middle-class garden is lovely. The sensitive-mother account also belies the fact that middle-class girls may not make that cosy transition to autonomy (see Eichenbaum and Orbach, 1982). Many 10-year-old middle-class girls are terribly anxious. What in all that security could have produced such anxiety? Sensible girls are rational: they have been pushed to achieve and to hide and gloss over the pain and anxiety of growing up, of transforming their terrifying emotions.

Many working- and middle-class girls expressed intense fears of school, associating it with growing up and leaving home. In the following extract, Jacky has gone with her mother to take her older sister back to school after lunch. When they return, Jacky plays with her dolly. Out of the blue she voices her fears about going to school in this fantasy episode:

C: She's sick, mummy.
M: Pardon?
C: She's sick.
M: Sick? What's the matter then?
C: She can't go to school.
M: Mmm?
C: 'Cos she's sick . . . again.
M: Oh, poor old thing.
C: She not big enough.
M: Isn't she? I thought you said she wasn't well.
C: No, she not well.
M: Oh dear.

It is interesting that Jacky first claims that the doll cannot go to school because she is ill, then changes to because she is not 'big enough'. Of course, illness and small size are powerful ways of remaining dependent and therefore of not facing the difficulties of growing up.

Penny is playing a fantasy game with her mother. She pretends she is a mother too, with children. Penny asks her mother what she has been doing:

M: Taken my little girl to school.
C: Who?

M: Penny.

C: Yes, what . . .

M: She likes it at school now.

C: Does she?

Penny's mother uses this conversation to bring up the issue of school. By her comment 'she likes it at school *now*', we get the impression that Penny may well have experienced the transition to nursery school as difficult. However, the sense of resolution is not complete:

M: How's your little girl getting on?

C: Um, all right.

M: Does she go to school now?

C: Um, yes, the same school.

M: That's nice, does she like it?

C: Yes, she just . . . she just started on . . . um . . . Wednesday. It's not Wednesday today.

M: Ooh, that's nice . . .

C: She doesn't go to playgroup.

M: No.

C: So she thought she would . . . um . . . go school every day.

M: Oh, I see.

C: Well . . . um . . . she doesn't want to go, grow bigger, so she can't.

M: She doesn't want to grow bigger? No.

C: She . . . 'cos she want to stay at the same school.

This example shows clearly how the issue of school, leaving home, is undeniably a site of struggle for the child. The transition *is* difficult; that cannot be overstated. But for Penny, a middle-class girl, as for Jacky, a working-class girl, the root of fear seems to lie in progressing from being a baby who can lay almost complete claim to her mother for several hours a day; who can enjoy the intimacy and owner-ship of her mother as a *dependent* child; to an independent big girl who must leave the home, and with that leaving lose the power of dependency: grow up, grow *big*.

We can no longer afford to view this 'difficult transition' as predominantly a working-class problem born out of deprivation and a lacking, inadequate mother. Such constructs both belie the immense complexity of working-class children's failure and explain it away, make it not 'our' but 'their' problem. By pathologizing working-class culture, working-class mothers, a particular, historically produced 'norm' can remain intact. The working-class girls of this study, even at 4 (and certainly by 10), are *failing* compared to the middle-class girls. But they are not deprived, their mothers are not inadequate, pathological (though we have shown how they are patholog*ized*).

We have criticized the view that mother–daughter bonding creates an inde-pendent girl who gradually separates to full autonomous status. We argued that girls do not leave their mothers for a vacuum, that patriarchal culture is not so easily banished. Going to school, then, is not simply going to a place where autonomous girls can skip happily towards independent and fully fledged entry into social democracy. At the 'big school' new meanings are created, new associations linking to old meanings in tortuous and complex ways. The meanings through which schools understand and identify pupils draw heavily on precisely those naturalistic, heavily gendered discourses which define mother and child. Here, then, the girls are to meet the full force of sexual difference as they are classified, not as good or poor pupils, but as good and poor, working- and middle-class white *girls*. Thers is no easy autonomy, no simple crossing the gender divide, thanks to the sensitive mother holding the safety net over the chasm below.

5   Power and Gender in Nursery School

Some of our earliest empirical work was carried out in nursery schools (see Walkerdine, 1981; Walden and Walkerdine, 1982). This is important, because so many approaches to the issue have indicated the nursery as the place where the supposed lacks of girls may be put right before it is too late. We have explored current thinking about nursery Mathematics elsewhere (Walkerdine, 1988). Here, we examine the emergence of new practices of Mathematics teaching in nursery and infant school; a move away from rote-learning and chanting tables, learning sums, to the idea that mathematical concepts are produced through action upon a physical and object world.

The routine tasks which form the basis for 'action upon objects' are commonly, as we have suggested, domestic ones, used as play in the nursery school. One scheme, *Early Mathematical Experiences*, usually takes such tasks to be the basis of Mathematics, and it could be argued that the transformation of women's domestic labour into a pedagogic practice which naturalizes development means that there is a certain 'femaleness' in the very domesticity of the early Mathematics curriculum. If this is so, it neatly coincides with the 'not enough experience' theory. We think that such a view is misleading.

Domestic work is *transformed* into play and into 'mathematical experiences', to become the basis of Mathematics and not of women's domestic labour. How is this shift achieved? We cannot discuss this in great detail here (but see Walkerdine, 1988). Women, however, play an important part in that transformation. As mothers and teachers of young children they create the possibility of 'knowing', if making the transformation involves laying the table becoming an exercise. Women are the environment which facilitates the exploration, not the knowers. They are deemed necessary for the path to rationality, but should 'know when to intervene but not to interfere' (primary school teacher quoted in Walkerdine, 1984). It is a difficult, if not impossible, path to tread.

Within this scenario, domestic examples are used, but their specificity is denied. This means that many children have problems with making sense of mathematical tasks precisely because they are *not* like the domestic tasks with which they are familiar. So what is it that has to be accomplished? It is characteristic of mathematical statements that they may refer to anything. In statements such as $2 + 3 = 5$ there are no referents. This absence of referents gives such statements their generalizing power, and it is this power which is of course so exciting. It is, potentially, the power to control nature: to make it act according to scientific laws and formulae. But to produce this power, certain things have to happen to the ordinary, everyday domestic examples which are taken to be its basis.

Let us choose two examples from some of our fieldwork which has been written up in *The Mastery of Reason* (Walkerdine, 1988). Both concern top infant classes. In the first, the group defined by the teacher as 'slow learners' is playing a shopping game. They pretend to buy items depicted on a pack of cards, which they take in turn from the pile. All the items — like a yacht for 2p — cost less than 10p, and the children have to work out how much change they would have left from 10p. They have a wonderful time precisely because the game allows them to pretend to be rich, buying expensive items like yachts for 2p. The game is not like real shopping, because the children get a fresh 10p for each turn, and this confuses one of them. The product of the game, however, is a mathematical statement on paper, of the form $10 - 2 = 8$ — not goods bought.

Various transformations have had to be made. You have to get yourself into shopping and out of it: in it enough to understand, but not so far as to be trapped into following the wrong rules. The object is to produce a mathematical statement which can apply to anything, not just to shopping. Yet the children in this example act going shopping to the hilt. They play at being middle-class shoppers, who behave outrageously with shop assistants. They play at being rich people who go on expensive holidays. But they do not play the other kind of power game: the game producing statements which have power over nature. The other group does. They get excited by the power and properties of the numerals on paper in an exercise on place value.

It is easy, then, to see the leap that girls are accused of not being able to make. If it is the leap which is supposed to leave the world behind the better to control it, it is also the leap which is said to leave girls working hard and following rules but without concepts — to prohibit them from mastery, autonomy or the motivation to succeed. We are back in the realms of the 'something wrong with girls' theories; and we must look at them and their evidence carefully, for they are very common indeed and likely to follow girls when it comes to evaluating their performance through their school careers.

How are non-mathematical practices transformed into school Mathematics? The children playing the shopping game had to shift discourses: move from shopping and buying things, change and wealth and poverty, into the production of a subtraction calculation on paper, where the only product is the calculation itself. This view of things is at odds with the common analysis which finds Mathematics 'in everything'. The invisible transformation of domestic practices into a naturalized mathematical development is quite different. Let us take this examination further by looking at what happens when domestic activities become a more formal pedagogy. In *The Mastery of Reason* we analysed several examples where mothers turn cooking into a lesson. There is a difference between a cooking lesson and a Mathematics one. We argue that specific transformations have to be accomplished to turn any practice into Mathematics: for mathematical discourse provides the kind of generalizing statement in which the referent is suppressed.

In another example (Walkerdine, 1988), the teacher got the children to do simple additions using wooden blocks. She made connections between signified and signifier, so that there was always a form of words to accompany the children's actions. She used a board with three circles joined by lines. As she moved the blocks from each of the two circles down the lines and into the third circle, she said: '— and — makes —'. Gradually she and the children replaced the blocks by drawings of blocks and then by numerals, so that in the end she and they achieved entry into the formal discourse itself.

What is accomplished here is not certain mastery over the physical world or discoveries which girls somehow miss because they lack the right experience or autonomy. Rather, this mastery is a discursive trick, another sleight of hand. It is a fantasy discourse, which has best been described by the mathematician Brian Rotman (1979) as 'Reason's Dream'. It is a dream of a discourse, in which things once proved stay proved for ever — a dream of a rationally ordered universe, run according to natural laws that can be mapped. But what if it is all a fantasy, a very powerful fantasy of control over time and space? Doesn't that put boys' sure possession of 'it' on an entirely different footing? And girls' lack? It is quite a different matter to consider a fictional discourse which inscribes the possessor with a powerful mastery rather than something which is unproblematically and empirically 'real'.

Early on in our work, we attempted to grapple with the idea that girls are lacking certain kinds of play experiences and that this led to their so-called failure in Mathematics. With this in mind, we recorded play in nursery classrooms. As well as failing to support the idea that there were huge differences in play, our recordings also signalled to us that the issue of girls' and women's power in the nursery had to be understood in a different way from the rigid stereotypes and poor, weak and defenceless little girls scenario.

Our fieldwork (Walden and Walkerdine, 1982) was carried out in two nursery classes. We made video recordings, an analysis of play activities in one nursery class and a task designed to examine gender identity. We shall outline the play tasks and comment on the way our work has been taken up in the literature because it keys into the issue of existing explanations, which argue that there is something wrong with girls.

In the play study we noted down the children's activities, every 10 minutes for 4 hours a day, for 3 weeks every 10 minutes. We used the following classifications:

1   Fantasy play: this included any creation of fantasy sequences using props, such as the Wendy House (or Home Corner), zoo, hospital, cars, or any other sorts of toys, to create an imaginary context.
2   Creative play: painting, drawing, pastry-making. Anything to do with the creation of an artefact.
3   Construction play with specific items: blocks of wood, Lego, shapes and puzzles.
4   Sand and water play: specific to those areas in the classroom and involving the use of shapes, buckets and spades, containers of different shape, size and volume.
5   Rough-and-tumble play: chasing, jumping, general running about.

6   Miscellaneous play: wandering about, sitting for milk or for a story, waiting to go out.

A statistical test on our results reveals a significant difference at .001 between girls and boys. However, let us examine this more carefully. The two popular activities with girls and boys alike were creative and construction play, but the orders were different: boys did more construction play and girls more creative play. Since this is what one might expect, it is easy to ignore the proximity of the amounts. It cannot possibly be argued from these data that girls do not engage in construction play, nor boys in creative and imaginative play. It is therefore important to see just what has been made of this difference. In an appendix to the prestigious Cockcroft Report (1982) on Mathematics education, Hilary Shuard wrote: 'A recent British study found significant differences between the spontaneous play of boys and girls in a nursery school; girls engaged in more fantasy and creative play, while boys chose more construction play and play with sand and water' (p. 280). Note how she manages to make the data say exactly what they do not say.

In relation to this, let us examine another small task which we gave some children in the same nursery classroom. Here, the idea that girls do not and cannot play with construction toys, particularly Lego, is questioned. We decided to get them to construct something with Lego, to see whether the girls would do so and to examine the complexity of the boys' and girls' constructions. The staff decided that it would be best if one of them sat at a table with Lego, because the children would be more cooperative with a familiar adult. It was the school's policy not to coerce children into doing anything, so they had to be self-selecting. It was, however, quite common for them to have specific activities put out on the table, with a nursery assistant seated there. We were able both to videotape the construction process and to examine the results. Five boys and five girls chose to complete a construction task. They tended to be the older nursery children, aged between three and a half and four and a half. We analysed the constructions according to size, shape, number and type of pieces, and asked each child to describe what they were making both as they started and when they had finished.

There was considerable scepticism amongst the staff about whether the girls would participate, yet we found no difference in the complexity of the structures built by boys and girls. All the children, apart from one boy and one girl, made houses. It is interesting that the boys' structures tended to be domestic interiors, complete with furniture, tables, chairs and beds. One girl said that her house was a dog's house. It was a solid structure of rectangular bricks, topped off with several flat pieces, leaving no space inside nor any entrance or exit. Of the two children who made different structures, the boy built a car and the girl a boat. This was the only boy who made anything resembling a tower (Erikson, 1965), as he put six rectangular blocks on top of a wheel and called it a car. The girl took a flat base, then put rectangular blocks on it and six Lego figures on the blocks. She said she had made a boat with captain and people.

The teachers admitted that the girls had indeed played and made complex constructions. What, then, are we to make of their strong conviction that girls would not play with Lego, despite their participation and their high percentage of construction play? However, this was not the only issue which came out of the recording of the Lego play. While we were videoing there was a distressing interaction between the nursery teacher and two small boys. An analysis of this made us question some of the preceding approaches to power and pedagogy.

Annie takes a piece of Lego to add to a construction she is building. Terry tries to take it away from her to use himself and she resists. He says: 'You're a stupid cunt, Annie.' The teacher tells him to stop and Sean tries to mess up another child's construction. The teacher tells him to stop. Then Sean says: 'Get out of it, Miss Baxter paxter.'

> TERRY: Get out of it, knickers Miss Baxter.
> SEAN: Get out of it, Miss Baxter paxter.
> TERRY: Get out of it, Miss Baxter the knickers paxter knickers, bum.
> SEAN: Knickers, shit, bum.
> MISS B: Sean, that's enough. You're being silly.
> SEAN: Miss Baxter, knickers, show your knickers.
> TERRY: Miss Baxter, show off your bum. (They giggle.)
> MISS B: I think you're being very silly.
> TERRY: Shit Miss Baxter, shit Miss Baxter.
> SEAN: Miss Baxter, show your knickers your bum off.
> SEAN: Take all your clothes off, your bra off.
> TERRY: Yeah, and take your bum off, take your wee-wee off, take your clothes, your mouth off.
> SEAN: Take your teeth out, take your head off, take your hair off, take your bum off. Miss Baxter the paxter knickers taxter.
> MISS B: Sean, go and find something else to do, please.

People who have read this transcript have been surprised and shocked to find such young children making explicit sexual references and having so much power over the teacher. What is this power, and how is it produced? Here, although the teacher has an institutional position, she is not uniquely a teacher, nor are the boys *just* small boys. Particular individuals are produced as subjects *differently*. A particular subject has the potential to be 'read' within a variety of discourses. Here the teacher is a woman, and while that itself is crucial, it is only because of the ways in which 'woman' signifies that we can understand the specific nature of the struggle.

The boys' resistance to her can be understood as an assertion of their differences from her and their seizing of power through constituting her as the powerless object of sexist discourse. Although they are not physically grown men, they can take the position of men through language and in so doing gain power, which has material effects. Their power is gained by refusing to be constituted as the powerless objects in *her* discourse and recasting her as the powerless object in *theirs* — 'woman-as-sex-object'. Of course, she is still a teacher, but it is important that she has ceased to *signify* as one: she has become the powerless object of male sexual oppression. The boys' resistance takes the form of a seizure of power in discourse, despite their institutional positions.

These two boys are not yet capable of physically assaulting the teacher, but it may be only a matter of time. Since they are both children and male, and she is both teacher and female, they can enter as subjects into a variety of discourses, some rendering them powerful, some powerless. It is also important to note how the boys refer to the teacher and to 3-year-old Annie in the same terms. They call Annie a 'cunt', so bringing the teacher down to size: she and a small girl are in discourse the same thing; sex objects. The power of their discourse renders all females typifications of the same qualities: in this case possessors of tits, bums and cunts. However, this argument is not just a concern for theoretical distinctions. The issue seems to have important consequences for practice. We can understand the boys as both subjects in patriarchal discourse perpetrating oppression upon their teacher and simultaneously as children oppressed/controlled by her authority. Are we, then, to choose action which wishes potentially to liberate them from their oppression, or are they to be suppressed as sexist perpetrators of a patriarchal order?

An important effect of this power struggle between teacher and children is the way the teacher interprets the boys' discourse so as to lessen its oppressive effect upon her, and to justify her failure to stop them as the correct strategy. To understand this we have to be aware of the psychological and pedagogic terms on which she views herself as teacher and the children as learners. What concerns us particularly is the discourse on childhood sexuality. The teacher did not wait so long to stop the children by accident, and it was no accident that her fairly gentle rebuke did not take issue with the content of their discourse.

When one of us discussed the incident with her later, she explained what had happened:

> The kind of expressions are quite normal for this . . . As long as they're not being too silly or bothering anybody, it's just natural and should be left . . . coming out with that kind of expression is very natural.

How does she come to 'read' the children's actions as a harmless expression of a normal and natural sexuality? What are the main strands characterizing childhood sexuality? To answer that question we must examine the formation of those discourses and practices which inform and constitute 'progressive education' and 'child-centredness', as we did in Chapter 3. We can understand it as the necessity to reformulate pedagogy to produce individuals who are controlled but not regimented.

The discursive formation which claims that boys are natural, normal children who should be left alone to develop at their own pace constitutes this teacher's pedagogy and experience. It is not 'knowledge' in her control, with which she can consciously oppress the children, nor transparent 'experience' which will give them access to knowledge which is liberating because they have produced it themselves. The knowledge is not inserted in the context of the school and set to work in the interests of the teachers to control the children. Conversely, its purpose is to produce better control through self-control and that, ironically, is what helps to produce the space in which the children can be powerful. In this situation, the children have the incontestable power to define what they do within the limits of the pedagogy. They recognize quickly that the magic words 'I don't want to' at once allow them to control the flow of events. Thus the discourse itself helps to produce powerful children. The space for their resistance is already there.

Similarly, the discourse of the naturalness of male sexuality, which is to be expressed and not repressed, produces and facilitates the teacher's collusion in her own oppression, for if she reads actions as normal and natural, and suppression as harmful, she is forced into a no-choice situation. She cannot but allow them to continue, and she must render harmless their power over her. We will explore in later chapters how the discourse of the natural constantly asserts certain aspects of boys' behaviour as normal and those of girls as pathological and problematic.

The pedagogy assumes that the 'natural' expression of emotions produces a rational individual by leaving children to 'grow out of' their base animal sexuality, their aggression and irrationality. These will be worked out and not pushed down to fester in the unconscious. Through this process children will come to behave in a civilized manner as agents, responsible for their own actions, whose interactions are based on rationality alone.

We shall now examine another interaction involving small boys, this time playing with girls in the classroom. We can apply the kind of model sketched above to understand the production of girls as subjects within pedagogic practices. Sex-role socialization accounts make girls reflections of traditional female sex roles. Women's economic dependence and oppression will produce passive and dependent girls: dominated, not dominant. Yet, as we have asserted, individuals are powerless or powerful depending upon which discursive practices they enter as subject. Work within the women's movement has shown that the oppression of women is not unitary and that different discursive practices have different and often contradictory histories. This means that women are relatively powerful, for example, where they signify as mothers (for example, in custody cases).

Children reproduce these practices in their nursery-classroom play. This means that the girls, like their mothers, are not always passive and dependent but are constantly struggling with the boys to define and redefine their play into discursive practices in which they can be powerful. To understand the power and resistance in children's play we must understand the practices they are re-creating. These both help to produce the children as re-creating the — often reactionary — discourses with which they are familiar and also constitute them as a multiplicity of contradictory positions of power and resistance.

This time the children in the classroom are playing hospitals. They have been given all the necessary equipment by a nursery nurse, who has ensured that all the boys get the doctors' uniforms and all the girls the nurses'. She helps to maintain the doctors' power over the nurses by asking the nurses to 'help' the doctors. One girl, Jane, changes this into a situation where she is to make tea for the patients. She goes into the Wendy House (Home Corner) and has a domestic conversation with another girl. One of the doctors arrives in the Wendy House:

JANE: You gotta go quickly.
DEREK: Why?

JANE: 'Cos you're going to work.

DEREK: But I'm being a doctor.

JANE: Well, you've got to go to work 'cos you've got to go to hospital and so do I. You don't like cabbage, do you? (he shakes his head) . . . well, you haven't got cabbage then. I'm goin' to hospital. If you tidy up this room, make sure and tell me.

Jane managed to convert the situation from one in which she is a powerless and subservient nurse to the only one in which she has power over the doctor: controlling his domestic life. It is important that her other possible route to power — for example, playing a more senior doctor than Derek — is blocked by the nursery nurse's action, and she is unlikely to be able to take that position herself.

Jane sets up the game as domestic so that she, like her mother, has power traditionally — though of course it is produced through contradiction and paid for by severely limited and limiting domestic labour. This indeed is precisely what is asserted by sex-role stereotyping arguments, but we think there are several important points which such arguments cannot explain. First, the girls are not always weak and dependent but appear to be engaged in a *struggle* with the boys to read and create situations so that they become powerful. The boys struggle equally to remove the play from the domestic domain, where they are likely to be subservient. It is interesting to note that in very few of the many play sequences recorded in these two nurseries did boys play powerful fathers *when girls were present*, though they did so when playing with other boys.

The fact that girls can and do take up powerful positions in play appears contradictory at first sight. Girls appear to struggle to obtain power in precisely those situations which are the site of boys' resistance. They try to manoeuvre the play so that it becomes domestic; the boys try to make it non-domestic. The domestic is a site for opposition and resistance to the power of women in the home lives of these boys. Neither at home nor in play, probably, would it easily be sanctioned for them to 'play mothers'. The girls, on the other hand, can identify precisely with their mothers' positions within domestic practices.

For these young children, however, the domestic is not the only site of apparent female power. Their school lives are controlled by female teachers. In many ways the teachers' discursive position is similar to mothers'. Indeed, in the nursery school good mothering and good pedagogy are seen as part of the same process — of aiding child development. We would argue that the power of women in this transitory situation, between the domestic and the academic, is precisely what permits the early success of girls. Girls take up positions of similarity with the powerful teachers. Indeed, the girls who are considered the 'brightest' do indeed operate as subjects within the powerful pedagogic discourse: taking the position of the articulate knower, becoming sub-teachers. Most of the boys in these exchanges are, by contrast, almost totally silent which is, of course, another way of resisting the discourse. Classroom practices, then, might be for the boys a site of struggle where they must work to redefine the situation as one in which the women and girls are powerless subjects of other discourses.

6   Entering Infant School

Our early work had established that issues of power and positioning were central to our account and had acknowledged the importance of fantasies and fictions in constructing the relation of masculinity and femininity to Mathematics performance. We had not taken very far, though, the idea that the discursive fictions of the natural create the subject positions for girls and boys, or that on entering these fictions they are measured against them, so that girls are always found wanting. In the chapters which follow we shall explore in more detail how this is accomplished — first, the discursive regulation of the *teacher* and the *child* as these position women and girls in primary classrooms.

We are faced not with an ideology of childhood which distorts the 'real' nature of children but with a 'truth' which regulates what 'should be'. The argument is, therefore, that there is no simple revelation — rather, multiply constituted subjects for whom the interplay of signs produces conscious and unconscious struggle. Central to this formulation is a shift in the concepts of power and resistance discussed in the last chapter. A crucial concept now is that of power/knowledge: teacher and child form part of a set of regulative apparatuses which define the truth of what happens in classrooms. We have already examined some aspects of the constitution of the truth about *the child*. Here, we shall examine the truth about the teacher of young children and its impact upon teachers' views of themselves and their relations with girls. Here are some interrelated statements about the primary school, teachers and children:

> ... the first essential for a teacher of young children is that she should have the right temperament ... such work as this will demand wide and thorough theoretical knowledge and also the ability to apply this knowledge with particular children. (Consultative Committee of the Board of Education [*The Hadow Report*], 1933, p. 153)

When children are materially, intellectually or emotionally deprived, teachers must strive to serve as substitutes for parents ... Much is asked of teachers in these circumstances ... to care tenderly for individual children and yet retain sufficient detachment to assess what they are achieving and how they are developing ...

> [Teachers] have to select an environment which will encourage curiosity, to focus attention on enquiries which will lead to useful discovery, to collaborate with children, to lead from behind ... *To a unique extent English teachers have the responsibility and spur of freedom.* (Department of Education and Science [*The Plowden Report*], 1967, p. 331; emphasis added)

These extracts, from government reports over 30 years apart, demonstrate clearly a set of relationships which we want to address. Summarized below are the ideal qualities suggested by these reports for the teacher of young children:

The right temperament
A thorough theoretical knowledge
The ability to apply this knowledge
The ability to stand in for parents
Patience
Tender care
Detachment
The capacity to:
     encourage curiosity
     collaborate
     lead from behind
Responsibility and spur to freedom.

This is a formidable list, yet a close reading of these reports would give us a clearer picture of what is expected from the teacher. She, with *the child*, forms a couple. Notice how training and knowledge of the psychological aspects of children's development combine with capacities for nurturance to make the teacher of young children the 'trained' and 'detached' 'observer'. She is like a mother, but she is trained in the science of observation.

Let us note briefly some of the characteristics she does *not* possess: she does not teach, but provides experiences; she does not discipline; she cares, collaborates, inspires, encourages. We could write a whole list of absences to counter the presence of the ideal qualities and find those absences constitute a dangerous voice from the past: the spectre of the old authoritarianism, overt power and regulation. Here there is apparently no regulation, only the teacher's 'responsibility and spur to freedom'.

The development of modern psychology, and especially the study of children, is central to the modern 'truth' about pedagogy. It seems central to modern regulation practices. The 'facts of child development' form the bedrock of modern pedagogy, and the teacher must know them. They form the basis not only of pedagogic monitoring devices but also of a modern form of pedagogic government. The female teacher is held responsible for this government and for the creation of a fictional space in which 'freedom' is to be assured. This places a terrible burden on women. Women as teachers, in the words of the Hadow Report (CCBE, 1933), have to have their 'capacities for maternal nurturance' amplified. We need to understand, therefore, how present practices come to understand teaching and learning as they want to and the consequences for women and children in schools today.

We can ask, for example, not 'How have women and children been controlled?', nor 'How has the family been shaped?' but rather 'How do modern pedagogic and family practices produce modern forms of government and modes of individuality?' Although Foucault was concerned with the relationships of modern capitalism, one aspect of his work on power and the human sciences allows us to examine the productive power of psychological knowledge in the regulation of the 'social'. What does this mean, and how is it lived out and regulated? Here we must show that scientific practices produce the social positions and identities through and by which subjectivity is created.

Foucault demonstrates (1979) that there was an important shift in the form of government as a set of knowledges and technologies arose for regulating the population. Particularly important for our purpose is the shift from government which relied upon sovereign and visible power to an invisible power invested in the very technologies designed to classify nature and regulate normality. For example, in relation to mental measurement, Nikolas Rose (1985) demonstrates how the calibration of the normal demographic distribution of certain capacities provided the basis not only for classification techniques but also for the division of the population into educable, normal, subnormal, abnormal, and so forth. Educational institutions and practices produced normal and subnormal children as their subjects. That is, the knowledge of mental measurement was itself instrumental in providing a system of classification, and therefore regulation, which observed, checked and monitored the form of 'individual'. 'Normal' was defined by the very practices of measurement. Such technologies acted powerfully to produce techniques and practices for the regulation of normality.

Foucault sites the development of the human sciences at the centre of modern government, of bourgeois democracy and its creation: the bourgeois individual. These sciences helped to produce methods of measurement and classification of the population newly contained in towns and cities. These methods were directly implicated in the new form of government, which depended upon techniques of population management to achieve a power which was not overtly coercive, like a visible sovereign power vested in the monarch, but was relatively 'invisible' and depended upon techniques by which people accepted government (apparently voluntarily). We wish to demonstrate that the modern primary school is an important seedbed for this 'voluntary' acceptance. In this sense we can begin to understand the teacher's position as 'responsibility and spur to freedom'. The freedom which she has to foster is the notion of bourgeois individuality. It is the fear of mass revolution which necessitates an apparently non-coercive form of government.

The teacher, then, is responsible for freedom. We can understand how important compulsory schooling (introduced towards the end of the nineteenth century) was for producing 'good habits' in the population (Jones and Williamson, 1979). However, while hard work and overt surveillance were at one time seen as good methods of regulation, it was later felt that overt forms of government — for example, education based on coercion — were likely to precipitate rather than inhibit rebellion because children might appear to learn their lessons, but secretly harbour resistance. To counteract this, a mode of 'covert' surveillance was introduced, based on 'love', not 'fear': lessons were to be learnt apparently by 'free will'. The centrepiece of the new pedagogy, with its love replacing fear, is the woman teacher (Hamilton, 1981).

Women, therefore, became the central prop of the new form of pedagogy. Teachers, trained in psychology, were to assume the entire responsibility for

children's 'freedom' and for the continued maintenance of the bourgeois democratic order. We want to show that women, as teachers, mothers, carers and caring
professionals, are absolutely necessary — and responsible — for the moral order.
This responsibility characterizes them as simultaneously safe and potentially dangerous (the bad mother), as responsible for ensuring the possibility of democracy,
yet deeply conservative (see Hall and Jefferson, 1976). Our argument is that women
of all classes have been placed as guardians of an order from which it is difficult to
escape. If you are told that you are totally responsible for the nature of the child and
with it, therefore, for the possibility of freedom, of democracy, how much guilt and
pain are involved in resisting such a notion?

Such a responsibility is a crucial issue for feminist engagement. The area of
theory and practice which defines children's 'needs' and women's 'responsibilities'
is often contested by recourse only to arguments about shared parenting. We seek to
take apart and examine the truth claims and positive effects of this concept of women
and children. This is the basis of a far more powerful argument.

The 'truth' of women's sexuality is constantly reproduced in the formation of
our identities: as schoolgirl, mother, teacher, psychologist, secretary. The regulation
of — and our identities within — those practices make us guardians of a fiction of
autonomy and possibility. How, then, do we go beyond such truth, as it continually
attempts to define us?

We have suggested that the power/knowledge relations produced in modern
government understand the school as an important site of social regulation. This
means that the 'good teacher' and the 'normal' and 'natural' child are defined within
the discourses and practices that regulate their production. To explain this, we now
discuss the term 'positioning in discourse'.

Our theoretical framework differs in several important ways from the idea
of 'social construction', which uses, for example, multiple roles, selves, or a struc-
tural/functional model. It also differs from other uses of the term 'discourse' (for
example, Potter et al., 1984) and other similar usages such as 'accounting systems'.
The concept of discourse, especially in the power/knowledge relation of Foucault's
later work, stresses the historical constitution of knowledge. It is therefore Post-
Structuralist, necessitating a shift beyond usages which rely on structural forms of
linguistics and, for example, Althusserian formulations, of ideology. Central here
is the historical creation of knowledge in forms of government. This allows us
to claim that such 'positionings' have powerful and 'real' effects, while acknow-
ledging that their 'truth' is itself historically produced, within certain specific possibility conditions. 'Social accountability' approaches also tend to get trapped within
a 'hollow concept of the human being' (Henriques et al., 1984; Ingleby, 1980). Foucault's work does not address the problem of subjectivity directly, but skirts it. This
leaves an important area unexplored: subjectivity cannot be defined as a 'sum total
of positions in discourse', but is far more complex.

We might also look to the critiques of Structuralism which have emphasized that the social 'totality' is not well-fitting and rounded, but more contradictory
than some models of simple causality suggest. Understanding the social domain as
a contradictory nexus of social practices (Hirst and Woolley, 1982) allows us to go

beyond a sense of smooth and coherent identity. We can envisage a set of identities or positions, produced within the discursive relations of different practices, which do not necessarily fit together smoothly: we have a notion of 'conflict' or 'contradiction' *between* positions.

The power of the regulation of practices is central. Regulation may take place through modes of signification, but it is more than a simple question of 'meaning'. Our model understands power not so much as a fixed possession (as in sovereign power) but as an aspect of regulative knowledge itself. For example, in defining the 'nature of the child', certain behaviours are felt to be produced and regulated.

Foucault uses the term 'veridicality' to distinguish the 'effects' of 'truths' from an epistemological or empirical sense of whether something is real. Let us explore some of the veridicality of modern pedagogic practices. If we explore the possibility that 'subject-positions' do not create unitary or coherent identities, then subjection can take place within a variety of contradictory practices. For women or girls, the designation 'teacher' or 'child' relates to positioning within those specific practices, and is coterminous with 'woman' or 'girl'. 'Woman' is not itself a unitary category but relates to different positionings — 'teacher', 'wife', 'mother', and so on.

It is important that in this scheme of things the idea of regulation does not imply that all children and women end up the same — that is, normal. It is the monitoring of normality and pathology which is important, for these categories are used to understand success and failure. In the following chapters we shall encounter the constant pathologization of girls' performance and the way in which teachers understand themselves in relation to that performance as well as to the behaviour of boys. We shall argue that while there is no simple positioning of children, positions are themselves replete with conflict which is traumatic for teachers and children.

For example, the teacher, guardian of the moral order and spur to freedom, becomes a facilitator. She must strive to counter the effects of bad mothering to secure democratic rather than rebellious citizens. This counts as freedom. The teacher must watch, observe and monitor development: certain qualities are required of her which are different from, and complementary to, those of the child. In this 'new couple', mother-substitute and child are the opposites and complement, not male and female, yet of course the qualities ascribed to 'the child' are implicitly defined as male anyway. As we shall demonstrate, only boys are natural children and only women are loving teachers. The teacher is both safety as facilitator and danger as morality. She, with mothers, is responsible for the production of the democratic citizen and the maintenance of democracy.

Teachers are responsible for the normal development of all children. They must monitor them, 'know all children as individuals' and 'know when to intervene but not interfere'. This impossible task is likely to produce considerable guilt at inevitable failure. It has particular gendered consequences for women teachers; and girls are caught in the multiple binds of having to be both natural children and potential women.

The positions of 'child' and potential 'woman' are in direct conflict whose root lies not in teachers, who are themselves caught up and trapped within the positions set for them, but in the power/knowledge arrangements within which apparatuses of social regulation define and monitor 'a child' and 'a teacher'. Those apparatuses are sedimented in practices through which normality and pathology are monitored. However, this means that the power accorded the teacher by virtue of her positioning within pedagogic practices has effects in defining and monitoring correct performance which, as we have already seen, is no longer a matter of obtaining the right answer or calculation; the proper and admissible evidence of success is activity and discovery. In this way 'child' slips easily into 'boy'.

Boys present ample evidence of 'activity', often through their naughtiness and violent behaviour, but it is easy to imagine how this might slip into a designation of 'intelligence'. Conversely, the literature on girls' attainment is full of the idea that they achieve only through hard work or by regurgitation of facts or following rules. Those activities are danger signals of the 'old pedagogy', of 'chalk-and-talk', of 'seeing and remembering' rather than of 'doing and understanding'. In that sense, then, no matter how successful girls are, their success may be discounted if they present evidence of rule-following and work, and it may be feared that the spectre of authoritarianism is entering the classroom through them. This danger is viewed as a pathology which must be corrected at all costs. In this context we can begin to examine what happens to girls when they enter infant school by presenting some data from one of our studies, this time of 6-year-old girls. Our fieldwork consisted of observing and audio-recording 8 girls in 5 different classes, and conducting interviews with children and teachers. Here we see a process which is present throughout the data, from 6 to 15: girls' good performance is treated as a problem, whereas boys' poor performance is not only excused but turned into a good quality. It is as if there were one law for girls and another for boys.

Both teachers and girls are caught in an oppressive double-bind. Female teachers are led to see boys as true children and therefore to approach with ambivalence the characteristics of girls and of their own femininity. They are not the villains of the piece, as some 'agents of socialization' arguments would have it. We must all examine how girls are led to become carers by the kinds of oppressive truths we have signalled.

While studies of primary schools, such as Ronald King's *All Things Bright and Beautiful* (1978) mention the relationship between femininity and definitions of primary school teaching, they do not examine what it means to be a teacher to the women involved, nor how they live the relationship between their positioning within infant school practices and their subjectivity. Teachers' definitions are often attributed to 'ideology', but then our subjective and psychic constitution remains far from clear. We saw in the last chapter how Ms Baxter took upon herself the responsibility for allowing the boys to insult her and felt that she had to 'know each child as an individual'. But what is the impact upon her sense of herself of the first, and how does she live the virtual impossibility of the second? Guilt is a constant and common feature of female teachers' accounts, for are they not made to feel responsible for the normal development of each child in their class and for a liberal rhetoric implying that all children could succeed if they were allowed to develop properly? They are supposed to be responsible for making the fantasy of a system of equality work. They serve to cover the vast inequalities in the post-1967 education system (see Holt, 1969; Kohl, 1971; Walkerdine, 1986a).

The school chosen for this phase of the work was in a London suburb in the process of 'gentrification'. Its catchment area therefore included some very poor and traditional working-class housing, together with some newly 'converted' houses owned mainly by 'professional' families. The school was chosen especially for this social mix. It had recently acquired a new headteacher and reorganized its classes according to principles of vertical grouping. This move caused some anxiety to the staff and, to a greater extent, some parents, who often spoke of not wanting their child to be the object of an 'experiment'. The effect was that the 6-year-olds, the object of our study, were not confined to 1 or 2 classes, but were to be found in all 5 classes. This meant a wider database for us and allowed examination of differences in practice between classrooms. The sample girls were selected, by a combination of test scores and teacher judgement, to represent the top and bottom of the range. We also attempted to ensure a social class spread.

All the teachers were women, but from diverse social class and ethnic backgrounds. Almost all, however, had an intense emotional investment in the children and a deep sense of caring. That this is engendered in women who enter the caring professions is not surprising. One of us talked of 'loving her inner-city children with a fierce passion' (Walkerdine, 1986a), while Carolyn Steedman (1985) said of her days as a primary school teacher: 'I loved my children and worked hard for them, lay awake at night worrying about them, spent my Sundays making workcards, recording stories for them to listen to, planning the week ahead' (p. 8).

We have already discussed how women are encouraged to bear the burden of responsibility for development and to take a lot of guilt into themselves. It seems that many of the teachers in this school have dealt with their own deep pain and neediness by taking into themselves the pain and needs of their children, especially of the girls. Many report deep unhappiness in their childhoods and school years, yet this very phenomenon consciously motivates their teaching and their empathy, especially with girls in pain. For example, the headteacher was abandoned by her mother as a young child and sent to boarding school. Now, her prime concern is to make children happy:

> I do have a . . . tremendous desire . . . to make kids enjoy school . . . I would still argue that the first thing is crucially important because as a person I was unhappy. OK, as far as the actual work was concerned, I performed, but how much better it would have been if I'd been happy. I mean, I'm not saying, you know, that I've got the gift of making every kid happy, but I mean I feel I have the sensitivity to pick it up.

This sensitivity to others' pain is a common feature and is certainly one for which women are prepared. But what is important here is not only this, but its linking with pain and unmet needs within the women themselves. Part of their unhappiness has been invested in looking after others. Teaching may be a caring profession, but it offers little caring to them. As one teacher puts it: 'I keep thinking, I'm ill too.

I want attention too!' She homes in on the pain of some of the girls in her class. One, with whom she had been angry, wrote a story:

> She said, here's a little girl and she's trying to fly her kite and the sun says no, no, no, you can't fly your kite and I said, what's the little girl saying, and she drew a bubble and it said, I want to fly my kite. And I said, who is that little girl, and she said it's me. And I said who is that sun up there, and she looked at me, and I said, could it be me, and she said it is you, like, don't be silly, it is you. And I said, oh I thought it was, and I said, what does it mean when the little girl says, I want to fly my kite and she says it means I want to be free. And I felt so horrible.

She also talks of another child, whom she frequently cuddles, who often complains of pains. Later in the interview, however, she tells of her own childhood and her dislike of her sisters when they were ill: 'Now, I can't stand it when people tell me they're ill.' What she can't stand are her own envy and pain and wanting. Out of guilt she then comforts — because she cannot stand — the pain of other girls. Caring for others is therefore more complex than it might at first appear. All the teachers have stories about the unhappiness of girls in their class, which they tell with feeling. One speaks of her unhappiness as a child and then of her difficulty in dealing with the fact that one of the girls in her class was murdered. She says: 'Teaching has left me the feeling that I'm not actually very good at being a worker in a grown-up place.'

She, like most of the others, did not positively choose teaching as a career but entered it because she did not do well enough to go to university and needed a job. Another became a pupil-teacher, when all she really wanted to do was 'never to leave school'. But where she grew up, her dark skin meant that other careers were closed to her. Another wanted to be a pilot, but became a teacher because it was the only form of higher education available where she grew up.

Inside these stories are unhappiness, pain and ambivalence, leading to complicated feelings for the girls and for themselves. It seems that the apparently altruistic caring involved in being a teacher covers emotions and histories which key into the history we have surveyed. So little is written about this forming of our subjectivity and our struggles to be powerful, ending up dealing with others' pain at the expense of our own and of our own freedom. To echo the words of the little girl with the kite, women want to be free too, but look how much guilt is carried within that desire: to be free and not to have to care for the pain of others? How could women want such a thing?

How do girls become teachers? What is the relationship between school years and wanting to stay in the classroom? We want to explore how these teachers viewed the girls in their charge and how the girls viewed themselves. The way the teachers describe and categorize the children fits clearly with their own histories. The two who grew up in the New Commonwealth reveal a clearer orientation to 'work' and to the stricter discipline of their own schooling. While both clearly key into the girls' pain, being a teacher for them meant the only available option and a tremendous amount of work, against fairly difficult odds. The others, trained later and in this country, display 'child-centred' attitudes, focusing far more on 'emotional needs'. All, though, see the school as a place where 'happiness' is to be ensured in an unhappy world. Maria and Sadie, the two women of colour, refer to good children as 'able', 'capable', 'grasping concepts quickly', able to work on their own, with 'good number concepts'. These two also laid most stress on being 'helpful' and had histories of being 'sub-teachers' themselves. In their two classes two of the good girls were indeed 'helpful sub-teachers'. The other two were not so designated. Only Sadie talks about children 'working hard'.

The other teachers, Anne, Christine and Hilary, use far more child-centred categories. All talk of the children 'enjoying' Maths and gaining 'pleasure' from numbers. The concern with emotional happiness is most noticeable in their discourse. They see many children — boys *and* girls — as experiencing anxiety and unhappiness (mostly because of home problems) and feel much more responsible for their emotional welfare. The level of their own anxiety and guilt is very high. They feel that they do not know enough about the children, nor help them enough.

For all teachers, good girls are quiet, capable and helpful, whilst poor girls are helpless, anxious and quiet. However, the younger teachers are far more inclined to concentrate on what they see as the emotional problems of the poor children, the older teachers on their 'language' problems. Boys are said to be naughty, distracted, unable to settle and lacking concentration far more often than girls. Naughtiness in boys is a marked feature.

The good girls come from three classes: Penny from Anne's class, Rebecca from Sadie's, and Satinder and Julie from Hilary's. There are considerable differences between them, which we shall explore later. These four are by far the clearest in their rationales for ranking children and for distinguishing between those whom they consider good or poor. Yet while Penny, Satinder and Julie employ criteria of 'right' or 'wrong', Penny and Julie are far more rigid than Satinder. Satinder and Julie refer to whether children get their number work right or wrong: all the time, mostly or sometimes. Penny, in addition, lays great stress on *speed*: the best children are quick and accurate. It is all right to be slow if you get it right in the end but there is no virtue in rushing if it produces the wrong answer. All four draw a clear relationship between being good at Maths and being good children — especially Penny, Satinder and Julie, who can say that those who 'get it wrong' are those who do not concentrate and 'muck about'. All four position more boys than girls as poor and describe them as silly, naughty and 'mucking about'.

Only Rebecca presents herself as a sub-teacher/helper, displaying considerable power in saying who is to be granted her help. She is also the only girl who refers to children as *clever* and *hard-working*. Teachers, however, characterize both Rebecca and Satinder as 'teacher-types': bossy, helpful, wanting to organize the other children. Penny, however, is described as 'mature' (without pejorative overtones) and of 'above-average' ability: 'too bright' to be a helper. Julie is too quiet and not outgoing enough to be a sub-teacher. It is interesting that all teachers stress their own likeness to the good girls.

All the girls except Penny rank themselves highly: as good at Maths, even if they sometimes get things wrong. Penny, however, ranks herself in the bottom group and says she is not very good because she is always chatting. She applies this criterion to other children. Penny is the only *professional* middle-class (probably new middle-class) girl in the sample. It is with such girls at 10 that we see most anxiety about not being good enough (see Chapter 7). It is unclear why Penny ranks herself so low. Her parents certainly stress intellectual achievement, and since she sees herself as 'chatting' it is possible that she believes herself to be not as good as she could be. However, it may also be important that she finds it difficult to admit to being good.

The four poor girls are from different classes: Veronica, Emily and Jo are all from Christine's class and Eleanor is from Hilary's. All but Emily, who comes from the petty bourgeoisie, are working-class. All rank themselves in the top group and therefore appear to have a very unclear view of their position. It is significant that the two girls who are experiencing the most complicated emotional problems, Emily and Eleanor, are most confused in their rankings and criteria. Eleanor cannot connect with the tasks at all, is unable to comment on anyone's performance in Mathematics and instead splits the class into who 'hit' her, 'tell on her' and 'tell lies about her'. She is a victim, but her interview also reveals that she does 'hit back' by 'telling on' people herself and by committing secret acts of violence, such as breaking the heads off dolls.

Emily simply says that everyone is good at Maths, without further elaboration. In contrast with Eleanor, Emily says that everyone is nice. She appears very caught up in personal relationships and with her own popularity. She positions herself as a nice, sweet, good girl who needs and remarks on children who help her and give her things. However, Emily is not as passive as she may appear; she is quite difficult at home.

By comparison, Jo and Veronica appear more 'aware' than either Emily or Eleanor. They both talk about children doing 'work'. Children who work are 'good' and those who do not — usually boys — are 'naughty', 'muck about' and are 'not very good'. Jo is almost obsessive about 'work'; she is the least comfortable in the interview and wants to go back to the classroom 'to get on with her work'. Veronica's comments are erratic: some children are simply referred to as 'good'; while she can articulate reasons for others' position, concerning reading and number work. However, like Emily, she is concerned about her popularity and remarks that various boys 'love' her. Both Emily and Jo say that they are good, while Eleanor cannot comment and Veronica reveals the most articulate anxiety. She says she gets annoyed and frustrated when she cannot do her Maths.

As we have said, only Penny had parents from the new middle class. Satinder and Emily were both petty bourgeois; Rebecca's father was a clerical worker and Eleanor, Jo, Veronica and Julie's fathers were manual workers: Veronica's skilled, a fireman, and Eleanor's a driver, Jo's a driver for a security firm and Julie's a milkman. What is important in terms of social class is that the girls span a continuum rather than divide into two neat groups. Especially with respect to the petty-bourgeois and lower-middle-class families, this makes the subject of upward mobility complex. However, it is significant that upward mobility for the good girls (apart from Penny, for whom this is not an issue) — that is, professional careers — is a major family concern. While the families of the poor girls share this concern they are, like their daughters, far more confused about what it entails. The girls all want to be nurses and teachers (all mentioning helping as a reason), except for Penny, who wants to be a violinist 'because my dad says I have to', and Jo, who wants to be a doctor. Nevertheless, they all aim for the professions — the caring professions at that, except for one.

All the teachers identified strongly with their good girls, but only two identified with the position of sub-teacher in the classroom. Rebecca and Satinder were bossy and both helped and dominated other children. All Rebecca's transcripts are filled with sub-teacher behaviour, and she is frequently called upon by the teacher to work with other children. She acts as moral guardian of classroom order, and as such has a powerful position as an authority. Satinder is similar, though more 'cantankerous' — frequently 'rowing' with the other children — and certainly forceful in her interactions. Rebecca and Satinder work throughout the recordings. Julie also works continually and is sometimes taken to be a sub-teacher by the other children, who ask her for help. However, she does not feel confident enough and says more than once that she wishes people would not assume that she 'knows'. Unlike Satinder in the same class, Julie is not noisy, and indeed makes sure that any 'unacceptable' comment which might tarnish her image as a good girl is kept to a barely audible whisper.

Only Penny is different. She presents herself frequently as 'an authority'. In one exchange with other children she manages to convince them that she knows what 'feature films' are; they are in black and white, are 'really scary', and are on television late at night. All this, and Penny's family do not even have a set! She does not act as a sub-teacher, frequently has long conversations and does not work particularly quickly. However, her confidence is striking and, like all the good girls, she can command the teachers' attention at will.

None of the good girls regularly gets all her work right, but they all get through it quickly and also obtain help from the teacher. They are often praised, although they do not spend a lot of time with the teacher, since they 'know how' to get on. By contrast, the poor girls are all relatively 'helpless', but in a variety of ways. Eleanor is perhaps the most distressing. On first putting on her microphone she spoke deliberately into it, repeating several times: 'Eleanor is stupid.' This was staggering in itself. The recordings were filled with Eleanor getting a lot of teacher attention, but failing to carry out the simplest of requests, such as finding a pencil. At first she appeared not to understand anything at all, and she certainly tried the limits of the teacher's patience. However, it became increasingly clear that she was 'vague' and 'distant' and in a state of what might be clinically described as 'detachment'.

Emily also commanded considerable teacher time and attention. She was very anxious and hardly did any work. On two occasions during the recording sessions she was greatly distressed at leaving her mother at the classroom door. Whenever she started to do a piece of work, she gave up almost immediately and went to the teacher, usually complaining of physical pains. The teacher then comforted her and told her not to worry or do any work and gave her instead a 'pleasant' task.

Jo was mostly silent and sullen in school and was not liked by the teacher. Subdued as she was, she frequently asked for help and was just as frequently rebuffed, constantly being told to 'go and ask someone else'. She often seemed lost, powerless and frustrated. The teacher remarked on her physical coordination. By contrast, Veronica, in the same class, was liked by the teacher. She generally had a 'good time' in school and spent most of it playing and working very slowly. However, she did express some frustration at not being able to do things and in her fantasy play she invented a character called 'Nicholas' who was sometimes her brother, her baby and herself. She did not approach the teacher often. She also enjoyed it when her parents, particularly her father, came into the classroom. During one recording he read the children a story, with Veronica sitting on his knee, looking pleased and excited.

Both Rebecca and Satinder have two older brothers, against whom they must 'hold their own' consistently. In this they appear very 'resilient'. Rebecca's mother spends most of the home recording doing domestic tasks. Although at one point she and Rebecca listen to favourite records together, they do not 'play'. Rebecca plays with friends in the street, where they hold a mock talent competition, with Rebecca being very bossy. She does not 'help' her mother, although it is clear that she is expected to do so. Her father too spends his time in 'work' tasks and in eating his evening meal.

Satinder, by contrast, spends all her time with her brothers. They are all very self-reliant. While both parents are working in the family shop the children watch television, argue and play board and ball games. They do not 'help' either, but are clearly used to looking after themselves. The mother's entire time is taken up with working in the shop and preparing the evening meal. During the weekend recording she cooks and chats to her family.

Julie also does not 'help' her mother. What is noticeable about all these girls is less that they behave like sub-mothers, than that they look after themselves and are 'no trouble'. Julie spends almost the entire first recording session at home in silent 'work' activity in her own bedroom: copying something into an exercise book and illustrating it. Her mother did play a board game with her and her brother, and the children also spent time reading. Outside the game there was a little adult–child conversation which was not regulative. Her father, a milkman, frequently fell asleep in a chair during the recordings and rarely interacted with them at all.

By contrast, Penny's father was self-employed and at home more frequently than her mother. Both parents admitted that Penny and her mother got on badly. Penny's father gave her violin lessons and ensured that she practised. He also cooked the evening meal. At other times, Penny played with friends in the garden. When her mother came home from work she sat and talked to Penny and on one occasion helped her and her friends build a wigwam. She was the only mother who actively 'played' and turned everyday activities into occasions for academic-type learning. Once she introduced a lesson about the growth of seeds on finding a pea which had germinated in a pod they were shelling. The 'lesson' continued until Penny ate the pea! Penny and her mother also made a cake together, but her mother did not spend most of her time engaged in domestic work.

Jo spent some time refusing to wear the microphone, but was later extremely boisterous. She also had two older brothers and was encouraged by her father to fight them; she did, and obviously got hurt. This 'sticking up for herself' was considered an important lesson. She spent far more time with her father, who was frequently at home, than her mother. They painted a stool together, and Jo was given a lesson in how to paint. They also watched two videos with the boys, and discussed them. During each recording her mother spent almost the entire time doing domestic work in the kitchen while the rest of the family was in the living room upstairs. The only exception was when she brought in tea and cakes and sat briefly with the rest of the family. Jo and her mother engaged in regulative conversations.

By contrast, Emily spent a considerable amount of time with her younger brother and her mother, who had enlisted the grandmother's help in constructing elaborate 'educational' games to fill the children's hours during the recordings. Clearly a lot of work had gone into them and they appeared to have been made for the occasion: reading and recognition games and a kind of obstacle race. Mother and grandmother seemed determined to be seen playing and interacting, since not a moment was left free. Her mother engaged in virtually no domestic tasks during the recording. Emily also played with her father, who showed her how to play a computer game. She had temper tantrums and was less 'passive' than at school.

Veronica played throughout most of the recordings, mostly by herself or with her younger brother, and she attempted to play with the researcher. Her parents were both at home and either did domestic work or sat chatting. She engaged in fantasy play with toys and some reading, though she changed tasks frequently.

Eleanor's home recordings were by far the most distressing. She had one younger and one older sister at home. Her mother was severely anxious and depressed and was being 'beaten up' by her husband, who was present during the second part of the recordings. Eleanor played with her sisters, quarrelling frequently, engaged in solitary fantasy play — where she held imaginary conversations, saying: 'No, my husband does not beat me' — and watched television. Her mother did domestic work, sat talking to the researcher and had regulative conversations with the children. Her father also did some domestic tasks and regulated the children. Eleanor's family was the object of intervention by a variety of social welfare agencies, although the results were distressing and depressing. All those involved had considered that Eleanor was 'all right' because she was the calmest, expressed no rage like her elder sister and did not cry like her younger one. However, there were grounds for inferring, from her symptoms of detachment, that Eleanor was the most profoundly disturbed.

All the parents expressed considerable concern about their daughters' education, though they displayed it in different ways, some of which were not understood by the school. All except Penny's experienced some sense of a barrier between themselves and the school and expressed the fear that either they or the school were not doing well by their children. Except for Penny's parents, fathers tended to express more concern than mothers about the value of education. They stressed the importance of gaining qualifications which would allow their daughters to have better jobs than they had. Education is seen as a 'golden opportunity' not to be wasted, particularly by the parents of the good girls. Most parents expressed the view that jobs were easy to come by when they left school, but that now qualifications were necessary.

Mothers, however, tended to express more concern about their daughters' 'happiness' at school, and most parents described their school experience as unhappy. 'As long as she's happy' was a common phrase. Many of the parents had done poorly at school and clearly felt upset about their schooldays, though the mothers of the good girls tended to say that they had been good at school, though none of them had had 'careers'. They were confused by the contradiction between working hard and 'getting on' and being happy.

Both Rebecca's and Satinder's parents stressed the value of success and of getting on and were less sympathetic to 'happiness' arguments. Satinder's parents discussed whether they should pay for their children's education. On the other hand, Penny's both emphasized development and did push Penny: she *had* to practise her violin daily and she was not allowed to fail. Their discourse was one of knowing and certainty: they expressed no fears about schooling, nor any sense of lack of knowledge about the school. Conversely, most other parents expressed worry about the vertical-grouping 'experiment', and often said that the school should 'experiment' on someone else's daughter.

Jo's parents, especially her father, talked much of 'fighting', a key term in his discourse. He encouraged his children to 'stand up for themselves', and saw himself as fighting to get a good education for them. Part of this fight had involved sending Jo to another school because the teachers refused to close hers when asbestos was found in the roof. The teachers, for their part, did not like his 'attitude', and the class teacher considered the parents 'rough'. Jo's mother was a shop steward in her union (she was a lavatory attendant), but said that she spoke in public only because she was forced to.

Julie's parents devoted their entire lives and money to their children. Her mother did no paid employment in order to be at home for them. Neither parent drank or smoked and they did not own a car. Instead, they spent all their spare money on books for the children and 'educational visits' at weekends. Their shelves were crammed with reference books and encyclopaedias bought especially for the children, who might use them for their work, as neither parent 'had time to read'.

Veronica's parents were much praised by her teacher for their 'laid-back' attitude: they were more concerned with her happiness than in 'pushing her'. She was therefore taken to be a 'well-adjusted' child. This hints at a double-bind, which applied especially to working-class children. If they were 'pushed' this would create 'anxiety', and only 'happy' working-class children who were less bothered about work were 'adjusted'. Yet the family's desire for upward mobility and educational qualifications could not be satisfied without 'anxiety'. Indeed, parents like Julie's put everything they had into their children's future. By comparison, Penny could be 'well-adjusted' *and* doing well because her parents did not display anxiety or 'appear' (to the school) to push her. The school, therefore, tended to disavow effort and to see it as potentially harmful if it caused anxiety.

The working-class and petty-bourgeois parents frequently bought 'educational' books and toys for their children, but they were not of the 'right kind'. Only Penny's parents had access to the current education discourse, bought the 'right' books and toys and engaged in the 'right' tasks. However, Rebecca's mother had taught her to read and Satinder's frequently helped her with Mathematics.

In some ways the parents of the poor girls were not unlike their daughters. All wanted their children to do well but did not know what to do about it. They tended to feel powerless and ignorant. The good girls' parents, while they may have done things which were antithetical to school practices, had clear strategies. However, the poorer parents' 'sacrifices' for their daughters' future were apparent. Thus, in conditions of relative poverty, much more was invested in these children to make the future happier and wealthier than the past: a difficult and salutary lesson.

We discussed in Chapter 5 how working- and middle-class domestic labour became the basis for intellectual development and how the pathologization of certain practices in which mothers specifically *taught* their children went with this. Alongside this notion is the common view that some parents, particularly white and black working-class parents, prepare their daughters badly for school and subject them to more rigid gender stereotyping. This view seems to come from white middle-class liberalism and carries with it a view that sexism and the oppression of women are produced by faulty socialization. We hope we have begun to demonstrate some of the problems with this approach: above all, it pathologizes domestic practices other than middle-class ones. It is simply not true that black and white working-class girls are doing badly at 6, though their strategies for success and evaluation by teachers are often quite different from those of middle-class girls. However, as we shall see in the next chapter, the problems for working-class black and white girls in national competition are enormous compared with those of middle-class girls.

7   10-Year-Olds

In this chapter we shall revisit the girls we met with their mothers at 4. We were able to follow up what had happened to 30 4-year-olds, who had originally been the sample for study by Tizard and Hughes (1984). We discuss elsewhere our reading and reworking of these data in relation to arguments about mothering (Walkerdine and Lucey, 1989). Here we examine in summary form some of the issues raised by what happened to the girls at 10 — in particular, the importance of class differences and how these cut across gender. All the girls were white, but Tizard and Hughes defined 15 as working-class and 15 as middle-class. We shall see how these girls fared, their teachers' views of them and their views of themselves. We also present a case study of two of them to exemplify some of the issues concerning the relationship of early experience to girls' later educational success.

At 4, all the girls were paired so that there was at least 1 working-class and 1 middle-class girl from each nursery school. By the age of 10 only one of the original pairs, Julie and Patsy (whom we will meet later) remained in the same junior school. Five of the middle-class girls attended preparatory schools belonging to the Girls' Public Day School Trust. The sample, apart from this, had become much more split along class lines. Basically, while the areas from which the sample had been drawn at 4 contained a mixture of working- and middle-class families, private, owner-occupied and rented housing and public housing, by 10 class differences in location had increased dramatically. The working-class families still lived in the same kind of housing, even if they had moved. The middle-class families, by comparison, had been far more mobile. Apart from those whose increase in living standards had allowed them to pay for their daughters' education, one had moved to Switzerland and others had moved to better and more expensive accommodation. In other words, the gap between the standards and lifestyles of the two groups had widened.

More dramatic and depressing, however, was the huge gap in educational attainment between the groups. The attainment of all the working-class girls (and of the other boys and girls in the same year at their school) was disastrous compared with that of the middle-class girls and their classmates. We have described how the responsibility for the academic attainment of working-class children and girls is laid at the door of the mother, yet it is evident from this study that even those mothers who transform their domestic labour into pedagogy in the acceptable way do not produce children who unproblematically succeed. There is something terribly wrong with this interpretation of the cause of women's oppression.

Some of the attainment figures for the different schools highlight the performance gap and demonstrate the complexity of the link between the psychic and the

*Table 7.1   Rank order of school means**

Test Scores	Middle-class		Working-class
124.48	Emily	(Private)	
119.08	Samantha	(Private)	
117.34	Helen		
116.25	Naomi		
115.91	Charlotte	(Private)	
112.44	Gill		
112.24	Penny		
112.15	Liz		
111.50	Amanda	(Private)	
108.36			Jacky
108.12			Jenny
106.65			Maureen
106.65			Teresa
104.70			Nicky
104.11			Susan & Katy
102.08	Diana		
101.97	Angela		
101.37			Anna
98.85	Julie		Patsy
96.64			Kerry
94.87			Dawn
92.15			Sally

* Two of the middle-class girls were not available for the follow-up study. On four occasions time was too short for a standardized test, so these results are not included.

social. Some of the working-class girls were doing well compared with their classmates. They were highly regarded by their teacher and thought well of themselves, believing that they were clever and good at their work. They also had high expectations. Yet if we compare their performance with those of the middle-class girls, often with lower self-esteem, it is like chalk and cheese. It will be many times harder for such girls to have professional careers than their middle-class counterparts. They are likely to experience pain and frustration in their struggle to meet their ambitions. This is important methodologically. It is quite common for attainment surveys to ignore data such as the position of the child in class and the teacher's estimate, in favour of national comparisons. But this skews the picture, which emerges as more complex and disturbing when all factors are considered.

The highest attainment was found in the public schools and in those state schools in upper-middle-class areas which were effectively regarded as state preparatory schools, feeding the nearby public schools. Table 7.1 gives scores from an NFER Standardized Mathematics Test.

Two working-class girls, Nicky and Dawn, were said at 4 to have fairly insensitive mothers. Their respective maternal relationships were judged to be fraught with wrangles and disputes. Now, at 10, we could therefore expect to find these girls failing dismally at school, but both are doing well. Their teachers evaluated them highly, as did the girls themselves. But there is a sting in the tail of this 'happy ending' from an unhappy start, which could have turned the developmental accounts

on their head. For while the girls are positioned as 'good' in their own schools —
and indeed their performance is higher than their classmates' — their scores in
relation to those of the rest of the sample schools present a different picture. Nicky,
ranked by her teacher as amongst the top in Maths and described as an 'ideal pupil'
is only average when she is placed on a wider scale. Dawn's position is much more
worrying. She came among the top three in her class in the test, completely fulfilling the expectations of her teacher, who regarded her as one of her top children and
evaluated her all-round performance extremely positively. However, Dawn's position in relation to the rest of the sample bears no real comparison. She, like all of
her class, perform appallingly — so badly that their top score, 103, is the lowest in
the sample.

The situation of girls like Dawn cannot be encompassed within a cosy 'equal
but different' explanation. She is not equal at all, and her difference — effectively
her class position — is not going to be changed by a rhetoric which attempts to
value 'working-class culture', as if exploitation and oppression simply did not
exist. The discourse of equal opportunities is shown here as the chimera it is. We
see that girls such as Dawn think well of themselves, and are thought well of by
their teacher. She does indeed do well compared with her classmates, but only massive changes would enable her to do anything other than fail within the British education system as a whole, to become one more figure in the ridiculous self-fulfilling
prophecy of working-class attainment. Conversely, how are girls like Patsy and
Katy said to have 'no ability' when they, of all the working-class girls, had —
according to developmental literature — the brightest futures, a head start, because
of their sensitive mothers? Given this insight, how can we now judge their performance so simply?

Post-war selection practices were aimed at syphoning off bright working-class
children (although almost all the studies of the period actually considered only
boys). This was the upward road to social mobility, but it led away from home. The
rhetoric of 'equality of opportunity' promised many things. Selection as the way of
catching talent was later frowned upon by the philosophy of progressivism, but
selection at 11 was not jettisoned by all education authorities. Some kept their
tripartite systems intact, paying only lip-service to the new god. From the data on
these 10-year-old girls, it is painfully clear that if selection at 11 is based on the
sorts of tests we gave them (and it is), then very few working-class girls indeed
could even *enter* the competition against the middle-class girls: they are complete
non-starters. In some of the working-class schools the children had rarely, if ever,
taken such a test and were confused by procedure and content. These children, not
surprisingly, did worst in relation to the other schools. Contrast this with the public
schools, where the girls were familiar with testing as a classroom practice, and even
laughed at the *easiness* of it. We do not wish to advocate more testing. We are
implying that oppression and inequality cannot easily be removed when a privil-
eged section of the population attend fee-paying schools and are coached to success.
As we shall see, however, even for these girls, success is not unproblematic.

How, then, were these girls viewed by their teachers and by themselves and
their classmates? We examined how teachers in all the schools categorized the

academic performance of girls and boys. Although they were not asked to make gender differentiations, all their judgments were highly gender-differentiated. In the middle-class schools they consistently used terms such as *natural ability* to describe the top pupils, but rarely to describe girls — even girls who were doing very well indeed in terms of the test score and the teacher's rating. Sometimes words like *flair* would be used, but it was far more common for even high-ranking girls to be called *hard-working*. This was used in opposition to terms such as *ability* and *flair*. In other words it had pejorative connotations, as where a classmate of Diana's said to be a: 'very, very hard-worker. Not a particularly bright girl . . . her hard-work gets her to her standards.' Take the teacher's comments about Diana herself: 'Technically she's very good, and creatively she has the ideas . . . she's not outstanding, no . . . but always does her best.' This phenomenon — of 'downgrading' the 'quality' of girls' good performance because it is thought not to be produced in the right way — is extremely common (Walden and Walkerdine, 1985). It has serious implications: any child who is seen to be working *must* be lacking in *ability* or *flair*: the qualities which produce good attainment without effort or work.

The effect for the girls in our study is devastating. We have already seen that many middle-class mothers pushed their daughters to intellectualize to a high degree. Here, however, we are presented with girls who are, for the most part, succeeding in the education system, yet something is taken to be wrong with their work. It will come as no surprise that the majority of the middle-class girls are themselves very anxious that their performance is not good enough — an anxiety that most of the teachers seem not to see. How can it be that girls who were brought up to be independent, rational thinkers, possessed of the independence and autonomy produced by sensitive mothering, are now categorized as 'hard-working' and not 'bright' and 'autonomous' thinkers?

Angela, a middle-class girl, scores the top mark in her class. When asked, she has a clear idea of why she ranks her classmates as she does, emphasizing the amount of work they do and thus how many 'right' answers they get, making clear the connection between effort and attainment. Angela's teacher, however, draws a distinction between hard-workers and those with flair, when talking of Angela herself: 'If she comes across something new it needs to be explained to her whereas some of these will just be able to read what they're to do and do it . . .' Angela does quite well, then, but she is certainly not 'brilliant': 'She's very hard-working, very quiet.'

Angela, then, is positioned classically as a 'good girl', an 'ideal pupil', but she does not have that elusive gift, 'brilliance'. She must rely on hard-work. But what has happened here? We saw how 'sensitive' Angela's mother was when the child was 4. She is articulate, one of the few children who found it easy to chat to her nursery school teachers. Why then at 10, even though she is outstanding in her class (surely coming top is an indication of achievement), is she designated a quiet, shy girl who comes top only through sheer hard-work? This judgment was never applied to any boy in any study — on the contrary, it was difficult for a boy to be judged a failure, even with the most appalling performance. Teachers talk, for example, about boys with very poor attainment still having potential or being bright.

While almost all teachers in working-class schools also described high-achiev-ing girls as hard-working, most of them viewed it as a positive phenomenon — in other words, it did not have the pejorative connotations it carried for teachers in middle-class schools. Hard-work was highly valued, and it is noteworthy that the high-achieving working-class girls did not share the middle-class girls' anxiety about the inadequacy of their performance. This may partly have been because the standard of attainment was much lower overall in the working-class schools, and the girls who were doing well were more likely to be picked out as 'good', partly because their position as 'helpers' is constantly reaffirmed, by the teachers and other children. Working-class girls whose performance is poor, and even those who are 'average', often refer to 'helping' as an attribute of those who came top of the class and will often put themselves in the position of needing help. For instance Sally, who is performing quite well, says of the girl she ranks as amongst the top in her class: 'Um . . . like if you can't do something you can always go to her because she'll help you.'

Whilst only a couple of the 10 middle-class girls who were top in their classes talk about 'helping', the issue of who helps and who *needs* help emerges as a recur-ring theme with *most* of the working-class girls, who also *put themselves forward* as helpers. Talking of a classmate, Dawn says: 'Sometimes she does need help, but she always asks me for it . . . Most people ask me.' Even girls who do not promote themselves as helpful are said to be so by the teacher, and this is highly valued. For instance, Anna's teacher deliberately sits her next to a poorly achieving girl, because she knows Anna will 'help and be kind' to her.

Another term applied to these girls was 'mature'. This term had many meanings, some of them pejorative. On the positive side, 'mature' girls have a good attitude towards their work. They are well behaved, they settle down quickly and quietly. They may not abound in confidence, but this, in girls, can be an asset. For example, Maura is said to be

> Very mature and understanding . . . and does her best all round in her work gener-ally . . . She is never pushy. She's not over-confident . . . That's part of her whole charm . . .

> She's very good, she's very mature and if you give her some information and say 'Go away and find out about it', she'll do it, even though she doesn't perhaps understand. (Dawn)

> Umm . . . quite mature really in her attitude to her work . . . But she's mature in her attitude to life as well really. She's totally organized. (Penny)

Maturity also signifies aspects of the good girls' positions in relation to their class-mates and their teachers. Being 'kind, considerate and helpful', they can also, whether of their own volition or because called upon to do so, become sub-teachers. But there is a curious double-edged element in the perceived maturity of some girls, who may mislead us into thinking that they have an ability which is not *really there*. For instance, Jenny is: 'quite big for her age and because she's able to talk and hold very good conversations with adults, I think we tend to believe she is capable of more than she really is'. The slippage is greater here; the meaning of 'mature' has shifted again. It refers specifically to Jenny's physical maturity and her apparently adult articulateness. It does not describe her work habits or position as a good girl. But her mature demeanour fools the teacher. Conversely, when we take the same characteristics in a boy in this class, they are read in a completely opposite way. Rather than overestimating this boy's 'real' ability, his apparent lack of maturity indicates for this teacher his hidden potential; how he is really 'not achieving as much as he could'.

Generally, boys were rarely said to be mature. More often their 'immaturity' was pointed out. While teachers of the working-class girls term their good girls mature and link this with hard-work, boys, on the other hand, high and low achievers alike, are referred to as *late* maturers, *late developers*. This juxtaposing of 'maturity' and 'development' implies a comment on boys' intellectual development, but a more worrying aspect of girls' sexuality underlies *their* maturity. This suggests that mature girls have already developed intellectually, whilst boys develop *late*. In other words, negative terms were often used to transform girls' positive attainments, independence and achievement, into undesirable qualities which, as we shall explore later, can be linked directly to the terms on which women's attainment and sexuality have long been feared. These may imply an active sexuality in girls who show independence of thought; this is an undesirable and unfeminine trait.

A different picture emerges from teachers' categorizations of poorly attaining girls. Remember that only one middle-class girl, Julie, was doing very poorly. All other poorly achieving girls were working-class, characterized by teachers and peers not as *working* hard, but as *trying* hard. All the poorly attaining working-class girls were viewed as unconfident by their teachers, but while there is a tendency to see them as 'sensitive', this is often viewed as a sham. For instance, Katy 'might look sensitive, but in fact it's like water off a duck's back'.

These girls may well be *acting* sensitive; underneath, they may be truly 'hard' — images of working-class women: 'hard as nails', 'tough'. Conversely, their interviews make it clear that they do feel a lot of pain, mostly expressed in the way all but one of them report victimization, and talk of (mostly) boys who hit, kick, punch, pinch and bully them. While other girls report bullying, it is striking that all these girls' categories are directed towards *themselves*. They all appear confused about why children are good or poor at their work, concentrating only on what those children are like to them and whether they will help them.

All the poor girls were much vaguer and more confused about the reasons why they and others achieved their position. They all conveyed a sense of not knowing or understanding why children are either doing well or failing — 'it's just that they are'. Some, notably Patsy, were so bound up with their position as victim that they could not engage with the exercise, nor distinguish between who was good or poor. Others did better. Katy, Kerry and Jacky were aware of their own and others' position in the class, but had no understanding of why or how.

Not all the girls viewed themselves as their teachers did. In fact, the working-class girls had a clearer impression of themselves, while some of the middle-class girls underestimated their performance, placing themselves in low groups and saying they were 'not good enough'. In contrast are the poorer self-evaluations of the middle-class girls, especially those attending private schools: 'Awful! Um . . . I don't know, I just am . . . Yeah, I just get nervous.' This is a girl who achieved the highest score in her class — indeed, in the whole sample! These girls tended also to be very anxious about their performance. All their schools laid great emphasis on testing, as they were being prepared for highly competitive entrance examinations to public schools: 'You have to keep it in their minds with the . . . tests . . . and just move on rapidly to new learning so that the tests are really to get them into the habit of learning quickly'.

Good performance was always praised, but not considered especially note-worthy in the middle-class schools, while the working-class girls were given status and praise for their good performance (although it is average or even poor compared with the rest of the sample). The middle-class girls were *expected* to achieve a high standard, so they were never sure they were 'good enough'. These character-istics are in stark contrast to the judgments made by teachers and girls of the boys in their class. Attributions about poor middle-class girls and about girls in private schools are remarkably congruent with judgments of boys, whatever their social class.

'Hard-working' was used less frequently to describe good boys than good girls. A majority of good boys were described as bright or as 'having ability', flair, brains. However, *most* were seen as potentially bright. Poor boys often behaved disruptively (and sometimes violently) in class, and were lazy and sullen. Yet they were taken to possess an inherent brightness:

> He's the one that went into a sulk . . . he can't be told anything, you can't even tell him to change places. But I'm pleased with the way he gets on. He's quite bright.

> [ ] can just about write his own name . . . not because he's not clever, because he's not capable, but he just can't sit still, he's got no concentration . . . very disrupt-ive . . . but quite bright.

Boys tended to be seen as displaying behaviour problems calling for the teacher's attention, but not as lacking ability. Their problem was, in effect, the teacher's: their behaviour challenged authority and control over the class. Conversely, the girls rarely challenged the teacher. They, not the teacher, were considered responsible for their failure.

Home circumstances were discussed in a similar way. Details about girls were often presented as information, whereas boys' family circumstances or history were usually cited to explain poor performance and bad behaviour. Most frequently the focus was on the mother, who, like the teacher, was singled out for responsibility in relation to boys. Conversely, girls were seen as 'coping' with difficult circum-stances and 'containing' anxiety, manifested as shyness and withdrawal: 'Break-up at home — is very quiet and withdrawn'. Boys' behaviour problems, however, were used to explain poor performance to the point of playing down violence to an alarming degree. Violence was frequently mentioned in girls' reports about boys, but few teachers regarded it as serious: 'always in quarrels, always kicking . . . a nice boy otherwise'.

Four out of the five working-class girls mention 'hard-working' as a positive characteristic of other good girls. Like their teachers, they see poor girls as 'trying hard'. In only one instance did they mention a boy who worked hard. However, while hard-work is a feature of success for working-class girls, only three middle-class girls mention work, and then in a different sense: a negative sense, of 'not working', applied to good and poor boys. Rather than being a feature of what girls do, it is an aspect of what boys fail to do.

For the entire sample (except the private schools, where there were no boys) the positioning of boys poses problems for the girls. Even girls whose categories are clear when referring to other girls become confused and ambiguous when talking about boys. While all are concerned that girls should be 'socially' good — nice, kind and quiet — good boys are characterized as not very nice: naughty, silly, lazy and aggressive. They also 'know': 'He knows things Miss doesn't know sometimes.' This is a clear statement about a good boy's authority. Good boys challenge the teacher *as* authority rather than *in* authority: they challenge her claim to know. This relates to their other challenge: they are viewed as disruptive. For all the girls, both good and poor boys display characteristics (naughtiness, not listening, talking) which are associated with failure in girls.

The other main feature of boys mentioned by girls is violence. Good girls speak of violent behaviour in general, whereas poor girls speak of it as directed towards them. We saw in Chapter 5 how naughtiness slips easily into violence and sexism, directed towards the teacher. We saw too how the teacher herself may feel that this is her responsibility *and* that its expression is a good thing. Teachers too are led to define naughtiness and violence in boys as contributing to the rule-challenging and -breaking they believe is part of the activity necessary for proper intellectual development.

Previous explanations of girls' performance have paid attention to anxiety; but that anxiety has been located within girls themselves. Here, girls' and teachers' discussion of anxiety contrasts with that of boys. Whereas boys are expected to be aggressive, naughty, anxious, but still to 'know', girls tend to be viewed as 'containing' anxiety, yet being more anxious about their work.

Counterposed to teachers' accounts of good girls' maturity, being able to cope, being quietly confident and well adjusted, the girls' interviews suggest that some are struggling — against frustration, aggression, violence and self-hatred — to maintain this façade. Most teachers seemed unaware of these girls' anxiety and negative feelings; this suggests that they concealed and contained them well. However, several girls mentioned that their 'bad' selves were exposed at home:

> Michelle [friend] always has a go at me at school, then I go home and get my mum and dad . . . I take it out on my mum and dad . . . and when I go home my sister winds me up and then I get in such a state I start hurting everybody . . . I just go to my room . . . and listen to my tape recorder . . . then I go downstairs and be normal again.

Of another girl who behaves impeccably at school, but is said to be troublesome at home, the teacher says: 'I was really shocked when I found out. I didn't believe it of the girl at all.' This same girl constantly refers to the other children as 'show-offs'.

Categories suggesting some measure of anxiety about Mathematics, however (such as unsure, unconfident, worried, gets upset), were applied three times as often to girls as to boys. It is not, however, poor girls who are seen as anxious. The terms are applied most often to 'average' girls, suggesting that teachers believe that these girls are held back by anxiety. They are said to become very 'nervy', 'frustrated' and often tearful when they cannot 'grasp' things straight away. The response to this is to offer such girls 'security' and not to push them. They are kept with work and in groups where they feel safe.

While there were certainly some boys who were seen as unconfident and anxious about Maths, different meanings and solutions tended to be attached to this. Boys are much less likely to be 'held back', and 'pushing' them may help. So, while 'self-confidence' is viewed as the key to girls' success, the mode of achieving it appears to be gender-differentiated. While boys may be described as 'abounding in confidence', 'overconfidence' in girls is a bad quality: 'She's never pushy. She's not overconfident. She doesn't imagine that she has amazing qualities or capabilities. That's part of her whole charm.'

It is perhaps important that none of the working-class girls described as 'quietly confident' mentioned anxiety. They were also more likely to mention 'helping', suggesting that they occupied sub-teacher positions. Since the 'anxious' middle-class girls who felt they were not good enough did not appear to adopt such a position, it is possible that they struggled to 'know' and to 'challenge', but that this form of power and authority may have been denied them. The power of boys appears to be both as *an* authority and a controller of the space of the classroom, where teachers feel responsible for their own lack of control. Conversely, 'self-contained' girls pose no threat. It may be relevant that only one (middle-class) girl in the entire set of teacher judgments was described as 'brilliant' in a similar way to some of the boys. This was not sanctioned or deferred to as it was with the boys, but was the target for pejorative comments. She was described as a 'madam'.

Anxiety is an important issue because we can see how many girls are put into a double-bind. They are designated more anxious yet expected to contain anxiety, while teachers contain the anxiety in boys. In our account, mastery in boys may be seen not as a sure achievement but as a defence against anxiety. We shall now pursue in more detail the cases of two girls whose mothers were 'sensitive' at four and who are now showing signs of acute anxiety and examine why this should be so, given that sensitive mothering is supposed to guarantee healthy autonomy.

Something has gone wrong. We have seen how much effort has stimulated discourse of sensitive mothering as the guarantee of liberal democracy. Yet when we revisited the girls six years later, we saw little relation to the predictions of developmental psychology and progressive education. There are no guarantees. The outcome is distressing, to say the least. For there are no autonomous middle-class girls who are not struggling with the consequences of sexual difference. There are no working-class girls who are not struggling with the consequences of class difference as well.

Julie is middle-class, Patsy is working-class. They are one of the few remaining original pairs of girls who are still in the same class. They raise some of the issues we want to explore.

Here is Julie at 4. The most striking feature of her afternoon at home with her mother and baby sister is the revelation of her intense and frequently expressed jealousy towards her sibling. She laughs when the baby cries, hits and teases her, and is clearly resentful of her claims on her mother's attention. She expresses a wish, at one point, for the baby to be there no longer, simply never to have happened! Her mother asks her what she would like for her birthday, and Julie replies: 'I'd like Annie [the baby] put back inside your tummy.' What should Julie's mother do with these difficult emotions? How should she react? Whenever Julie expresses violence and hatred towards her mother and sister, her mother attempts to convert them into 'nice' feelings. She often uses the terms 'happy' and 'sad' in her efforts to deflect conflict between Julie, herself and the small baby, and in trying to foster a more sympathetic attitude in Julie. She deals with these emotions by rationalizing or ignoring them, apparently leaving Julie with little option except to escalate her violence, vainly attempting to make her mother notice, until the inevitable occurs and her mother threatens to send her to her room. In this way her mother no longer has to confront her violence. So where can it go? No matter how 'sensitively' Julie's mother may point out that such emotions are not 'nice', no matter how much she may be 'meeting her needs', Julie's violence has to go somewhere — somewhere underground, since it is completely unacceptable in the social world. At ten Julie expresses extreme self-hatred, which seems to cohere around her experience of herself as 'too big' and 'not nice enough'.

We asked the girls to imagine that they could be like somebody else if they wished. Who, in their class, would they most wish to be like? Julie, when asked why she picked a particular girl replied: ''Cos she's small and nice,' while she perceives herself as 'big and fat'. (She is in fact neither particularly big nor fat for her age.)

Julie describes herself as 'horrible' and adds that the only good thing about her is that she feeds all the pets in the house. In other words, the only aspect of her behaviour she finds acceptable is looking after others: nurturant femininity. Not only is everything else unacceptable, it has to be hidden. For at 10 she voluntarily goes to her room, especially when she feels violent towards her sister:

> Michelle always has a go at me at school, then I go home and get my mum and dad . . . I take it out on my mum and dad . . . and when I go home my sister winds me up and then I get in such a state that I start hurting everybody . . . Because Michelle winds me up at school and then when I get home . . . I just go to . . . my bedroom and listen to my tape recorder . . . Then I go downstairs and be normal again. The only thing nice about me is I feed all the pets in the house.

Julie has to deal with these unacceptable feelings alone. No one sees them because she has made sure they are hidden inside the privacy of her room. However, the relation of her self-hatred, her size and her nurturance provide grounds for worry about her future. She now presents classic femininity: the mother who feeds others, but is afraid of being too big, too heavy herself, who hides difficult emotions. All these are sites for the production of anorexia or bulimia. Indeed, so intense is Julie's desire not to be grown up or capable of intellectual work that she is the only middle-class girl in the sample who could really be said to be failing at school. Her Maths teacher admits that she and her parents have 'done all sorts of things to try and tempt her to enjoy Maths'. This means that Julie has been put under considerable pressure to perform and, like other middle-class girls, she expresses anxiety on the subject, describing herself as 'stupid [at Maths] 'cos I get all worried up with it'. Her one resistance, then, is to refuse to enjoy Maths, to refuse to intellectualize, which is the one thing her mother and teacher have stressed more than anything else. This refusal gets her noticed, it gives her power in her intellectual powerlessness: it is her only remaining weapon in the fight in which she has almost entirely turned against herself. Here Julie can persist in being the thing she has, in fantasy, always wanted to be and remain: a baby, getting attention. It is not surprising that since middle-class practices value educational success highly, this is the site of Julie's resistance. Here, then, we can see resistance used in both a social and a psychic way. It is a defence against her terrible pain, a strategy for coping, a way of sending the symptoms underground.

If we now turn to Patsy, the working-class girl, we also see extreme anxiety at 10, but in a different form. Patsy's mother also is sensitive. Although she was very busy preparing for the family to go away for the weekend, cooking and packing, Patsy was with her most of the time. They chatted and sang together; sometimes Patsy 'helped' her mother. One analysis of this pair is that they achieve an affectionate intimacy, a space in which the child can 'puzzle' over complex concepts, past events and, through the mother's sensitive responsiveness to her struggle for expression, meanings can be made clear, expressed, understood and shared. At the same time, the educational content of their exchanges should not be undervalued, for *new* concepts, *new* information, are being imparted by the mother.

What is important from our point of view, however, is Patsy's wish to be a baby. She does not want to take the place of a younger sibling, but is upset when her mother tells her that her older brother was a baby first, before her. She replies: 'I want to be the baby first.' Although on one level the meaning of that is clear, there are associations with wanting to be baby first and foremost and to be *the* baby.

Her mother attempts to deal with Patsy's obvious distress by telling her that she will have a baby of her own one day. She is not excited by this encouragement. She goes to a baby's crib, lies in it and sucks her thumb. Her mother's advice suggests that the nearest she will get to being babied again is to be nurturant, to be a mother and look after a baby: the needs of others. Her mother presents growing up, at least in this instance, as becoming a mother. Patsy therefore has no way out except to retreat, and retreat she does. While she is willing to help her mother in domestic tasks where she earns the praise 'good girl', she wants to look helpless in physical tasks, especially those her mother defines as involving being 'big':

M: Do you feel like being a big girl enough to fill the water carrier up?
C: No.

For Patsy, growing up is linked with physicality, not intellectuality. It is presented as becoming the nurturer, the responsible one; forfeiting the position of cared for, for carer. This Patsy resists forcibly: *she* wants to be helpless, to be looked after. She will not engage with this physical task of filling up the water container, of helping mum, if it means she has to become a big, responsible girl. However, if her mother redefines the task as one which 'clever' girls can do, Patsy is then more than happy to do it, for to be designated clever does not present a threat to her position as baby. Her mother often abandons her strategy of resisting Patsy's infantile desires by entreating her to be a big girl, and switches to praising her as 'clever' or 'good'. During this episode of the water carrier, Patsy, designated a clever girl for filling it up, is spurred on, for the *first* time in the recording, to insist that she does something by herself — something, importantly, at which her mother has failed! Her mother is trying to screw the top on the full water carrier, but cannot manage it:

> c: Let me try it, Mum.
> m: It won't go on.
> c: Let me try.
> m: Go on, you try.
> (Patsy has a go and successfully screws the top back on.)
> m: Oh, you've done it. You're cleverer than I am, right?
> c: Mmm, I know, I'm very clever . . . aren't I?
> m: You are.

So the impetus for Patsy's development (wanting independently to attempt a task and succeeding) is not any desire on her part to gain praise for being a big girl, nor is it spurred on by a desire for discovery of — or intellectual mastery over — her physical world. Rather it is that she will be seen as a clever girl: this presents no threat to her position as the baby.

It is evident in the transcripts that mother and daughter have a warm and rewarding relationship, and we would not wish to deny this. But this closeness produces a fantasy, lived as reality, of having her mother all to herself, a fantasy that her needs can be met. After all, her mother knows her so well that she helps her to express meanings that can barely be formulated. Patsy's mother is in no way to 'blame'. Rather, we want to point towards the possibility of certain positionings for working-class girls which may affect their strategies for coping at school.

Education can represent a way out for working-class women. Some of the members of the Girls and Maths Unit were positioned as clever by our families; this marked us out as 'special', and even at an early age hopes of escape were being invested in us. But that specialness was a fantasy, and though created out of a desire for us to get out, produced painful difference. How does a girl who, since she was a small child, has been positioned by her family as the brainy one, the special one, cope with consistent failure to live up to any of these expectations at school? Imagine Patsy then, on going to school, where there are many other children, and teachers who expect you to do things by yourself without saying that you are clever for the least little thing. Moreover, school is culturally different from home. Teacher is nothing like your mother and all the rules seem strange, the demands different.

At nursery school Patsy acts as a helpless baby; she cries and wants her mother. What does it mean for her to leave home and go to school? For what it's worth, Patsy has a high score on an IQ test at 4. She is remarkably similar to two other working-class girls with high IQ scores whom we shall discuss in the next chapter.

At home at 4 Patsy was positioned as the clever baby. At school at 10 she seems to experience no positive recognition from anybody. In her interview she categorized her classmates in terms of whether they were nice to her or hit her:

> I don't like him a lot . . . He pushes me and calls me names . . . He's a bit like Tanya. They both . . . keep punching me and keep kicking me and all that . . . He's terrible because he sits next to me and punches me a lot.

She positions most other girls in the class as 'nice' or 'friendly': 'Deborah is quite nice and quite good at a lot of things and um . . . she's quite friendly too.' She has become the classic victim: violent emotions have now been displaced on to everybody else. They may be nice to her or take it out on her. It is shocking that Patsy has apparently been transformed from a happy 4-year-old to a 10-year-old social isolate with paranoid fantasies.

Further exploration of the problems of leaving and the issue of difference entails seeing what the class teacher has to say about Patsy and Julie, two girls in the same class who are both failing. As with most of the girls at 10, the teacher has trouble recognizing their anxiety. She attributes Julie's failure in Maths to 'a block' but nevertheless categorizes her as 'bright', while Patsy is perceived as basically 'nowhere near as bright as the rest of them [the class]'. We gave all the children a standardized Maths test and both girls achieved equal scores, yet the teacher does not view them in the same light. Julie has a block that could be resolved by coaxing and coaching. Julie, in other words, is basically bright. As with all the middle-class children, the teachers tended to give them the benefit of the doubt and to assume that they were bright. If the brightness was not visible, it just needed bringing out. This is also a typical teachers' view of boys. On the other hand, Patsy's teacher saw her as stupid and babyish: 'She does things like sitting under the table and that kind of thing . . . she falls back on that sort of infantile behaviour . . .' As with judgments on other working-class children, the teacher was not prepared to aver that there really 'was something there.' So here were two girls, with similar attainment, judged by the teacher in class-specific ways, and in neither case could she see their distress and anxiety. It is quite startling that Patsy, so able at 4, should, at 10, be classified as stupid. The teacher also assumes that Julie's 'block' can be cured, but that nothing can be done about Patsy's stupidity. However, the picture is not exactly rosy for Julie. Intervention may engender even more resistance. Both girls' symptoms at 10 are profoundly disquieting. Both have problems with violence which go unrecognized.

These two girls, both with sensitive mothers, are 'failing' at 10 and demonstrating considerable anxiety and distress. Socialization has not worked. Both Julie and Patsy resist, but in different ways. They are understood differently by their teacher, and this affects them differently. In both cases violent emotions are externalized, located elsewhere. There is some continuity from what happened at 4, and some transformation. Finding antecedents does not mean blaming the mothers — far from it. The pain of growing up for these girls cannot be located directly in their mothers' 'failure' to meet their needs. Rather, we have seen that it is the meanings ascribed to actions, the fantasies linked to them — of Patsy's investment in being her mother's clever girl, of her mother wanting that and condoning 'her baby'; of Julie's mother having 'another' baby now, displacing Julie in all her fury. These are complex events, in no way simply attributable to empirical presence or absence, nurturance or sensitivity.

Let us examine more closely what this positioning in school means. The importance of apparatuses of social regulation is clear: two girls with the same test scores, but inscribed within different views of how those scores were produced. This reminds us forcibly of the complex plays of difference and division within regulative strategies. There is no simple materiality, no behaviour, which is either correctly understood or not. Julie's and Patsy's scores are taken to be caused by different things: one remediable, the other not. In that sense, then, the production of their difference through fantasies of otherness is crucial. Patsy is basically said to be 'stupid'. Let us then think about the relation between the complex causality of their attainment and how it is read and acted upon in school, so that they are produced as (different) subjects. Patsy displays all the signs of 'infantile' behaviour: for example, crawling under tables. Yet it is clear that — whatever it means — she had a high IQ at 4 and her mother, who was not insensitive, made constant reference to her 'cleverness'.

Julie and Patsy are both distressed, but not in the same way nor with the same effects. Do we not need, therefore, some account which examines and can cope with the complexity of their constitution? Three working-class girls, who had high IQ scores at 4, are not only failing at 10 but are regarded as 'stupid'. All in some way present themselves as victims of other people's violence. Why are they so frightened? Other girls certainly do not fail to mention boys' violence, but do not see it as directed at them. Why? Let us reconsider separation. If the early environment, the meeting of needs, is right (so the story goes) the child will be able to leave the mother for independence and autonomy. Yet when boundaries are crossed, when the home is left, school is attended. These girls are positioned at home and at school and there are certainly differences in the way they are subjected. Crossing the boundary, then, involves differential regulation: the meanings inscribed in the school are bourgeois, patriarchal. How is Patsy's otherness understood? Might not her fear of violence have something to do with this?

If a child is infantile, frightened and silent in school, the humanist discourse blames the mother and then tries to set about curing the pathology by therapy. But what if the pain Patsy feels — which does indeed create fantasies, defences, paranoia — means that she is frightened in an alien world she does not understand, which claims all too easily to understand her? She cannot rise up against her oppressor. She cannot unleash her anger against those she needs so desperately to call her 'clever'. She has to locate the violence in them. This painful splitting means that the vital tool of her anger remains untapped. It is this fragmentation, having to be 'somebody different' at home and school, crossing over the divide into complex differences, which must be explored if we are to cease blaming mothers. Such splitting is central to accounts of a subject constructed only in the gaze of those oppressive others. What would it mean for us to have the strength and courage to fight, without isolating our mothers as the only way forward?

When some of us went to school, especially to grammar schools, we learned very quickly to split off home from school, to see our families as ignorant, our culture was stupid. We wanted so much to be liked, to be clever. It was, after all, what was expected when we had been chosen. We achieved it, but only by learning what to say or not to say, what to do or not to do. We learnt it by painful splitting and fragmentation, which had difficult consequences for us. To reduce this to unmet needs is a simplification of oppressive proportions, since a discourse which claims to understand us is all the more painful because it does not. It is oppressive to produce a mode of regulation which denies the effectiveness of power and oppression.

For all the girls at 10 growing up is difficult. For the working-class girls who are coping, we are presented with the sham of their equal opportunities. It is perhaps salutary that almost all of them expressed the desire to join the helping professions, mentioning helping people as a rationale. Perhaps, then, a small percentage could have equal opportunities to join the professions inhabited by the mothers of the middle-class girls. Are these girls being educated simply to be sensitive mother-substitutes? But as we have said, things are certainly not rosy for the middle-class girls, for most of them are put in a double-bind: they are good but not good enough, because they are quite simply and starkly not boys.

Teachers' classifications of girls are no mere rhetoric. These 'truths' are as likely to lead to practice as any which shape domestic and mothering practices. Feminist accounts of mother–daughter bonding suggest that it leads to autonomous and independent girls, who can separate from their mothers. This means that autonomy and mastery-orientation are produced through early experience with the mother and that girls' supposed lack in this area can be confirmed and laid at their mothers' door. Other feminists have stressed the breaking of the dyad by the father: that separation is never simply leaving the mother. The classifications of girls and boys, differentiated as they are, place certain capacities 'in' boys. They possess some capacity, some potency, as yet invisible but known to be there. The bourgeois male is also endowed with 'reason', and woman must guard and contain irrationality, leaving him free to hold it.

The channelling of irrationality on to women is central to an understanding of the fictions and fantasies inscribed in difference. Mothers become not knowers themselves but nurturers of knowers: caring and the caring professions together make possible the autonomous children who will become free, liberal, rational thinkers. Women's bodies are stripped of their active sexuality, of their passions, to become nurturers of knowers. Teacher after teacher tells us that boys 'know' and that boys' violence (their passions) are just the road to knowing. Small wonder, then, that the girls — like Julie and Patsy — split off from their violence and displace it on to boys.

If teachers invest boys with invisible capacities and deny that they see such capacities in girls, there is again no simple empirical 'real' for us to find — instead we find fictions, fantasies, splittings, and everywhere sexual difference. No matter how well their mothers prepared them, this is what the girls have to face. They may manifest the same behaviours as boys until they are blue in the face, but they will never 'mean' the same thing. If they are independent, they will be a 'madam'; if they are strong, they will be 'selfish'.

We are arguing that the proof of masculinity as rational, as possessing knowledge, as superior, has constantly to be reasserted and set against the equal and opposite proof of femininity's failure and lack. This is not to collude with the idea that women, working-class people, black people, really 'are' lacking, but to demonstrate the investment made in proving this. Such 'proof' is based, in this analysis, not on an easy certainty but on the terrors and paranoias of the powerful, who are always afraid of the loss of what they have conquered. It is necessary to understand, then, how those others, and those other narratives, become a constant threat. Disproving them, without showing up the fantasies for what they are means fighting a losing battle.

Girls do not grow up to autonomy but on one side of a sexual divide already replete with myth and fantasy — myth and fantasy with material consequences. They will be discriminated against because they are not men. Some will want to prove that they are like men, others will resist in other ways. The struggle girls face is not easy and it raises many contradictions for the women teachers with whom they come in contact, who see in their female pupils many of the difficulties they faced themselves. This can be painful. Many women teachers in this study were contradictory about the girls in their charge. Sometimes they would admit to girls being like them, but there was always ambivalence and pain:

> She's basically a big softie [like me], y'know, in some ways she's not like me, she's not as outgoing as I can be, but she's going to have to be careful she doesn't get walked on.

> I hate[d] having to be spoken to in class. I absolutely hated having to be the centre of attention . . . She used to be like that. I found myself very easy to relate to her, and if ever she was pulled out by the headmaster, she used to sort of . . . she used to panic — 'I don't want to go, I don't want to go' — I can imagine myself being like that.

At other times teachers would go out of their way to deny that girls were having any problems. We would be confronted by girls who talked of their anxieties, while their women teachers denied them.

By contrast, the teachers found anxiety in boys all the time. Moreover, they 'contained' it; they took it upon themselves to alleviate it:

> He's the one that went into a sulk . . . and he can't be told anything, you can't even tell him to change places. But I'm pleased with the way he gets on. He's quite bright.

We have seen that similar splitting and denial occur with violence in boys and girls.

There is no simple sense in these data in which boys really 'have' something (brains, flair) which girls lack, yet socialization approaches operate as though they do. They assume that girls fail at school because they are 'stereotyped', they cannot break out of rigid roles, they have not had the right play experiences at home. This implies that boys really are 'the Law'; really do possess what history, culture, science, have accorded them; and that girls are lacking and must be more like boys if they are to succeed.

If teachers deny anxiety in girls, they fail to give them support while feeling that they must shoulder the burden of responsibility for boys' failures and violence. Thus anxious and violent girls become pathologized in practices which help to produce sexual division. At 10, the girls are struggling towards a fragmented and divided adulthood and a harsh world outside. It is not uncommon within feminism to see girls (usually working-class girls) who do not make 'non-traditional' choices as beyond the pale. The voluntarism of such a view denies the terrific struggles in which these girls have to engage. It is not easy to face racism, to leave one's class or to cross the gender divide. Rather than a feminist moralism that blames girls, teachers and mothers for failing to live up to some rarefied notion of a feminist consciousness, isn't it about time we faced the complexities of that struggle — a struggle, though differently lived, for all of us, all the time?

8   Junior–Secondary Transition

We shall now meet children and teachers from the top classes of two junior schools. In order to examine the idea that girls' performance, while good in primary school, declined in secondary school we decided to follow a group from the top of the junior school to the first year of secondary school. This idea of a falling-off in performance was not supported by what we found, and we realized that a reworking of the whole debate was necessary. This aspect of the research has been written up in Walden and Walkerdine (1985). We reproduce some of that work within the context of our research as a whole. It was here that we consolidated various ideas about 'positioning'.

In both our primary schools, classes were given a Mathematics test, which we devised with the teachers to give us a measure of performance against which to compare teachers' judgments. It is important to understand these data in relation to the discussion of quantitative analyses in Chapter 3.

The test was similar to the comparability test used at age 11 in Inner London schools (see Walden and Walkerdine, 1982, for more detail) and drew on the Assessment of Performance Unit's five categories of Mathematics (APU, 1980a and 1981a): geometry, measures, number, algebra and probability and statistics. Neither test was timed, since as the APU puts it: 'pupils would be more easily able to demonstrate what they knew if the test was short and they were not required to work against the clock.' Both concepts and skills were tested. By the APU's definition (1980a) a concept 'involves the recognition of a relationship', whereas 'skills are learned routines'. Thus we hoped to obtain, on a much smaller sample, results which could be assessed in the light of the APU's analysis. As we pointed out in Chapter 2, it has been suggested (Shuard, 1981 and 1982; Sheffield City Polytechnic, 1983) that there are sex differences in responses to various types of questions: girls are better at computation (rule-following), whereas boys are better at geometric (spatial) problems. We included both types of question. There were 23 questions, with a possible maximum score of 40; all 66 children in the top junior classes of the two schools took it as part of their normal Mathematics lessons.

Each question was coded: answered rightly, wrongly (attempted and wrong), or left unanswered (not attempted at all). The results were then analysed by school, by sex, then by school and sex, according to how the question had been answered.

Type of Response

When all the results were analysed there were no sex differences in the numbers of questions answered correctly, answered wrongly, or left unanswered. The mean for boys and girls on the three categories is shown in Table 8.1.

Table 8.1   Sex: Type of response

	N	Right	Wrong	Unanswered
Girls	37	23.8	11.4	4.8
Boys	29	23.8	11.3	4.9

However, if we look at the same analysis by question answered (see Table 8.2), but broken down between schools, we find interesting differences:

Table 8.2   School: Type of response

	N	Right	Wrong	Unanswered
J1	30	23.8	9.6	6.6
J2	36	23.8	12.8	3.5

Whilst the number of questions answered correctly remains the same between the schools as it had for the sexes, the interesting variations occur between the other responses. School J2 has nearly a quarter more wrongly answered questions than school J1. J1, on the other hand, has nearly twice as many questions unanswered as J2. If we break the figure down further by sex, school and type of answer we see that for correct answers the girls of J2 and the boys of J1 have nearly identical mean scores.

If we look at the test items in more detail, the pattern becomes clearer. Out of 40 separate items only 3 show any statistically significant difference between the sexes. These are: Q.2: 'Draw in the lines of symmetry on these shapes.' Part 1, which required the respondents to draw the lines of symmetry on this shape,

revealed a significant sex difference in favour of boys. Table 8.3 shows the answers broken down by sex and type of answer.

Table 8.3   Test items: Sex and type of answer

Sex	Right	Wrong	Unanswered
Female	(4)	(31)	(2)
%	10.8	83.8	5.4
Male	(14)	(14)	(1)
%	48.3	48.3	3.4

This is significant at p < 0.001 and coincides with the first APU Primary Survey Report (1980a), which gave boys the edge on the symmetry sub-category of the geometry section. However, it is also interesting that this question was the first of a three part question on symmetry: the other two parts involved drawing the lines of symmetry on the following shapes as well as the one above:

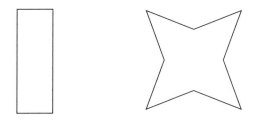

The answers to these last two parts reveal no statistically significant differences between the sexes.

Let us look at the other two items which reveal significant differences in favour of girls. These were the first part of Q.6: 'These clocks are all ten minutes fast. Write the correct time under each one.'

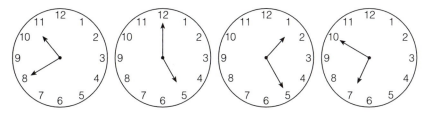

None of the other parts revealed any sex differences at all. Answers to Q.4: '60 per cent of a class can swim. What percentage are unable to swim?' revealed a statistically significant greater number of girls than boys getting this wrong, or leaving it unanswered, as did the replies to the question '315 divided by 6 = ?'

How can we understand these responses? Only 4 out of 40 items yielded any sex differences at all, and these were divided equally between boys and girls. In analysing the questions used in 'Mathematics and the 10-Year-Old Child', Shuard (1981) suggests that girls do better on the questions which teachers think are important, and that primary school teachers tend to rate 'easy' — presumably computation — questions higher. However, our work seems to suggest not that girls necessarily do best in easy or straightforward (computation) questions, but that the way in which differences are assumed between what could be defined as easy or hard questions, or verbal and spatial questions, implies a theoretical basis which we examined in Chapter 3. What seems even more important is that there is little difference in responses between sexes. In addition, as we shall explore later, it is not true that teachers in our study valued 'easy' questions in any simple sense.

Equally important is that the between-school differences were greater than those between sexes. Searching for a particular sort of difference can prove invidious: anything indicating a similarity then tends to be dismissed as not worth investigation or written up in such a way as to suggest doubt. In our view that is one weakness of the interpretations made of the data collected by the Sheffield Polytechnic research team in their report *Mathematics Education and Girls* (1983). Having decided to look at (and for) differences between the sexes, they are obliged to try to find them. As they say: 'The reason for the greater emphasis on attitude during the later years of the project was that little difference in boys' and girls' attainment had been found initially' (p. 9). They are clear that: 'the between-sex differences were small compared with the variation within the sex and between the same sex in different schools' (p. 31).

The pattern of negligible — often non-existent — sex differences persists throughout the report, yet the very fact that the research was designed to shed light on a 'problem' for girls meant that all analyses must relate to that. The biggest differences between girls and boys was their reaction to fractions: 'Many girls were still at the conceptual level of one-half whereas the boys could understand any fractions.' On the basis of interview data (pp. 41 ff.) and of the responses to questions which the pupils worked out separately with the interviewer (pp. 59 ff.), they go on to make statements about classrooms:

> The girls were more patient in their work ... This is not altogether a good characteristic. In a lesson the girls take more care than the boys and so work fewer problems ... It is, perhaps, in the reaction to difficulties that, perhaps [*sic*], there is a difference between girls and boys. If a girl finds difficulties in Mathematics does she think of the folklore 'girls cannot do Maths' and so give up, whereas a boy feels it is part of his male image to persevere ... ? (p. 68)

This, we would suggest, leads to the problem of trying to confirm what is denied in the data. This is not the first time it has been suggested that setting out to find differences often leads the researcher to ignore data of more importance, which may suggest similarities (Maccoby and Jacklin, 1974; Gubb, 1983).

The relationship between performance and attitude is at the heart of the question of girls' performance in Mathematics. For example, the Assessment of Performance Unit's six surveys on mathematical development — three on the primary sector and three on the secondary — suggest that whilst at 11, performance differences between the sexes are slight, and often not statistically significant, girls do feel less confident than boys about Mathematics. By the time of the third published survey (1982) the APU suggested that although the actual differences between boys' and girls' mean score on their tests were slight, they could be seen as foreshadowing larger differences, which appear at 15 (1982a, pp. 118–19). Yet the APU found it difficult to suggest an explanation for this, other than that girls felt less confident than boys about the subject. Earlier in the third survey, however, they had made it clear that at 11 'general attitude had little relationship to performance' (ibid., p. 96).

We now examine the data from teacher interviews. Given our emphasis in earlier chapters on the importance of classroom practices and teacher evaluation, our analysis will focus upon the issues of practice and judgment. What terms and categories did teachers use to describe themselves, their practice and their pupils? Whence are such understandings derived? How do they affect what happens in their classroom and therefore the performance of their pupils? How far and in what way are evaluations and practices similar and different — from teacher to teacher, from school to school, from primary to secondary school?

We need to establish here our critical position on the concept of the 'hidden curriculum' and its importance in raising the issue of the classroom production of gender. The implication is that processes, usually unexamined, are at work beneath the apparent curriculum and do much to shape the kind of behaviour and responses produced by girls and boys. Some areas which have been studied to show how this works are segregation by sex, illustrative material in books and patterns of interaction. We feel that the explanatory power of such approaches is limited precisely because they split off hidden from overt organization, content and processes.

Let us give an example. The hidden-curriculum approach would examine 'sexist bias' in the content of the Mathematics problems on which the children in each classroom worked. From such information, processes would be extrapolated and taken to produce norms of feminine and masculine behaviour, roles and stereotypes. Related behaviour demanded by teachers might well be similarly stereotyped. However, while it is important to examine such processes, a focus on content alone leaves other issues about the Mathematics curriculum untouched. In Chapter 7 we cited the commonly held assumption about girls' superior performance on low-level computational questions and boys' on higher-level problem-solving, alluding to the debate about girls being capable only of lower-order activities. While we suggested that the evidence did not in any simple sense support such conclusions, it is important to examine why the distinction between rule-following and proper conceptualization (a) has considerable force and (b) is applied to girls.

We have already argued that particular important distinctions are central to some psychological assumptions about learning and cognitive development, and to modern theories and practices of Mathematics teaching and learning: for example 'rule-following' and 'proper conceptualization'. These have important effects for defining what counts as attainment. If girls are judged successful, but their success is said to be founded on rote-learning and not on proper conceptualization, certain adverse consequences follow from this mismatch. Clearly it is not just a matter of hidden processes reinforcing roles and stereotypes. We must examine theories, practices and teacher judgments to understand the complex interplay of conditions by which girls' and boys' performance is produced, monitored, evaluated and regulated.

All the teachers and children were interviewed. Before their interviews our teachers filled in questionnaires about their backgrounds and thoughts on teaching Mathematics, to give us some common ground for discussion rather than information about any particular children. We asked three teachers in the primary and ten in the secondary school to rank the children in their classes according to whether they considered them good or poor at Mathematics. This provoked some hostility and anxiety from all teachers at all levels. They did not wish to commit themselves to an admission that they did, in fact, classify children. The work which has been published on teacher expectation had obviously influenced them in this. However, despite expressions of concern, which we noted, no one actually refused. These classifications form an important part of our data when related to both classroom practice and the children's views of themselves as learners of Mathematics.

Our interviews with primary school teachers whose classes we observed revealed that they saw primary Mathematics in much the same way: conceptual understanding was its bedrock. The main aim should be to provide tools, lay foundations, for later life. Both female teachers (one from each school) saw differences between boys and girls. Ms C from J2, said of one of the girls she felt was poor at Mathematics: 'She is very dicey on Maths in that she doesn't have any confidence at all.'

> *RW:* Do you think confidence is important in tackling Maths?
>
> *MS C:* Yes, very important. I think you've got to be confident about your ... about the situation you're in and how to handle it ... in terms of problem-solving ... you can't take off at all, start thinking necessary to solve the situation when you don't have confidence. [Lack of confidence] seems to stop people starting their thinking patterns in Maths. You might be able to start it in writing things down and cover that up so they don't get into the subject properly, but not in mathematical situations.

What, then, were her views on differences in ability between boys and girls?

> *MS C:* No, I wouldn't have said outstanding differences, but what I have found interesting with this group of children is that at the end of the third year the boys started to think in more abstract form.
>
> *RW:* What do you mean, they began to think in more abstract form? How did you notice it?
>
> *MS C:* When we did the calculator work they were able to think in terms of what you were doing with the numbers rather than in terms of what was added on to what. They were more interested in the processes ... than worrying about whether they got it right, and to be able to be free, to free themselves from that ... and it was natural.

Ms A from J1 had similar feelings about the girls: they worried more, they were academic, capable and hard-working, but anxious. In her view 'they perpetuate the stereotypes by choosing to do tasks, to help'. Boys, on the other hand, were 'more creative, divergent and tangential ... see more opportunities to explore'. Asked to think about the bright boys and girls in her class and then the slow ones, and about differences and similarities amongst them, Ms A replied that the highest-scoring boy and girl (on our test) were

> ... sort of convergent thinkers. Very much directed. Get on well in formal directed atmospheres. She is terribly diligent, but she [the next highest scorer] ... she's basically better at Maths because she thinks and she's interested and she finds it fascinating and she's interested in the odd bits of it. She's untidy and slapdash but she does things. But she's [first girl] very nervous about Maths ... she always finds security in the formal bits, computation and patterns and her work is always beautifully meticulous and typical of her personality.

Both these teachers tended to see boys as more interesting — annoying, certainly, but with that extra spark that the hard-working, anxious girls lack. A common theme picked up from their responses is the counterposing of the active, enquiring, rule-breaking child with the well-behaved, passive, rule-following child. The ways in which teachers phrased their responses almost always meant that active children were boys and passive ones girls.

We have considered the importance of the relation between theory, practice and teacher evaluation. We argued that the criteria through which good and poor performance are understood often lead to evaluations of girls' performance as incorrectly produced. In considering why girls display characteristics which teachers read in these particular ways, it is important to consider the children's understanding of themselves. We shall demonstrate how girls struggle to maintain those very characteristics which lead to teachers' pejorative evaluations of their work.

We chose to work with 'repertory grids' (Salmon, 1976) because they permit an exploration of a child's particularity and at the same time, by aggregation, a method of looking at commonalities amongst groups in a common context. The grid itself consists of elements — in this case people, particularly those considered significant in either positive or negative ways — and constructs: categories used by the participants to make sense of their world. The children were all asked to write about people they liked and people they disliked, and videotapes of classroom sessions were analysed. Five main themes common to both schools emerged, which were treated as dichotomies:

1 being nice/not being nice;
2 being popular/unpopular;
3 being clever/not clever;
4 being annoying/not annoying;
5 like me/unlike me.

These were supplemented by four constructs concerned with being good at the subjects which occupied most of their school days: Mathematics, English, art and sport. These nine constructs were elicited and used for all the interviews. Each child was allowed to choose her/his own elements in a process known as triadic elicitation, whereby each element was chosen according to its similarity to or difference from either the interviewee or others. 'Self' had to be included and a construct called 'ideal self' (someone you wished you were like) was opposed to 'negative self' (someone you were glad you're not). As Phillida Salmon has put it (1976):

> The adaptability of grid techniques to individual situations also means that it can be used for the assessment of interpersonal relationships. The assumption of common areas of construing . . . is perhaps particularly relevant to the fields of personal interaction where each individual involved must have some understanding of the others' subjective world if communication is to be effective.

The results were aggregated and analysed in various ways. All quotes are taken from the interviews conducted when the grids were filled in. There were 14 children in the original sample; the other 16 were chosen as being good or poor at Mathematics on the basis of their test results. The final total included 18 girls and 12 boys, reflecting class proportions of sexes.

Most children chose others in their class as their 'ideal self'. Boys usually chose peers whom they considered good at sport, particularly football. All the boys who wished they were like famous people chose sportsmen; all except one was a footballer, the exception was a boxer.

Without exception the girls chose other girls within their class as people they wished they were like. Their reasons ranged from 'she's nice, pretty, kind', to one girl who was not good at Mathematics, who said: 'Nearly everyone likes her, Miss, 'cos she can do her sums properly — sometimes she helps you.'

The choices of 'negative self' showed an even narrower range of choices. Twenty-one out of the 30 chose someone in their class. At both schools all the children chosen performed poorly in class, suggesting that children's definitions of 'good' and 'poor' performance were situated within the same nexus of relationships as those of the teachers. Two boys and two girls chose the 'opposite sex' as people they were glad not to be. Why were the girls glad not to be boys?

> ... because they're dirty and spiteful ... They're brutes ... they're hard on girls sometimes.
> *RW:* So you're glad you're a girl?
> Yeah, they're softer than boys. They're more intelligent in some things. Most things.

Another girl has a different reason:

> 'Cos if you buy clothes girls get more choice and things like this.
> *RW:* There aren't things that boys have that you wish you had?
> Yeah ... fun ... yeah, I think they do [have more fun] 'cos they play football and games like that.
> *RW:* Why don't you play football?
> It's not reasonable, none of the girls in my class plays football.

One way in which these children make sense of their lives is through gender differences. There was clearly little cross-sex friendship. No girl at either school chose a boy as someone to whom they related in a positive way. Only one boy at school J2 chose a girl, and his comments underline some of the themes we shall take up later. He said: 'Well she's a girl, right, she just makes me laugh. And right, if I get into a fight or something she always tries to stick up for me.' Boys' reasons for disliking girls were not as clearly articulated — unlike the girls' reasons for disliking boys — but an analysis of the interview tapes shows different worlds, constituted by sex.

For boys, sport is important and defines each boy's place within class relationships. Life is lived freely in the playground and other spaces, and girls are mysterious and peripheral. For girls, the important people at school are nice, kind and helpful, and there is little mention of outside activities except for those to do with the family. School and not-school come together only with regard to another set of practices around pedagogy in the classroom.

When the grids were compared, the most interesting data bore on the relationship of the construct 'clever'/'not clever' to the subjects the children studied. For boys, cleverness and being good at Mathematics were close. Girls linked cleverness and being good at Mathematics with being good at English and popular. This relates to the sets of practices observed in the classroom (at both schools) and to the data from the interviews. Girls seem to link being good at their work with being a nice, kind and helpful person. The following extracts are from the interview with Patricia, a girl in the sample, considered poor at Mathematics:

> Well, I mean she's nice and all that 'cos I didn't know an answer and she goes 'What's the matter?' I go 'I'm stuck' she goes 'What number?' . . . and she told me the answer . . . She helps me with my Maths.

So, people who are nice within the classroom tend to be those who are good at their work. They fit within two frameworks, one to do with being female, the other to do with accomplishment. This can be expressed in another of Patricia's statements about the opposite sort of girl — one who cannot do her work:

> She doesn't do nothing, that's why she wants to sit next to me so she can copy all my work. I don't let her no more . . . I used to let her 'cos I didn't think . . . She got it all wrong 'cos I got it all wrong.

This shows how children understand the teacher's pedagogic frameworks about learning by doing things for oneself, and are prepared to apply them to themselves and others.

'Nice', 'kind' and 'helpful' are seen as feminine characteristics. Cleverness is associated with these, but helpfulness seems to be the most important and can be substituted if a girl is not understood as clever.

When the consensus grids for all the children (boys and girls) chosen as good and poor were analysed, it seemed that for all children being good at Mathematics was related to being clever. Poor children of both sexes tend to see Mathematics in a cluster with other unanticipated constructs. For example, two boys from J2 who were poor at Mathematics linked being good at it to the construct for 'annoying'. One said:

> . . . sometimes I find the sums quite long and that, and I can't work 'em out so I just leave 'em . . . I am bothered about Maths but if it comes to a hard sum and I can't do it I leave it and go on to the rest, but when I've finished if I can do it I do it, but if I can't I just leave it out.

Several of the girls at this school linked 'annoying' with 'being good at games'. A consensus grid produced for J2 showed a close relationship between 'self' and 'being good at games', suggesting that at this school it was important for positioning. At J1 being clever was close to the construct about the subjects, suggesting that here there was more emphasis on class work.

We have argued in previous chapters that a particular combination of classroom practices and understandings of mathematical learning produces failure in girls; in consequence, girls are positioned as successful but not succeeding. Here we shall examine some of the production parameters of this situation, illustrating them with examples from our own study. Since there is a vast amount of data, case material and observation, we can provide only a glimpse. We decided that the most effective method of presentation would be to set out some of our more important analytic categories and then illustrate these with reference to particular children (girls and boys) who represent specific polarities in the positionings we describe.

In both primary and secondary classrooms our fieldwork consisted of notes, observation of classroom practices and videotapes of the specific performance and interaction of the children in our sample, each of whom was videotaped for one hour. Together, the field notes, test, interview, grid data and videotapes form a massive amount of information on children and classrooms. Here we concentrate on fragments from our transcripts which illustrate particular concepts derived from our analytic framework. We shall begin by elaborating these.

Our pilot study identified certain concerns which we felt offered potential explanations for the apparent phenomenon of discontinuity in children's attainment. We did not uncover any simple discontinuity; rather, continuities which support our previous work on early successes, and make explanations of later performance more of a problem than was previously envisaged.

We have argued against an analysis which understands girls as powerless because they are feminine and against a model of girls simply 'squeezed out' of academic performance. Relations of dominance and subordination, power and resistance, can be explored in terms of social relations in the classroom. Girls are not subordinate in any simple or once-and-for-all way but can fall from powerful to powerless from one moment to the next. Femininity and academic achievement are not, in this analysis, incompatible, but their relationship, as we have been trying to show, is neither problem-free nor without specific effects.

A particular site or positioning which, as our pilot work demonstrated, allows girls to be powerful in the primary classroom is that of sub-teacher. By being like the teacher and sharing her authority, girls can be both feminine and clever. This gives them considerable kudos and helps their attainment. In many ways the relations of power and powerlessness, helping and being helped, exist between teachers and children and between children. Some girls will be helped by one set of children and be helpers to another; powerful in one set of relations and powerless in another: for example, a girl may be popular but not academically good. By examining those practices and contexts described in Chapter 7 we can see that there are relative (and to some extent cumulative) powers. A girl located as powerful in helping and in sport, for example, has a very high status with other children. However, she may still be considered not to have 'flair', or not to be 'really' or 'naturally' bright by the teacher. There is, then, a difference between the pupils' and the teacher's estimations, which in turn relates to issues of femininity and classroom attainment. They may be complementary or contradictory. These different positionings produce and affect different girls differently, but their total effect helps to shape and interpret classroom attainment.

Although the positioning of mathematical success in terms of rule-following and challenging interacts with the femininity and masculinity dimensions, we have argued against a simple reading that independence and autonomy in girls are produced by making them more like boys as a prerequisite to academic success. We shall explore the effect of a certain kind of confidence in rule-challenging procedures on the teacher's evaluation of performance. The classroom relies on both behavioural and organizational rules, but there are also those rules — described in Chapter 2 as propositional — which are internal to the organization of mathematical knowledge itself. To be successful, children must follow the procedural rules. However, teachers perceive breaking set as the challenging of the propositional rules. They read it as 'natural flair'. In the first instance, 'naughtiness' (most often in boys), breaking behavioural rules, can be taken as evidence of a willingness to break set, to be divergent. Consequently, girls' good behaviour is evidence of passivity, rule-following and hard work. Later, however, bad behaviour in class tends to be expressed as anti-intellectualism, which can no longer be read as playful but as oppositional (Willis, 1979).

To challenge the rules of mathematical discourse is to challenge the authority of the teacher in a sanctioned way. Both rule-following and rule-breaking are received — albeit antithetical — forms of behaviour. If there are pressures specifically on girls to behave well and responsibly, and to work hard, it may prove more than they can bear to break the rules. They would risk exclusion for naughtiness and would need confidence to challenge the teacher. Such contradictions place them in a difficult, if not impossible, position. For example, to understand the contradictions involved in rule-breaking and the problems attached to speaking out is very different from an analysis suggesting that girls have simply 'got something missing' or have been forced out by a patriarchal conspiracy: currently the most favoured forms of explanation.

We start with Patricia — chosen by her teacher in school J1 as poor at Mathematics — to show how she is produced and maintained as helpless. She was one of a group considered 'much of a muchness'. She herself chose as her ideal a girl whom she considered 'just like me really, not very good at things'. The transcript shows her, with her classmates, doing an exercise on numbers. They have been asked to add all the numbers from 1 to 5, then from 1 to 10, from 1 to 15, and so on. Consonant with primary school practices, the teacher never gives explicit instructions. First they do some examples. Then, if they do not understand the proposition, he explains it. Eventually he talks about triangular numbers, which is what the exercises have been leading to, but at this point the class are being given practice at manipulating numbers.

It is apparent that Patricia has misunderstood the teacher's instructions to add all the numbers. Her friends have to help her, and she becomes steadily more anxious. At the beginning of the second tape she tries to get the teacher's attention to see whether or not she is doing the correct thing:

> What do I have to add it to, Sir? [to Jo, her friend] He's just shown me how to do it. I'll find out, I've gotta add it, haven't I? Sir, is this right? I've got it, I think . . . Here you are, look here, here's the answer I got, Sir? Sir? Is this right?

The teacher ignores her to talk to another child. Patricia continues to try to attract his attention:

> Sir? Is this right? I'll go and have a look 'cos if . . . if he's showing us how to do it I'll go and have a look . . . Sir, is this right? . . . Sir, I can't do these.

The teacher's response, on looking at her work, is to suggest that the task is too difficult and she should do something which has been written on the board and explicitly marked as easy. This is his attempt to help her: work she can do may leave her feeling less demoralized. But all it succeeds in doing for Patricia is confirming her position as not very good, offering her security in her helplessness. Her position as powerless is underlined by each of the dimensions mentioned earlier. The teacher felt unable to intervene with Patricia except to give her more practice on lower-level work, which he hoped would help. Patricia's problem in attracting his attention meant she had to rely on her friends. In the following exchange, Patricia constantly asks her neighbours Ann and Jo for help:

> J: (to Ann) She's done it wrong.
> A: Who?
> J: Patricia.
> P: Well, how do you do it? . . .
> A: You're still doing it wrong.
> P: (to Jo) Am I doing it wrong?
> J: Yeah.
> P: Why?
> A: 'Cos you're not copying the board.
> J: You're not meant to copy the board. You're meant to work it out for yourself.
> A: You're not.
> J: You're meant to work it out yourself . . .
> P: 1 to 3 equals 4, right? (she looks at Jo's book). Yeah, oh God, talk about thick. (She rubs out her work.)
> J: You're doing multiplication. It's add.

In fact Patricia has been adding the numbers, but has failed to understand that the task is to add all the numbers from 1 to 3, not to add 1 and 3. In this episode Jo establishes her superiority in several ways: by talking about Patricia to a third party, whilst ignoring her; by offering no advice on how to correct the problem, merely stating that she knows what to do, whereas Patricia obviously does not. Ann's response is also dismissed, since the children 'know' that within the pedagogic framework learning is achieved by doing, not by copying. Jo is able to dismiss Ann and deliver the *coup de grâce* at the end by nonchalantly 'spotting' Patricia's problem. From this point in the tape Patricia asks for help eight times: she is therefore always put in a position of the one who is helped. Jo is dominant in the exchange and understands both the immediate problem and the rules of the classroom. She acts as a sub-teacher to Patricia (and to Ann).

Let us now take an example of a good girl in the primary school. Elizabeth is in a difficult position. At the same primary school as Patricia (J1), she was considered good by her teacher: 'She's interested and she finds it fascinating and she's interested in the odd bits of it.' Elizabeth likes Mathematics and considers herself clever. Unlike Patricia, she rarely asked others for help and tended to work independently. In the lesson we taped she was getting bored with the work set and could not work out what to do: '. . . still came out wrong. I'm tired of this. I'm not doing it any more if I get it one more time wrong . . .' Immediately after this the teacher approached and singled her out for praise: 'Children, look at this neat and very good work. I want work like that . . . I want work at that standard.'

Without trying, Elizabeth was able to attract the teacher's attention, and at a particularly crucial time. This stopped her from becoming disheartened (she continued the task) and reaffirmed her position as a good child, who did her work in the 'correct' way. This made her powerful in classroom social relations. All the others considered her good at her work and she was sought out for help, although she gave it unwillingly.

Thus classroom practices situate each girl in a quite different position: Patricia as powerless and Elizabeth as powerful. Moreover, Elizabeth's position helps her to deal with problems. Even when she does not get her work right, her problems are dealt with in an opposite way from Patricia's. The teacher treats her as able; she therefore knows that if she tries, she will succeed.

The helping/sub-teacher positions occurred in both primary schools, J1 and J2, but resulted from different ways of teaching Mathematics. At J2 the children were organized into groups to do specific pieces of work, while at J1 the whole class worked on tasks together for most of the time. At J2 group members talked to and helped each other, and specific children were told to help others — Sally, for example, is told to help Molly:

> *T:* Now Sally . . . that page is a page that you did very well. Do you remember organizing that? I'll give you a chance to organize with her, all right?

The teacher returns later to make sure all is well:

> *T:* So you understand what you're doing? Do you? You don't. Well, Sally, I thought you'd explained it to her. All right, you explain it again and I'll sit in on what you're saying.

Later the teacher continues to discuss the question, which is about sets, but as the conversation continues her exchanges, although nominally with Molly, are actually with Sally:

T: So here you are, you had 24 rows of bushes. I want your help (to Sally). You've got 24 rows of bushes and you set them out . . . how? Is that how you set them out? Is she copying this example or not?

S: No, Miss, she's not.

One of the examples from this school involves two boys helping each other. This next exchange, whilst partly humorous, is indicative of how George approached his task of helping Ray. They had to find the area of three pieces of carpet. First they had to estimate it, then measure it and compare the two sets of figures:

G: Right, just tell me what the length is?

R: From there to there (touches top two corners).

G: From there to there (top to bottom corners of one side).

R: Correct (Stewart pretends to 'nut' him). What's area?

G: Area? The whole.

R: Right . . . You're learning.

This extract also expresses how Ray accepted the parameters being used to define himself, George, and the way of working. We include it to show that these positions are not *essential possessions* of boys and girls. They may relate to the production of femininity and masculinity, but this means they have different effects when displayed in the two sexes. It is important, however, to show that they can — and indeed do — overlap.

In Chapter 9 we shall explore what happened to these children in their first year of secondary school, focusing particularly on the continuities and discontinuities in their performance and positioning.

9   Entering Secondary School

The children we met in the last chapter all transferred to the same comprehensive. We followed their transition and monitored what happened to them in their five Mathematics classes. In this chapter we shall examine some of the transitions and explore the continuities and discontinuities between primary and secondary. Early in our work we were led to the conclusion that since girls were relatively good in primary school, there must be a falling-off in secondary school to account for their so-called failure which is so loudly announced. We hope that by this stage it is clear that we do not accept the kind of explanation that has hitherto been put forward. In none of our secondary work did we find simple falling-off. We concluded that the phenomenon had to be accounted for differently.

This school (S1) had a long commitment to comprehensive education. It was amongst the first in London, and its ethos was in favour of mixed-ability work and the ideals of a balanced education for all. The pupil catchment area was mixed in its diversity and range of both class and ethnic background. The school tried to ensure that the composition of the 10 first-year tutor sets allowed as far as possible for an adequate and representative selection of sexes, social classes, racial backgrounds and ability groupings.

The Mathematics Department in this school was committed to teaching in mixed-ability groups up to the fifth year. Then, however, it selected O level and CSE groups. There was a move afoot to continue mixed-ability teaching up to the examinations, with different provision within the same class for pupils taking different examinations. Implicit in the idea of mixed-ability teaching is the view of pupils as individuals, with different rates of development and different needs. There is a wish to avoid streaming according to ability as defined by some sort of test — this labelling is seen as an inevitable corollary of the testing process — and to provide more flexibility for teachers and pupils (Kelly, 1978). However, as we have seen in relation to arguments about child-centredness in primary schools, this approach demands a rethinking of teaching methods. It becomes impossible to teach a whole class the same topic in the same way, because of the diversity of ability. Our secondary school was involved, almost from the beginning, with the development of new methods evolved specifically to deal with mixed groups.

Throughout the school, Mathematics was taught using SMILE (Secondary Mathematics Individualised Learning Experiment). The acronym is indicative of the orientation of those involved in its development: they wished to make Maths enjoyable. SMILE began in 1972, after a meeting between the originator of the Kent Mathematics Project — the first mixed-ability scheme for teaching

Mathematics in comprehensive schools — and several heads of Mathematics Departments in London schools. The scheme was devised on a matrix comprising all the areas of Mathematics to be covered at various levels. Teachers can choose to work horizontally, covering different topics, or vertically, pursuing one topic in depth. All the areas are covered by a graded series of work-cards whose numbers are noted on an individual matrix comprising 10 tasks which each child in a class is given.

Record-keeping is an important part of the teacher's task: monitoring progress and development. It is also an important part of the child's role: each child is expected to mark and self-correct work. Only when this is done for each task can the child be given new work and signed off. Comprehensive schooling seems to have been accepted as the best social form of secondary education by those at the 1972 meeting. As usual, however, any fundamental social reorganizations were met in certain quarters with criticisms about falling standards, particularly in those areas seen as basic. Mathematics teaching is notorious for coming under fire at these crucial times. Consequently the literature on SMILE, which began to appear from 1973 onwards, was concerned to give the teacher's-eye view of the scheme and its rationale. The main strands are:

1   Children work at their own pace and at a level suitable for them;
2   The teacher guides them through it;
3   The scheme is flexible and in a constant state of development.

It was felt that the old chalk-and-talk methods created passive pupils waiting to be fed. True to its unacknowledged, theoretical background in cognitive developmental theory, SMILE's aim was to motivate children to work because they were enjoying it and could take responsibility for it. Ronnie Goldstein, its originator, wrote (1973): 'and when they [the pupils] have learnt to use it properly they enjoy the total responsibility they are given for organising their own activities'.

One of SMILE's strengths was that the teacher, 'freed' from mundane organization, would be able to teach. As Goldstein put it:

> ... with the teacher relieved of all routine classroom organisation he is freed to attend to the rather more important matter of education — tutoring individuals and also temporarily formed groups. (ibid.)

The warden of the Ladbroke Mathematics Centre, where the scheme was devised, developed and still has its headquarters, wrote that the teacher's role was that of adviser rather than 'dictator'. Rachel Gibbons (1975) saw one of the scheme's strengths as enabling the teachers involved 'to grow in stature . . . become more self-critical in their work and of the quality of the material they put in front of their pupils'. The introduction to the SMILE scheme states:

The project features individualised learning, mostly with mixed-ability classes of thirty children, with each child (a) working on one of 1,400 tasks; (b) working at her own level of ability; (c) working at her own speed; (d) choosing, with an assignment, her own order of working; (e) marking her own daily work; (f) working in a group when appropriate; (g) writing an appropriate test after each assignment; (h) responsible for materials/equipment needed.

The teacher's role varies tremendously, according to personality, but the common features are to: (a) provide a working environment with learning materials and equipment; (b) develop the child's responsibility for her own work; (c) check how pupils have done on individual tasks; (d) teach to a group or the class if appropriate.

So we can establish that teachers operate within particular frames of reference, derived from their conception of learning in the classroom. This in turn may be related to the rationale of the methods used.

Before going on to discuss the teachers and the classrooms, it is important to examine arguments from quantitative data: children's performance. This paves the way for a more detailed discussion of what happens in each tutor set. We devised this test using the APU's five broad categories. This time we also incorporated aspects of the entry guide to SMILE.

Using the two guidelines in conjunction with one another, we produced a test consisting of 25 items, graded according to difficulty and in the APU areas. Like the SMILE entry guide, it was further subdivided according to levels of difficulty. So the first five questions were at level 1; questions 6–11 at level 2; 12–17 at level three; and 18–23 at level 4, the most difficult. Questions 24 and 25 were miscellaneous applications of number questions and verbal problems. So it was anticipated that when the results were analysed the questions' progressive levels of difficulty would produce fewer correct answers. The answers were coded right/wrong/unanswered. Analyses were done by sex and by classes to gauge the various effects of different teachers.

If we first analyse the answers by sex, there were 96 children in five classes, half the entry intake: 54 girls and 42 boys. Out of 25 questions — some with more than one part, making a total of 38 items in all — only 4 items showed any statistically significant sex differences. Three were parts of questions; the other parts did not reveal any differences in response.

The first item, the first part of a level 2 question (Q.6a), revealed a statistically significant sex difference in favour of girls, 92.5 per cent of whom answered correctly. This consisted of a café price list of 12 different items: tea, coffee, cake, chips, and so on. Someone was seen to ask for 'Coffee and cake, please.' The question was: 'How much will you charge?' This money question involved finding and adding up the relevant prices. Certainly the majority of the children answered correctly, but significantly more girls than boys did so. The second part yielded no difference: 'What change will you give from 50p?' These can be no simple explanation for this sort of response. In both parts the question was relatively simple, once the prices had been extracted from the superfluous information. It could be that girls felt happier with a familiar, verbal problem, involving only the simplest mathematical calculations. The question then arises: Why did more boys not answer the question correctly, given its simplicity?

None of the discussions about differences in response to questions (APU, 1980a, 1980b, 1981a, 1981b, 1982a, 1982b; Shuard, 1981, 1982; Sheffield City Polytechnic, 1983) has considered why girls do best on 'easy' questions. If these questions are 'easy' (see Shuard, 1981) it would be reasonable to assume that all children, regardless of sex, would do well on them. If, as Shuard says, girls do best on questions the teachers think are important, why do boys not understand that these questions are 'important', 'easy' and, presumably, worth succeeding at? To divide questions into categories and then to assume that only one sex is capable of doing well in them is to beg all sorts of questions about why the other sex — considered better — does less well. Once analytical distinctions have been made between 'easy' and 'hard', it becomes impossible to explain the mismatch. Have boys skipped a stage? Are these questions so easy that they get them wrong? Why use such a dichotomy in the first place? And why, therefore, is boys' failure so rarely the object of scrutiny?

The next question showing any sex differences was Q.12, a level 3 question about angles. Three angles were shown, and the question was 'Which of these angles is a right angle?' Eighty-eight per cent of the boys answered correctly; 62 per cent of the girls. Only 7 per cent of the boys got it wrong as opposed to 30 per cent of the girls. This question could be considered 'spatial', but it also required knowledge of the properties of a right angle.

The first part of Q.16, a level 3 question based on a Venn diagram, showed a small difference in favour of girls: 'Which number is inside all three sets?' However, the second part, 'Which numbers are inside just two of the sets?' showed no sex differences in response.

The final item where there was any statistically significant sex difference was in Q.23, a level 4 question (the hardest) on statistics: 'Five pupils take a test. These are their marks: 23, 2, 1, 17, 27. What is the mean mark? (the mean is the ordinary average).' Seventy-nine per cent of girls and 90 per cent of boys attempted this part of the question, although only 26 per cent and 41 per cent respectively answered it correctly. The sex difference appeared on the second part: 'A sixth pupil takes the same test. The new mean mark is 16. What is the sixth pupil's score?' Only 3 pupils, all boys, got it right, but the difference appears in the girls' response. Fifty-five per cent left it unanswered as opposed to 27 per cent (about half) of the boys. Of those who attempted it all the girls (45 per cent) got it wrong; 27 (or 65 per cent) of the boys. So more boys than girls attempted the question, even if the answer was incorrect. If we look at the results by sex we see that the overall mean mark was 21.8. The girls' overall mean mark was 21.5; the boys' 22.1. There are wide discrepancies in the scores between tutor sets (see Table 9.1). Differences from the overall mean are in brackets:

Table 9.1   Secondary mathematics tests: Overall results by sex and tutor set

	all 5 tutor sets	t1	t2	t3	t4	t5
overall mean boys A girls	21.8	24.5 (+2.7)	20.4 (−1.4)	20.6 (−1.2)	22.2 (+0.4)	20.9 (−0.9)
Total Chdn	(96)	(21)	(20)	(19)	(20)	(16)
Girls	21.5	26.2 (+4.7)	20.9 (−0.7)	20.4 (−1.1)	20.9 (−0.6)	19.1 (−2.4)
Total Girls	(54)	(11)	(12)	(9)	(12)	(10)
Boys	22.1	22.7 (+0.6)	19.6 (−2.5)	20.8 (−1.3)	24.1 (+2.0)	23.8 (+1.7)
Total Boys	(42)	(10)	(8)	(10)	(8)	(6)

The strongest group in the first year are the girls in set 1: far ahead of their nearest challengers, the boys of set 4. The weakest groups are the boys of set 2 and the girls of set 5. Tutor set 2 is the weakest overall, and set 1 the strongest. The only real conclusions to be drawn from this table are that the first-year intake at school S1 was certainly mixed and that differences between sets may relate to differences in teaching. Analysing the answers by set, we see the expected statistically significant differences: set 1 does better overall and set 2 worst. Again as expected, the higher the level of (the harder) questions, the fewer the right answers.

In answers to level 1 questions, set 2 showed the most difference, leaving Q.3b (whole-number computation: ? − 16 = 34) unanswered and splitting 50–50 right and wrong answers on Q.5, a fractions question: 'What fraction of the shape is shaded?' On the next two items, a generalized level 2 arithmetic question (? × 8 = 96) and a symmetry level 3 question (two lines shown with a diagonal labelled 'mirror': 'Draw the reflection of the lines in the mirror') — show set 2 getting significantly fewer right answers from the others.

As in the primary data, it would appear that differences between pupils are caused by their reaction to questions which look unfamiliar: whether they are tackled regardless or left unattempted. This seems to reflect a difference in confidence, which has more to do with what is normally expected of the pupils in their classes than with sex. It could be related to social class, but our evidence is too scanty to corroborate this.

Again, as with the primary test, there are few statistically significant sex differences but differences between classes, so there are differences between tutor sets in the first year of secondary school. It is important, therefore, to examine wider aspects of social relations and discursive constitution.

In primary schools, children's first introduction to education, there is concern to teach the fundamental rudiments of knowledge on which later education may build. At secondary school, however, 'real' learning begins. The day is divided between subject areas, with different teachers, usually in places specially designed for the purpose. The curriculum becomes circumscribed — formal syllabuses abound. The teachers' training is often different. Whereas primary teachers tended to come from Cert Ed or B Ed courses, with an emphasis on developmental psychology, secondary teachers were specialists in their own subject, with a degree and a post-graduate qualification in education. PGCE courses are more intensively geared to teaching practice, with less educational theory than on full-time, four-year B Ed training courses; but every qualified teacher has some background in educational theory. Mathematics teachers, however, often have no experience or qualifications, but are accepted because they are in short supply. Any educational theory may have been acquired on an ad hoc basis.

The Cockcroft Report (DES, 1982) categorized the Mathematics staffs of 500 maintained secondary schools at four levels of qualification, based solely on academic criteria, with the caveat that good paper qualifications do not make a good classroom teacher. The four levels of qualification were:

1   Good — basically anyone with a first degree in Mathematics or a related subject plus a PGCE or BEd with Mathematics as main subject.
2   Acceptable — Mathematics graduates with no teaching qualifications or those with Cert Ed in which Mathematics was a main subject.
3   Weak — graduates or those with a Cert Ed with Mathematics as a subsidiary subject or those trained for primary schools or those with a degree in a Mathematics-related subject.
4   Nil — teachers with no Mathematics specialism or without status in any Mathematics-related subject.

If we look at the qualifications of the teachers we interviewed we can make informed guesses as to the source of their perspectives on teaching and learning Mathematics. In fact, three of the nine had 'good', four 'acceptable' and two 'weak' levels of qualification. Six had pursued some form of teacher training, usually postgraduate.

We asked them all about their opinions of the SMILE scheme and about the differences they observed between good and poor children, boys and girls. The 'good' teachers, all of whom had Mathematics degrees and PGCE qualifications, felt quite positive about SMILE except one who had serious reservations, which will be explored later. All three said SMILE was valuable because it began from the individual's own standpoint and allowed for a programme to suit each child. This attitude exemplifies the child-centred concept of education: learning through doing, each child with an individual starting point.

These teachers found that the only problems with such an individualized learning scheme were administrative. Equipment went missing, cards were written in difficult language, lazy teachers could use it to introduce mixed-ability teaching without considering the implications . . . Through the replies ran a wholehearted commitment to mixed-ability Mathematics teaching. This develops from the child-centred approaches of the primary school; its rationale is the possibility of catering for all needs and abilities in one class by providing graded and structured materials. This is why SMILE is divided into various levels, both of topics and of difficulty.

As one teacher put it, mixed-ability teaching provides 'the possibility of different children interacting to mutual advantage, the bright children learning more through explaining to others, children not being irrevocably stereotyped'. He has reservations about the scheme, and his criticisms help to clarify its foundations. We shall quote from him in full and then discuss his statement:

> The illusion is that children learn from reading the work-card set, testing their understanding by answering questions ... All too often children ask for the teacher's help, not having read the card or ... not able to read the card with understanding ... children want to know 'how to do the card', not learn what it means and how it fits in with previous work. The cards are seen as individual tasks, the overall rationale or topic is rarely perceived ... Children's retention is diminished through a failure to teach them to communicate what they are doing ... this verbal experience is essential but not part of the scheme.

The scheme's underlying rationale is that children learn better by 'discovering' for themselves. Like the primary teacher, therefore, the Mathematics teacher becomes a facilitator, a provider of context, not a leader or instructor. However, as in the primary school, it becomes important for the children to complete as many cards/matrices as possible, and learning becomes secondary to accumulation. Also fragmentation of topics disrupts continuity: children may not recognize similar areas of work in different contexts. Discussion, although not discouraged, is not actively encouraged, so children have little opportunity to explain areas and make sense of the work.

To sum up, then, the teachers with the 'best' qualifications rely on a psychological model of the child as learner which presupposes that knowledge is internalized activity. This model draws for its overall rationale on the encouragement of mixed-ability teaching in 'progressive' educational ideas, focusing on each child as a learner with different sets of experiences, abilities and aptitudes, all of which must be capitalized on. How do these teachers classify their good and poor pupils? All characterize the good children as competent: '[They're] not afraid of getting something wrong ... They're prepared to try and answer, because if it's wrong then they just try the next one or another approach.' Good children show 'confidence', 'perseverance', 'solid background': both boys and girls 'have the ability to get on by themselves and also initiate new ideas'. They have solid foundations of expertise, and are interested in the Mathematics for its own sake. The teachers liked this. All these three teachers' most outstanding pupils were girls. This is how they described them:

> [She] would be largely talking about Maths ... the main part of it would be to learn something about the Maths.

> [She's] intelligent and intellectually confident ... lots of good ideas and initiative.

> [She] can do anything given to her, a really outstanding mathematician.

Poor children lacked confidence and teachers could not distinguish them from one another. They needed a lot of support. As one teacher said:

> They're actually kids who don't think of themselves that their job in life is to grow and learn and that that's possible for every human being. They think there's another game to play in which they're at the bottom of the ladder and therefore they don't engage in the game.

Achievement was judged by behaviour, and it was felt that disruptive children achieved least and needed most help. One boy's achievement was seen as 'a function of how much help I give'. This child-centred approach leads teachers to see failure or success as a product of individual biography/psychology. There is little recognition of social setting and pressures which are not noticeable: expressed through disruptive behaviour or poor language skills.

The four 'acceptable' teachers also said that SMILE was a useful integrated programme of individualized learning, ideal for a mixed-ability class. The teacher's role is mentioned: 'SMILE allows the teacher to become an adviser rather than being the sole source of information and knowledge.' Freedom and autonomy for pupils constituted another plus, including the freedom to choose topics, work rate and peer groups. These teachers reiterate their colleagues' feelings about the strengths of the system and echo the child-centred primary teachers in their psychological and individualized view of learning.

Criticisms had little to do with the learning process, but focused on administration. The main complaint was that if SMILE was used without a break by a teacher who did not understand it or was not committed to it, it could become boring. Again, the complicated language was criticized and the fact that it was not possible to do class or large-group work, since not every child would have done the necessary groundwork.

These teachers distinguished the good children by their ability to understand and pick up explanation or concepts quickly. They were well organized, thorough and systematic. One teacher felt that they were distinguished by solid Mathematics backgrounds, both at their junior schools and at home. The home background was important: 'that helps and will stay with them for a long time. Gives them a tremendous start.' Poor family background was an excuse for poor achievement. One teacher contrasted children with 'flair' with those who worked hard, particularly girls. On the one hand there were children who 'seem[ed] to have a natural flair for it. They seem to be able to argue the concepts out with themselves and come up with some interesting ideas.' On the other is the girl who 'works damned hard . . . it's obviously through damned hard work that she's discovering.'

All the teachers seemed to counterpose the interested children with 'flair' to those who were workhorses, or had neither interest nor ability. Poor children were disorganized and slow to understand: of 'low ability at Mathematics anyway'. Just as one teacher compared girls in terms of flair and hard work, two of the four discussed them in terms of presentation. One, who considered organization important and differentiated between good and poor children on their ability to organize and write their work systematically, took his analysis one step further and claimed that poor children overemphasized presentation: 'to compensate for lack of mathematical understanding'. He claimed that one of the poor girls overdid the presentation: 'all that kind of detailed work, of course, hides the main mathematical concepts'. A good boy was still considered good even though 'he won't bother about presentation, but I can see that he understands the mathematical ideas and he proceeds very well on that basis.' Yet this same teacher claimed that the ability to write work systematically was vital to making sense of it.

The other teacher agreed about overemphasis on presentation, but also noticed what was mentioned earlier: that some of the girls considered poor just 'tend to rush through . . . they just want to get the matrix finished and carry on with another one . . . they give up very quickly . . . and they can't be bothered to sit down and work it out carefully.'

Last were those teachers in the 'weak' category who had degrees in Mathematics-related subjects but no specific teaching qualifications. They mentioned the importance and value of SMILE for mixed-ability teaching: its flexibility 'and its ability to usefully employ most children at a level of work suitable for them', and the fact that the weaker children were neither exposed nor stigmatized for not 'keeping up'. As for weaknesses, the organizational problems cropped up again, but with a different emphasis. Whereas one of the other teachers had welcomed the reduction of teacher's role to that of an adviser, a teacher in this category considered this reduction a problem, especially since this implies that SMILE is invested with total authority. The scheme needed more than mere distribution to children: it needed thought, and topics which were not well structured should be taught differently. So there are teachers who do not necessarily accept the rationale of SMILE uncritically. They feel it has weaknesses, albeit remediable. This may be because they have not shared the access to the 'educational' discourse of learning theories which shapes the practice of qualified teachers.

These teachers' categorizations of good and poor children were different. One thought his good children came from good backgrounds, where they had gained their knowledge about mathematical concepts, so that they picked them up and capitalized on them quickly. The other saw them as confident and enthusiastic, if not always accurate. He was disappointed by the children from middle-class backgrounds as he did not feel that their initial promise was borne out in practice. One teacher described the poor children in terms of their Mathematics ability: they had poor presentation and writing, and failed to understand the terminology or to relate their skills to similar problems in unfamiliar contexts. The other described his poor pupils in terms of their social backgrounds: 'socially isolated', 'social problems in relating to people so severe that they distort [her] potential'.

What has happened to the children now they have been subjected to the new practices of the secondary school? Apart from the size difference, the backgrounds and framing of the staff are different. Most of them are subject specialists, with a variety of views on teaching and learning. Most of our sample had two

Mathematics teachers splitting three periods a week in a 2:1 ratio, so another dimension was introduced: the differences between teachers in their readings of the children's performances.

Patricia's position at secondary school did not change much. Both teachers (Mr G and Mr H) considered her weak, and one repeated the primary school's description: she was in a group considered 'much of a muchness'. She still had difficulty attracting attention and was often dispossessed of her place in the queue by more aggressive or dominant children. The taped lesson was about learning Braille and attempting mathematically to discover the possible combinations of dots. At the end of the first tape the teacher came to see Patricia and again explained the task to her: her only response was 'Yeah'. As in primary school, she was constantly asking her friends what to do: 'Can you do that one?' . . . 'Tell me what to do.' The teacher saw her less than the others, and for shorter periods of time. She rarely questioned him or seemed satisfied by their exchange. Mostly she sat quietly — one teacher called her 'non-noticeable'. She spoke to the others only to discuss her small nephew or to ask for help.

For George (from school J2) the position was reversed. He was the one in need of help. SMILE as operated by his teacher meant mostly individual work. George's only sustained contact throughout the taped lesson was with another boy, John, whose sub-teacher relationship to him had developed as a result of the way in which work was structured. George was constantly questioning him: 'What page did you start from? . . . Have you done these . . . What's that one?' Throughout the tape John helped George, but in a way that affirmed his superiority: 'You're gonna have to do it, you're that stupid.' This relationship clearly shows the sub-teacher/ helper asymmetry. Both George's position as helper in the primary school and his position as helped in secondary school derived from the teacher's power in setting up class relationships.

At secondary school Elizabeth was considered 'obviously fairly competent' by one of the teachers and by the other 'confident . . . keen and eager. She wants to learn and she knows it takes some work on her part'. Elizabeth found it easy to command attention from both her teachers. The rules of Ms R's classroom were fairly explicit: children were praised for concentration and rebuked for lack of it. They were also praised for good work, although the teacher often said that neatness did not matter; she was more concerned with understanding written texts. Idle chat, gossip and aggression were frowned on, and the girls were often told off for being trivial.

Elizabeth appeared to have none of these faults, although she was often aggressive to her neighbours if they could not follow her explanations or were being silly. She was easily discouraged when work was not going well (as we saw when she was at primary school) but claimed to be bored because it was easy. Ms R told the children that what they produced was the measure of what they could do, and Elizabeth was often 'fed up' if she could not perform as she wished. In Mr P's lessons, especially SMILE, Elizabeth more often claimed to be bored. Her confidence was manifest: she could approach the teacher and demand that a specific card be put on her matrix. Again, she helped others and was sought out for this purpose, though she was often not very welcoming and could be rude. She seemed to prefer

Ms R's lessons, taking a dominant role, answering and asking questions, putting her head down and seeming to concentrate hard on the matter in hand.

If Elizabeth needed help she could obtain it almost instantaneously by demanding attention and she often adopted the strategy (most favoured by boys) of just calling out answers. She acted in what could be termed a 'masculine' way, in that she actively — even aggressively — participated in all classroom interactions. She was confident, especially about Mathematics: 'I like it, I enjoy it, I can do it.' Nevertheless she did not want to be like a boy, nor did she like boys. In both primary and secondary school she chose them as the people she most disliked. A masculine strategy of academic practice does not, therefore, mean a wholesale or unitary masculinity. Elizabeth succeeded precisely by managing a 'balancing act' between a 'masculine' positioning for academic work and a feminine one in helpfulness and non-work contexts, ensuring a stable feminine position. For many children this is neither easy nor successful.

Here, as elsewhere in learning Mathematics, it was considered important to be able to 'break set', to 'free' oneself from the confines of rule-following or rote-learning. Our teacher interviews — both primary and secondary — are full of the distinction between mechanical and creative work: between flair, or natural ability, and hard work. We shall now demonstrate how teachers 'read' certain types of behaviour as exemplifying these dichotomies. Girls are never unproblematically allowed to enter the categories teachers consistently castigate them for not belonging to: they may be admonished for not 'breaking set' or 'having flair', but in fact teachers make it very difficult for them to do so. We can compare Helen, one of our sample children, with another girl in her class, Kay, considered by her teachers, Messrs J and K, a good girl.

Mr J said: '[Kay] registers most with me . . . because she does have a very precise interest. She likes to get things straight, she's almost officious about it.' She was one of the few children able to make 'connections between the different areas of their work': an ideal pupil in that she could 'combine presentation with a thorough understanding of the mathematical ideas and in some ways that's an ideal combination'. With this mention of presentation we see a clear dichotomy between the rule-challenging and rule-following which polarizes girls and boys. For example, Mr K's best children were able 'to organize . . . write down their work systematically . . . so that they can make sense of what follows'. Later, however, he categorizes his poor girls, of whom Helen is one, as having a 'tendency to overaccentuate their presentation'. He feels 'all that kind of detailed work . . . hides the main mathematical concepts.'

So there is an immediate contradiction between the importance of presentation and challenging the rules, even though the former is considered an important part of Mathematics. A good boy did not 'bother about his presentation, but I can see that he understands the mathematical ideas', so Mr K chooses (as he himself says later) not to complain about the untidiness of his work, in case it hinders his progress. This teacher's stress on presentation is unacknowledged, so that it creates a double message and also a double-bind for those who wish to do what he wants. Helen was considered not only to overaccentuate her presentation but also to be 'very well-mannered and polite and rather than push herself forward to understand more Mathematics she'll sit back'.

Helen said about Mathematics: '[They] try to explain . . . but there's always someone 'round . . . waiting and I feel I've got to hurry and I get in a mess.' Her diffidence and uncertainty caused her problems, and she was the only person interviewed who mentioned being bullied. Other children in her class corroborated this. All the children, however, saw Kay very positively. She was the only first-year child out of the 32 interviewed who could successfully bridge the sex barrier to be accepted by boys and girls — on their terms. She was able to take part in masculine activities, particularly football, and still be seen as feminine, as Ruth affirms: 'She enjoys a game of football and all this as you see, but the thing is . . . she don't wear trousers. She's just like a boy but she don't wear trousers. I'd like to be like that. She's fun.'

Kay was powerful in the class, liaising between girls and boys, teacher and pupils. Here, for example, is Julie: 'Kay, she doesn't grass if you do something wrong. She's a good friend, she sticks with you . . . she's not stupid.' Boys described her and their male friends in the same terms. Willy likes Kay for pragmatic reasons: '[She] supports the same football team as me . . . she's good at football . . . she's a brilliant defender . . . if the ball goes past her she'll bring you down.' Helen showed more acerbity, claiming that although the basis of Willy's and Kay's friendship might be football, 'she goes 'round with him for things she doesn't know'. Both teachers mention Kay as a visible, strong-minded child who insists on what she wants from teachers and pupils. So she is more powerful than any other girl so far because she can place herself in relation to the teacher, the other girls and, unusually, the boys, without any loss of 'femininity' or being considered 'odd'.

Nasanthie — who, from an analysis of the video data, appears to be working quietly throughout most of the Mathematics lesson — has the following conversation with her teacher. She is working on a SMILE task. At one point, whilst her teacher, Mr L, is attending to a pupil near her, Nasanthie informs him that she is finding the SMILE cards boring: 'Oh these cards are boring, Sir.' He looks at her, then returns his attention to the pupil he was originally 'advising'. Shortly after this, however, he indicates to Nasanthie that he wishes to see her, so she brings her book to his desk and he begins to mark it.

In this extract he evaluates Nasanthie's work positively. His constant reference to her neat presentation is particularly interesting. To find a possible explanation for this, the teacher interviews were analysed. Mr L comments:

> A bit more complicated . . . a sort of . . . on her own a bit in the class . . . almost chosen to be sometimes which is a bit worrying . . . very careful presentation. I'm a bit of suspicious of it. I meant the sort of work that would only come from . . . it's got to be a girl really to work at her level that carefully . . . not quite sure of her ability really. I think . . . I think again she had a . . . I don't know what her initial profile was, I can easily find out actually 'cos I remember thinking that I won't really be in agreement with it . . .

T: (to N) That's nicely done. That's all right — 22 . . . 26 — yes. Oh, you've done your letters as well — beautiful — which were your guesses?

N: Pardon?

T: You haven't written down your guesses.

N: Oh, do you have to write them down — Oh . . .

T: What were they? What did you guess for your . . . Do you remember what your guess was for the first one?

N: I can't remember now.

T: Did you guess numbers C and A? Yes — beautifully presented as always.
(T marks book, occasionally looking up and around.)

T: Where's your matrix — is it in your other book?

N: Yeah, it's in my other book. I'll bring that on Tuesday. I'll have to do my test now.
(N picks up book and starts to walk away.)

Despite the fact that Mr L maintains that he is 'suspicious' of Nasanthie's neat presentation, in the classroom he evaluates this positively, which can surely only encourage her to continue. Neat presentation can be an asset; it certainly makes the teacher's task of 'correcting' it that much simpler. However, as we have seen, many teachers suggest that an overemphasis on presentation can also be a strategy for masking any difficulties pupils may be experiencing with Mathematics. This could be true of Nasanthie, as her test results are much weaker than the teacher expected them to be:

T: That's funny [Lydia did better on the tests]. I was beginning to think that it wasn't fair on Nasanthie, that Lydia's a lot weaker and that I'm depressing Nasanthie's performance . . . That's surprisingly weak. Oh, Nasanthie did terribly. I'm quite surprised.

Mr L, who is 'not sure if she's [Lydia's] getting anywhere at all', is surprised that she achieved a better result than Nasanthie. It would appear therefore that not only is Nasanthie's neat presentation misleading her teacher (despite his comments), but there is a strong possibility that it may be masking difficulties she is having.

During the lesson related to Braille, the teacher asks the class to work out as many combinations as possible using a total of six dots. A boy informs him that the number of possible combinations depends upon whether a blank is considered in the numbering.

x: Sir, depends if you count the blank one.

T: All right, I think that's — I agree with that. It depends whether you leave the total blank one, whether you call that nothing or not.

Charlotte, who is involved in a number of conversations with her teacher, is responded to as follows:

c: No it's not.

T: Charlotte, what . . .

c: Sir, you said count the dots.

Shortly after this exchange, Charlotte asks her teacher a question relating to the same issue:

> c: How do you know whether it's top or bottom?
> t: Well, I think that's probably what the Frenchman Monsieur Louis Braille, in the last century, thought to himself: how do you know whether it's top or bottom?

The teacher obviously considers this an insightful question, as he uses it to continue class discussion. However, he prevents Charlotte from working through the answer herself: 'All right, if you don't need 63, you can leave some out. So somebody, other than Charlotte. What would it make sense to leave out, using what Charlotte just said?' When considering the Maths problem Charlotte appears to be 'one step ahead' of the class discussion. This understandably creates problems for the teacher. When she asks a question that has not yet been raised, her teacher attempts to halt her immediately:

> t: Who's gonna . . . anyone got any more? Yes, Charlotte . . .
> c: See 'J', do, if that can be like that . . .
> t: We 'aven't done that yet.
> c: You can't do that like that, can you?
> t: You can actually. All right. You can. Blind people can feel that that is different and that is, in fact, the letter.

When Charlotte challenges the teacher's authority to know, he uses knowledge outside the class discussion (or rather the limited amount of knowledge the pupils would be expected to have about Braille) to establish his point, thus appearing to move outside the problem's mathematical framework. He is confronted with a very difficult situation: Charlotte's individual challenges and demands for attention require extra time that he does not necessarily have. As this particular exercise requires class participation, he must attempt to allocate his time 'equally'.

> t: All right, I agree, but I think it's just as good Maths if you count this one as long as you know what you're doing, OK. Anyone not got that, anyone stopped a lot fewer?
> c: Sir, you can't really . . . I mean, you didn't say anything about . . . We were talking about the dots.
> t: Right.
> c: If you say count no dots as well, and we're talking about [emphasizes this] *dots* . . .
> t: All right, I'm quite happy for you to take this attitude. I'm not arguing with you, but I'm also prepared to agree with somebody who's taken . . . Right, so in case anybody wasn't here . . . (t then goes on to explain the purpose of the exercise to the rest of the class.)

The teacher's use of terms such as 'Right' and 'I agree' would be considered positive assessments of Charlotte's answers. However, there is a far more complex process within this interaction. Resisting Charlotte's challenges to his authority to know does not offer her an adequate explanation of the alternative method of answering this mathematical problem. He says of her:

> *T:* I think there are always going to be individuals who react against any system — especially if the system is stressed, actually. I think there are individuals in 1:2 [his class], Charlotte in particular.

Mr H, who was interviewed after this particular Maths lesson, when the homework relating to its topic had been marked, said how impressed he has been with Charlotte's homework: 'Her way of classifying the problem struck me as surprisingly good.' He also suggested that Charlotte had 'mathematical thinking that hasn't been tapped by me'. The 'untapped mathematical thinking' that was resisted in the classroom was 'safely' praised in homework.

Another of Charlotte's Mathematics teachers makes some interesting remarks about her. Although no transcript material of classroom interaction between Mr G and Charlotte is available, a summary of his comments is worth considering: 'Tremendous abstract thinker. She's a great explorer — She's great at the Maths that . . . perhaps we don't recognize enough. Probably won't end up doing many matrices this year as she thinks SMILE is very routine.' He also suggests that Charlotte is discontented with SMILE, and whilst he appears to recognize her mathematical ability, continues:

> *T:* Charlotte's quite selfish. Um . . . if she has an idea she wants it to be voiced, she wants it to be publicized. I don't think there's any — for the good of the class, or to see if the others are interested. I think she's constantly trying out ideas all the time, and that's why she finds SMILE a bit of a constraint, really.

Both these teachers are unsure about these two particular girls' abilities. Nasanthie's is surprised at her low test result, and Charlotte's describes her as 'a curious mixture — most of her written work is weak, but she shows verbal signs of not being weak.' Whilst femininity is never *overtly* mentioned, the teachers' responses to Nasanthie's and Charlotte's 'activities' may show how certain 'truths' about acceptable feminine behaviour enter the classroom. Certainly Nasanthie's teacher, Mr L, would appear to have some of these ideas. His comments on her neat presentation — 'I mean the sort of work that would only come from . . . it's got to be a girl really to work at this level' — indicate this. The SMILE scheme maintains that one of the teacher's roles is to encourage individual motivation in participating pupils. Nasanthie's test grades would suggest that her present motivation is not challenged in the right direction if she is to achieve success in Mathematics; therefore, it can only be suggested that her teacher's praise of her neat presentation (which may serve to encourage this, possibly masking her problems) is also somewhat 'misguided'.

As we have seen, a distinction is generally made within developmental psychology when knowledge and thinking in relation to Mathematics are being considered — we cited Buxton's (1978) apt distinction between 'knowing how' and 'knowing that': the former is understood as rule-following — knowing how but not necessarily understanding the rules' effectiveness and range of application; the latter can be taken to imply the application of a procedure with a deeper under-standing of its meaning and rationale. We have also discussed the interaction be-tween teachers' perceptions and practices, masculinity and femininity. We have suggested that whatever methods girls adopted in their pursuits of mathematical knowledge, none appears correct. If they are successful, their teachers consider that they produce this success in the wrong way: by being conscientious, motivated, ambitious and hard-working. Successful boys were credited with natural talent and flexibility, the ability to work hard and take risks. Both successful girls and boys were considered confident in approaching Mathematics. Anxiety, lack of confid-ence, and feelings of insecurity were attributed to the less able girls — who, more-over, were on the one hand 'accused' of overpresentation (masking difficulties) and on the other of being disorganized, rushing through and not bothering to organize their work. Teachers considered that boys who were unconcerned with presenta-tion nevertheless understood the mathematical ideas. Further, as we have also seen, teachers tend to think that boys fit the role of 'proper learner' — active, challenging, rule-breaking — 'knowing that'.

Charlotte appears to display attributes of the 'proper learner'. As her teacher Mr G suggests, she is a 'tremendous abstract thinker'. When she displays confid-ence and *actively* challenges the teacher, she is met with resistance. Pat Mahony has discussed the suggestion that girls exert a stabilizing influence in the classroom — teachers frequently have problems with discipline when attempting to control a male-only class. A number of authors (French, 1984 and 1986) have also suggested that boys demand a far greater amount of the teacher's attention than their female counterparts. If, then, more girls were, like Charlotte, as demanding as boys, it does not necessarily serve the teacher's best interests to encourage such time-consuming behaviour — this may account for Mr H's attempts to halt Charlotte's question-ing. Furthermore, Charlotte's behaviour patterns are not necessarily expected from a female member of the class; they do not accord with teachers' preconceptions of 'correct' femininity. This could explain Mr G's comments suggesting that Charlotte is selfish. Whilst Mr G appreciates Charlotte's mathematical thinking, he is critical of her strategy in seeking mathematical knowledge.

Irrespective of the teachers' ways of dealing with the girls' 'discontents' with the SMILE scheme, the consequences for Nasanthie and Charlotte are the same. Nasanthie's 'passive discontentment' is solved by 'keeping her happy'; praising her neat presentation. When she informs the teacher that she is bored, Mr L makes almost immediate attempts to attend to her; however, the possible problems sug-gested by her test grade are ignored and unresolved. Charlotte's 'active discontents' are resisted, despite her 'forceful' manner. Her ultimate demands for attention are not satisfied. Neither teacher is sure of the girls' 'true' mathematical ability.

Both girls are placed in difficult double-binds. Nasanthie is bored, but far from pushing her on to other work, the teacher uses precisely the strategy which he dis-parages: to praise and encourage her neat work, thus keeping her firmly within the position in which she has been placed, because neatness becomes for her a source of power. Although at first sight Charlotte seems to fare better, in fact she is thwarted in her attempt to challenge the rules of mathematical discourse. In our detailed analysis of conversations between teachers and pupils, boys' challenges were frequently elaborated and extended. But even if a girl took the risk of challenging, as Charlotte did, there was not one example in a Mathematics lesson of a teacher elaborating or extending her utterances. Instead, teachers appeared threatened by them.

Our argument throughout has been that attainment in Mathematics is more complicated than an ability/performance model would imply. We have suggested that attainment in itself (or lack of it) is not a unitary possession of individual children. We have shown how teachers conceive of ability or attainment in ways which relate to their ideas about teaching and learning, and how social relations within the classroom serve to build up positions for children. In this way children are constructed as good or poor at Mathematics; this has material effects on their view of themselves in relation both to their own work and to their peers.

We have theorized this in terms of a nexus of positions which children take up. We can therefore see similarities between children and the specificity of each case, not as exceptions, which can only be explained as such, but rather as explicable in terms of this network. Let us look at two of the girls we have already mentioned.

Patricia's position in the primary school was one of invisibility. The teacher considered her not good enough and rebuffed her when she was finally able to make contact. His view of her trapped her into reliance on her friends. She was revealed as anxious about her work. The other children saw her to be in need of help, which they provided, whilst all the time cementing their positions as better pupils. She was powerless, on the periphery of the class, into which she could not fit.

Elizabeth, on the other hand, filled the 'ideal' position at primary school: she fitted squarely into the teacher's framework for understanding good performance. Her work was neat, she answered questions correctly and did not constantly need help or reassurance. This gave her confidence in her own ability vis-à-vis both her work and her peers. It is interesting that in the secondary school both these children replicated their primary school positions, and for the same reasons. Elizabeth fitted within the framework of classroom relations, while Patricia did not.

Helen, on the other hand, was in a different set of positions in secondary school. At her primary school she was considered good at her work (contradicting her secondary teacher, who thought her poor) and although she was often, unlike Elizabeth, forced to seek help from the teacher and others, she had few problems coping with the work. It is interesting that in her case study at primary school this prediction was made about her transfer: 'Helen might find the transfer to secondary school more difficult because of her reliance on the definitions of others than, for example, Elizabeth, who is much more self-contained.'

We shall now examine the interviews conducted with children in the first year, to compare them with the teachers' positionings and examine how their views have or have not changed since primary school. As we said in Chapter 9, repertory grids are used to elicit how individuals — and, in our case, groups — construe and make sense of their immediate social world. Information is solicited about significant people and activities (or constructs) through triadic elicitation: the child chooses people she/he considers like or unlike her/himself and explains why. The significant activities (or constructs), used for the whole sample, were elicited by getting as many classes as possible to complete sentences about activities and people at school. Two examples were: 'My favourite subject at school is . . .' and 'My friends are . . .' In this way eight constructs were chosen which seemed to encompass most of the choices. Of these, 8 and 5 were to do with the most frequently mentioned subjects: sport, science, French, English and Maths. The remaining three constructs were concerned with 'personal' positive or negative attributes: friendly and understanding, boring and clever. Thirty-two children from the 5 classes (a third of the total number) were chosen for interview; 18 girls and 14 boys, reflecting the proportions of the first year. They were also divided by whether they were good or poor at Maths (apart from our sample children, this was based on their respective classes). In general, a third of the class were interviewed, but in some cases this involved 7 children (class size 21); in small classes (16) only 5 were interviewed.

When the grids were completed we decided to concentrate on an analysis of consensus grids as showing differences or similarities between groups. Consensus-grid comparisons were drawn between boys and girls; good girls and good boys; poor girls and poor boys; poor and good girls; poor and good boys. Each child's individual grid was analysed in relation to her/his sex, her/his school class. From more detailed analysis we can see the relationship between the different groups *on the constructs offered and the particular time when they were administered.* This is important: these analyses provide a snapshot of how certain children felt, at a certain time, about specific events and people. It cannot be taken as universally applicable.

Comparing the boys' and girls' grids it seems that although there is a fairly high degree of correlation between the two at 0.84, closer analysis reveals differences between the self-perceptions of boys and girls. Boys rate themselves more highly than girls on the construct sport, science and friendly and understanding, and as less boring. The importance of sport to boys is reflected in their ranking of their ideal selves as good at sport, usually better than themselves. Girls do not rank more highly than boys on any construct. This suggests that boys tend to see themselves more positively than girls, especially on these constructs. The comparisons between the grids for those girls and boys who are good at Maths shows an interesting divergence: boys rank lower than the girls on prowess. Good boys do not think they are as good at Maths as good girls. From the rankings of the girls' and boys' ideal selves we can summarize the areas which the sexes felt were most important, because they gave them high ratings. Girls' ideal selves rated much more highly than both girls and boys on the constructs for friendly and understanding and for science, whereas the boys, inevitably, came higher for sport.

Both boys and girls who were poor at Maths, when compared with those of their sex who were good, came off worse in the comparisons. Poor children seemed, regardless of sex, to have much lower opinions of their own worth in relation to these particular constructs than good children, regardless of sex. The only other set of comparisons which produced different results was between poor and good boys. Poor boys rated themselves more highly for the constructs for French and Maths than did the good boys. Poor girls rated much lower than good girls on all constructs. This suggests that prowess at Maths is not important to boys, or that it is less important than it is to girls. It also suggests that boys do not consider ability at Maths so important to their self-perception.

An analysis of the choice of elements reveals which qualities are considered positive and which negative. Each child was asked to select an ideal self — someone they admired or wished they were like — to provide us with some notion of the sort of people they considered significant. Eighteen out of 32 chose people they knew as their ideal selves — 12 of them classmates (7 girls and 5 boys). The girls' reasons were diverse: 'She makes friends easier than I do' or, as Debbie, one of our sample children, said, 'She's just like a boy but she don't wear trousers. I'd like to be like that. She's fun.' Another, Kim, said: 'She's so clever, she understands the cards [SMILE] straightaway.' Another chose a girl for a variety of reasons: 'a nice girl . . . a nice name. She's nice-mannered, she has nice clothes and she's helpful. The very opposite to me.' This comment suggests that this girl is aware of what an ideal girl should be: her list of this girl's qualities is a list of female stereotypes which she cannot attain, because, as she puts it sanguinely, 'it's not in my nature'. Girls tended to choose classmates they admired for their personal qualities, whereas boys chose classmates whose achievements or performance on school activities surpassed their own. Michael said about his choice: 'He's good at a lot of subjects at which I'm not.' Or it was just 'personality', or because the boy was 'good at nearly every sport and he's clever' — an enviable combination! None of the boys chose a girl or woman as his ideal.

Whilst none of the girls chose boys, two did choose men, mainly because of their occupations. One was a doctor — this girl's ambition — the other was a male Maths teacher, 'because he's clever'. There are no similarly highly valued female characteristics. Only boys chose famous people as those they aspired to be: men who excelled in fields which attracted them — a judo expert, a scientist and a guitarist — and related to important outside interests. Girls, on the other hand, tended to pick people with characteristics they valued, suggesting that girls' out-of-school activities are either less important to them or even non-existent. Boys and girls in the first year of secondary school are still leading quite separate lives, with a quite separate sense of what is important. On the other hand, there seems little envy of boys by girls, or wish to be more like them. Even Debbie's comment about her friend being 'like a boy but she don't wear trousers' suggests that girls may want to be like boys in some respects but not all.

If we look at the choices made for negative selves — those people one was glad not to be like — 14 out of 18 girls chose people they knew and 5 of those 14 chose boys. Reasons included their meanness, bullying and showing off and causing trouble. Six out of 18 girls mentioned how silly and irritating the boys' behaviour was, while others mentioned their stupidity and selfishness, but in fact all these negative personality traits were also used with reference to girls. Five out of 7 boys also chose a classmate as someone they were glad not to be like, but only one chose a girl as 'bossy'. The rest were all boys and the reasons were similar to those of the girls: silliness and meanness. Half of the boys (7 out of 14) mentioned girls as possessing the worst negative qualities: from blaming the boys and getting them into trouble to bullying and being boring, disruptive and noisy.

Niceness was the positive characteristic most often chosen (16 out of 32). When asked to explain further what this meant to them, 10 children said it was to do with being friendly and understanding; the rest saw it as being popular and getting on well with others or related to cleverness. Nice is a catch-all term most often used by and for girls; it embraces a wide range of attributes from looking good to having good manners, being able to get on well with others. Generally it embraces a set of female stereotypes and is not often applied to boys. The other two most frequently chosen characteristics were also exclusively applied to one sex or the other. Only girls chose helpfulness after niceness and boys chose prowess at sport. Other characteristics exclusively chosen by girls were quietness, responsibility and funniness, while only boys chose being good academically.

The most common negative quality chosen by both sexes was being 'flash' — showing off in class — or boring. Twice as many boys as girls chose bullying and mucking about. Girls had a greater variety of negative characteristics, including being soppy (this in relation to boys), meanness, telling tales, not being clever, being shy or rude or selfish. Only two mentioned bullying directly, but another mentioned being mercilessly and hurtfully teased by boys, which suggested that the same behaviour was called different things. If the two categories were taken together, twice as many girls as boys mentioned that sort of behaviour.

As in the fourth-year junior interviews, cross-sex positive choices were rare. Both boys and girls chose the opposite sex as negative elements. Only in one class (1.5) did boys and girls choose members of the opposite sex as people they liked or would like to be like. In this class the most positive and popular person chosen was a girl, whose combination of cleverness and prowess at sport made her universally popular. Otherwise, boys and girls seemed to coexist in separate worlds. However, when the individual grids were correlated with those for class and then for sex (regardless of performance at Maths), 26 out of 32 had higher and therefore more positive correlations with their class than their sex, suggesting that at this stage children tend to feel less differentiated by sex than by their class, in which they spend most of their time. This solidarity could also be enforced by the newness of everything else in the school and by the first-years' particular position as the lowest of the low, the smallest fry in the pond.

Of the six children who felt more part of their sex than class group five were boys and three were poor at Maths, suggesting a slight measure of unhappiness. There were fewer scapegoats in this sample than there had been at primary school — not surprisingly, since the children had not been together for very long. They were asked about their feelings about the school, and 69 per cent (22) said they liked it. Reasons fell into three categories: the place, the people — children and teachers — and the work.

The place was perceived as nice and friendly. As expected, its size (1,500 pupils) drew the most comment. Those children who liked the school felt its size was a positive aspect: it meant better equipment and more and varied opportunities, especially for sport. Conversely, the size and the noise were what most disturbed those children who disliked it — mostly girls who were good at Maths. They formed the largest group who disliked the school (four out of nine), whereas only one out of seven of the good boys shared this feeling. The boys tended to talk positively about the scope and range of things to do at secondary school, whereas the girls who were unhappy tended to prefer the small-size security of one classroom and one teacher in the primary school to the movement and change of the new place.

Several children mentioned bullying, but not as a central concern and only one, a good girl, seemed concerned about it. Most mentioned how nice the teachers were and how good it was to be treated as adults, not children. For children who were happy the school's size provided a variety of new friends to be made, whereas unhappy children felt they had had more friends, and more opportunities to make friends, in primary school.

'Interesting' and 'varied' were frequent as comments about the work. One picturesque reason for preferring lessons here to lessons at primary school was that since they were longer, there were more opportunities to mess around. One girl (considered not good at Maths) felt the teaching was better, since at primary school 'they didn't learn you what you really want to learn'. The children were asked about Maths specifically and also about the Maths scheme used — SMILE. Nineteen out of 32 children, or 59 per cent, liked Maths: 61 per cent girls, 57 per cent boys. The most positive sub-set were the good boys, of whom six out of seven claimed to like Maths. It is interesting that 60 per cent of this same group disliked SMILE. It was overwhelmingly the good children of both sexes who liked Maths (85 per cent). A majority of poor girls also claimed to like it, but only 28 per cent of the poor boys did so (2 out of 7). The reasons given ranged from finding Maths useful and interesting to because one was good at it and it was easy — this latter reason was from a boy. Most of the girls who liked it did so because it was interesting. Of the 13 children who said they disliked Maths, 7 were girls. Their reasons fell into two categories: they felt they could not do it and were no good at it, or they did not like the subject or the teacher. Six of the boys claimed not to like Maths but were still prepared to see themselves as quite good at it (as the consensus grids showed, poor boys still rated themselves as better at Maths than good boys, despite their performance). Three girls and two boys, all poor children, claimed to know they were no good at Maths.

To SMILE there was a more positive response: 22 out of 32 children said they liked it. Comparing the figures, it seems that the first-year pupils do not see Maths and SMILE as synonymous. SMILE certainly evokes more positive response than Maths, except for good boys. Broken down by sub-sets, the figures for Maths and SMILE are as follows:

89% (8) good girls liked SMILE compared with 66% who liked Maths.
67% (6) poor girls liked SMILE compared with 55% who liked Maths.
43% (3) good boys liked SMILE compared with 85% who liked Maths.
71% (5) poor boys liked SMILE compared with 28% who liked Maths.

So this surprising set of figures shows that good boys who felt overwhelmingly positive about Maths felt much less enthusiastic about SMILE. Their dislike centred on the boredom of doing the same or similar work. They felt it was childish, like being back at primary school, and that it was as easy as primary school work. One of 10 poor boys disliked what others found challenging: the variety of work-cards. He would have preferred to work through a book and thus to have seen his achievements more tangibly. All the boys who disliked SMILE would have preferred to do other kinds of work: either from the blackboard as a class lesson, or (three requests) in groups. Certainly exploring other teaching strategies may help to keep the interest of those children already feeling disaffected in their first year. Reasons for liking SMILE, on the other hand, included variety, interest, being enjoyable, being easier than other Maths.

The most interesting difference seems to be that the group who felt least happy at their new school (the good girls) felt happiest about working in what was to them an unfamiliar form, whereas the boys, who seemed to welcome the changes at secondary school, disliked SMILE precisely because it reminded them of their primary school, a stage they felt they had left behind. In the next chapter we shall examine how these issues have been consolidated in the fourth year at the same school.

10   The Fourth Year

The data from our study of the fourth year in the same school substantially confirmed and extended what we had gained from our work with younger children. However, it is particularly important here that the teachers' positionings had effects on examination entry.

Although girls are still doing well compared with boys, they have less chance of entering O level Mathematics and are less likely to pursue Mathematics because they find it boring. We explored these areas further not only by observing the children in Maths, but also by following them in English lessons. We shall see that girls' performance and chances in English and in Maths are very different. Although this is recognized, it is usually attributed to girls' superiority in arts and languages. We suggest instead that teachers' methods and judgments position these girls quite differently: a difference which allows them to succeed while they are continually thwarted in Mathematics. First we shall see what happened to the fourth-years' test scores and then related those to teacher judgments and children's own views, together with an examination of their progress in English and Maths.

Fourth-year Secondary Mathematics Test

The fourth-years were tested during the terms when we did our fieldwork to decide which pupils would take which examinations (O level or CSE). We decided to analyse the results of the school Mathematics examination for several reasons: (i) the school was unwilling to test the children again so soon; (ii) the test was wide-ranging and covered quite similar areas to APU secondary surveys 1 and 2; (iii) the pilot nature of the fourth-year work and the smallness of the sample meant that we had little or no knowledge of fourth-year classes other than the one in which we did the fieldwork. These test results provided a wider database.

The test was divided into two sections, A and B. There were 20 questions in Section A covering, in no particular order, all areas of Mathematics. Section B was divided into six sections, all dealing with specific areas such as Sets, Cubes, Triangle Transformations, Money Matrices, Centigrade and Fahrenheit, Journeys. The first section was worth 40 marks, the second 60. In Section B the four best marks out of the sections were taken, and the mark out of 100 was scaled down to give a mark out of 40. A total mark was then achieved by combining (i) the seam mark, (ii) the mark for course work out of 40 and a mark out of 20 for investigations. Since this test was preparatory for public examinations and so designed to be held in similar circumstances, it was timed. For our purposes, however, we re-marked the scripts for five out of the ten fourth-year forms, giving each answer a score (as for the first-years): right, wrong or unanswered. Scripts by 62 boys and 35 girls were marked. This does not include all the children in this half of the year, since 15 boys and 6 girls were persistent non-attenders and had not taken the examination at all. Unlike the first-year and fourth-year junior samples, in the fourth year at secondary school boys outnumbered girls by almost 2:1 (76:41), whereas in both the other age groups, the figures were reversed in favour of girls.

When the printouts were analysed for type of response by sex there were no statistically significant differences in Section A. In Section B — on sets — the last three questions were answered by proportionately more girls than boys, regardless of whether these answers were right or wrong. Answers yielded no statistically significant differences by sex — rather by type of response. Certainly in the second section fewer of the last questions in each part were answered. Of the temperature questions only one part yielded any difference: converting O degrees Centigrade into degrees Fahrenheit. Significantly more girls than boys left this question unanswered. Of the five questions in this section, only this question showed any significant differences.

Analysis of questions by tutor set showed far more statistically significant differences. Set 1 mostly got the entire cubes section of Section B wrong, suggesting a lack of familiarity with 3-D diagrams, mapping diagrams, volume, area, and so on. In fact the greatest differences are between set 2 and set 1's right and wrong answers: set 1 lag behind. We also had details of the pupils' scores in the other parts of the total work marked. The final mark in this examination comprised not only examination results but also results of class work (course work and investigation work; open-ended problem-solving). Tables 10.1 to 10.5 show the respective fourth-year marks by sex and set — first, the average marks for all areas (Table 10.1). These marks include those for course work (out of 40), investigations (out of 20) and examination (out of 40). As we have said, there were 35 girls and 62 boys. Overall, girls did substantially better than boys and scored higher marks in all sets except set 2, which contained a group of boys who scored the highest overall mark. Tutor set 1, as anticipated from the analyses of the examination results, has the lowest overall mean score (see Table 10.2). As we can see, one girl and two boys were absent for this work. Again the girls in all classes did better than the boys and the four girls in set 3 have high scores. Table 10.3, for course work, shows this pattern. Again, the boys from 2 score the highest for boys, but the girls of set 3 score exceptionally high out of 40. Apart from set 2, the girls consistently outrank the boys. The final set of marks are average scores for the examination results, by set (see Table 10.4).

Table 10.5 shows which sets did best and worst on all dimensions. The boys' scores are clear — those in set 2 came top in all areas; those in set 1 came bottom. The girls in set 3 did best in all areas except investigations, which could be considered the most open-ended and least structured. Those from set 1, whose overall total marks were the lowest of all the groups of girls, came top here. Otherwise, the lowest marks in other areas were shared by other sets — each presumably showing a particular weakness.

Table 10.1   Fourth-year secondary mathematics test: Marks by sex and tutor set (total figs in brackets)

	Overall Average	Tutor Set 1	Tutor Set 2	Tutor Set 3	Tutor Set 4	Tutor Set 5
Boys and girls Total (97)	57.9	48.9 (23)	63.9 (19)	59.9 (15)	62.3 (23)	56.5 (17)
Girls (35)	62.5	56.9 (10)	58.4 (7)	74.5 (4)	68.1 (9)	59.8 (5)
Boys (62)	55.3	42.8 (13)	66.1 (12)	54.5 (11)	58.6 (14)	55.1 (12)

Table 10.2   Fourth-year secondary mathematics test: Investigations marks

	Overall Average	Tutor Set 1	Tutor Set 2	Tutor Set 3	Tutor Set 4	Tutor Set 5
Girls and boys (94)	12.4	12.2 (22)	14.2 (19)	11.7 (15)	11.9 (23)	12.1 (15)
Girls (34)	14.4	15.2 (10)	14.4 (7)	14 (4)	13.6 (9)	14.8 (4)
Boys (60)	11.3	9.8 (12)	14 (12)	10.9 (11)	10.9 (14)	11.1 (11)

Table 10.3   Fourth-year secondary mathematics test: Course work marks

	Overall Average	Tutor Set 1	Tutor Set 2	Tutor Set 3	Tutor Set 4	Tutor Set 5
Girls and boys (97)	24.3	22.5	25.6	24.3	26.3	22.5
Girls (35)	26.3	25	24.3	30.3	29	23.6
Boys (62)	23.2	20.6	26.3	22.1	24.6	22.1

Table 10.4   Fourth-year secondary mathematics test: Examination marks

	Overall Average	Tutor Set 1	Tutor Set 2	Tutor Set 3	Tutor Set 4	Tutor Set 5
Girls and Boys (97)	21.9	16.6	22.7	23.9	24.5	23.3
Girls (35)	23.5	21	19.7	30.3	25.6	24.4
Boys (62)	21.1	13.2	24.4	21.5	23.8	22.8

We present our material in this way to make the point that the test data alone provide no complete explanation of the scores. It would be difficult to make statements about how these scores are produced if we had no data on classroom practices and the constitution of teachers and pupils within them. If we are to consider intervention it is important to know what goes on in classrooms (the end results of which are the test scores) as well as the effects for policy.

Table 10.5 Fourth-year secondary mathematics test: Scores on all results by class and sex (The total scores refer to the results of all the items added together)

	Investigations	Course work	Examinations	Total
Highest score GIRLS	Tutor Groups: 1	3	3	3
BOYS	Tutor Groups: 2	2	2	2
Lowest score GIRLS	Tutor Groups: 4	5	2	1
BOYS	Tutor Groups: 1	1	1	1

In December 1982 the fourth year took a mock examination to decide for which public examination they would be entered. Out of the entire year's intake of 229 pupils, 31 were entered for O level. Of the rest all but ten, who were entered for Mode 1 CSE, were entered for Mode 3 CSE. Mode 1 is set and marked by the examining board; Mode 3 is set and marked internally by the school and moderated by the board. Here the examination was based on SMILE and coordinated by the SMILE centre. Mode 3 was most frequently chosen, since it depended on course work as well as examination performance. Mode 1 was suggested only to those children who, for whatever reasons, had not done much course work.

In the school's — very reasonable — opinion Mode 3, incorporating class work and examination work, gave a fairer assessment of competence than Mode 1 or O level. However, O level was, at that time, still the most prestigious examination, more acceptable to future employers. Only Grade 1 CSE was equally acceptable.

The average mark this school demanded for entry into the O level set was 82.5 (three girls and seven boys were entered, despite lower than average marks). Of the 28 (out of 31) children whose sex was known (by us) entered for O level, 20 were boys, 8 girls. Despite the fact that in the mock examinations, which we have analysed in this chapter, girls performed generally better than boys, in four out of five tutor sets hardly any girls were entered for O level. Our interpretation of the data suggests, conversely, that despite their success in the fourth year relative to boys, girls are not being entered for O level in anything like the same proportions.

While it is quite common to treat test results as a picture of incontrovertible fact about performance and — by implication — ability, these results suggest that something is happening in the school which downplays girls' superior performance by practices which discriminate against their entry for O level. As we have suggested earlier in this chapter, it is not uncommon to use very slippery criteria when interpreting test data. Scott-Hodgetts (1986) criticizes our interpretations and implies that we impute girls' failure to teachers' prejudice. We hope it is clear from earlier chapters that we are concerned with teacher and pupil subjectivities as constituted within modern pedagogic power/knowledge relations, and not with prejudice. We hope our approach shows how differently we interpret the 'real'.

In the next section we shall demonstrate that teachers' arguments for entering girls for CSE rather than O level are based on characteristics displayed in the classroom, which tend to be read as 'lack of confidence'. Teachers feel that they should protect rather than push the girls in question. However, it is hardly surprising to find that, in consequence, girls' CSE results are not bunched at the top end of the attainment range. Although test results are often understood as hard data and classroom data as soft (even feminine), if we ignore those practices through which subject positions are produced and subjectivities created we cannot possibly make any sense of the complex causality involved in the production of test and examination results.

Mr N's categories in describing his fourth-year Mathematics set were similar to those by which he described his first-year group, and to those used by other teachers. Good girls, for instance, were conscientious and confident, able to grasp new ideas quickly. They had solid mathematical backgrounds, which had stood them in good stead. A word which was only ever applied to good girls in the context of their Mathematics lesson was 'ambitious'. It was used on two separate occasions and seemed to hint at their motivation for being good, although there was no real clarification. The teacher's description of one gives the essence of what he felt about all of them:

> Very conscientious, very well motivated, ambitious, wants to do well, not terribly interested in the subject for its own sake. Just tremendous perseverance. Lots of support from . . . family . . . so is pretty successful.

Good boys were good at 'visual things'. Again, they benefited from a good Mathematics background and had 'flair' and 'natural ability'. They were also interested in Mathematics for its intrinsic worth, rather than for any instrumental gain, such as an O level or CSE Grade 1 pass. Here the teacher contrasts a good boy in his class, whom he described as

> [A] stereotypical boy, you know, interested in science and so Maths and aeroplanes and stuff like that. So would see Maths as important and intrinsically interesting.

with poor girls, who were unsure all unwilling to take risks. In fact the typical girl was:

> . . . very unsure of herself, unwilling to volunteer things that might be wrong, wants to take it away and look at it carefully and spend some time going over it again before actually committing herself . . . she'll apparently have no confidence in her ability.

Poor girls lacked confidence and needed considerable help and support to grasp ideas. Poor boys, on the other hand, tended to bluff and cover up their faults. They were lazy, although some were excused because of the poor self-image they derived from a poor family background.

Confidence, flexibility, thoroughness, the ability to pick up new ideas quickly and with a minimum of teacher support, are all highly praised. This suggests that the secondary teachers, like the primary teachers, felt positive towards those children who understood explanations readily and did not, therefore, seem to challenge their teaching ability. All the qualities mentioned as positive reflect the ideal pupil: lively and interested (not too lively and therefore disruptive!), conscientious, little trouble in class, producing a lot of work to a high standard, with a good grounding in the basic areas of Mathematics which can be capitalized on.

'Poor' children have 'low ability', are 'unable to grasp mathematical ideas', 'unsure of themselves' and 'nervy', cannot remember what was learnt before and apply it to the present. They fail to make connections. It is not clear quite why the teachers should characterize the children in these terms. It is often thought that such children do not understand because they have language, social or behavioural problems. Essentially the problem is not seen as susceptible to change at school. All the poor children are considered to have behavioural problems which preclude the things children need for success in Mathematics: an interest in and curiosity about their surroundings, perseverance and enthusiasm.

Looking at the characteristics specifically ascribed to boys and girls, good girls persevered, were sharp, had flair and confidence, backed up by a solid primary school background. The boys, especially good boys, showed natural talent and worked hard, were confident, flexible and took risks. They too had solid backgrounds. Poor girls were more likely to be considered lacking in confidence and anxious, rushing through work because they were insecure. They were also accused of overemphasizing presentation and being disorganized. Poor boys were mostly seen as having behavioural problems: disrupting classes or hiding their inadequacies with annoyance. They, too, lacked confidence, but needed more support, presumably because if denied it they would be more likely to disrupt the class.

By the fourth year the children were established within their classes, in both their relationship to their peers and to Maths. Throughout the school the emphasis on individual work and individual credit meant that by now they had become totally individualistic. As we showed in the last chapter, the older children felt that they were less part of the school group. We could surmise that working on individualized Mathematics schemes for so long left them more concerned to get on than to discuss and/or help others. Also, it seems that by the fourth year they were doing such different things that there was little common ground for discussion.

It is significant that the girls seen as good by the fourth-year teacher rarely sought help. The teacher could therefore see them as both good and hard-working. They both helped other pupils and were seen by others as good. The teacher called both 'conscientious', even though one had been truanting.

Amongst the poor girls Yong was thought to work hard but not to be very good. However, she rarely went to the teacher for help, because she was timid and felt that she was not very good, since she found Mathematics a struggle. Again, as in both the lower classes, it seemed to be the ability to attract the teacher's attention which differentiated good from poor pupils. Yong expressed her feelings in this way: 'I'm not very good at Maths . . . I haven't talked to him much about Maths. I haven't asked him much . . . Sometimes when I'm not good at Maths I don't ask.' 'I always struggle,' she said of herself. She felt trapped, afraid to ask for help. This gave her a sense of powerlessness in her Mathematics lessons and she was forced to turn to other children for help and support. In the videotaped lessons she spent nearly twenty minutes reading and re-reading her work-card. She tried to work back from the answers in the answer book. At this point the teacher came beside her:

T: Let me see . . . you might . . . where you've got a difficult graph like this, you might find it better on proper graph paper. Do you know what I mean?

Y: Yeah. (The teacher moves away, leaving Yong rubbing out her work.) I was all wrong. (She tries again and attracts the attention of a visitor to the classroom, who goes to help.) I don't get this (reads from work-card). You are driving 200 ft behind Bruce. It says: 'What is your maximum safe speed?'

V: Right, so you just read that off the graph . . . I've not actually seen this card before. Do you read off the graph? The maximum safe speed is 55 it looks like, isn't it?

Y: Oh yeah . . . D'you get what this means? Do you think the curve should go through the nought?

V: Your curve does actually go through the nought . . .

Y: Oh.

V: Think about what nought means. If you're no distance at all behind the car in front, that means you're actually touching the car in front . . . your speed actually has to be nought for it to be safe, doesn't it?

Y: Mmm . . .

This extract exemplifies some of the dilemmas mentioned earlier, experienced by both teachers and pupils. The pupil had no access to — or was afraid to express — the terms on which the activity was conducted. The teacher wished neither to push nor to do all the work, preferring to let the girl find the answers for herself. This trapped both participants and contributed to the girl's pessimistic view of her ability.

Good children, regardless of sex, helped others. Michelle, asked to help a boy, claimed, however, 'I've forgotten how I did it.' When the teacher came to ask what the problem was, she replied: 'I can't do it anyway. I doubt if I'll be able to understand it. I don't understand any of this.' This girl, at the intersection of the constellations 'clever' and 'helpful', wanted to abdicate some of the responsibility which this implied. She may also have felt pressure to get on and to complete as many matrices as possible.

As we have noted, it was vital for these pupils to be seen as capable of handling social relations properly. Helping/being helped therefore took on other connotations to do with being 'boring', 'unable to do it' and not an interesting person. It was as 'uncool' to help as to be helped, except casually as in this sequence between Vivienne and Michelle:

V: I don't get that.

M: (who has been sitting on top of a store cupboard) What?

V: 'x' equals 2.

M: 'x' 've gotta do it on? Where? Where does it say that? Is 'x' going along the bottom?

v: So I put 'a' on 2.

m: 'x' equals 2.

v: I don't get that. First of all I thought it meant a [untrans.] axis and put 'a' here, along the 'x' axis.

m: No . . . that's wrong, that's 2, that's . . . It's 'x' equal 2, that line there.

v: Oh God, I always get this wrong. 'x' equals 2 would here.

m: Yeah.

v: Oh, I get it now, thank you.

By this stage, it seems, many children have decided that Mathematics is 'boring', yet few seem able to articulate why, apart from blaming themselves. Michelle seemed to understand her friend's problem, but made no attempt to explain it. Equally, her friend seemed content to assume that it was her fault ('I always get this wrong'). At this stage, power is invested in those who have access to Mathematics as a body of knowledge, and they retain their power by not letting others into their secret. Those who are good have understood the rule-governed nature of the inter-action and can work within it successfully. There was much discussion about the amount of work done, and this was related to examinations, since a school-based CSE Mode 3 course derives 50 per cent of marks from course work, for which a minimum number of matrices need to be completed. Rule-challenging or following seemed, at this level, to apply more to those who challenged behavioural rules. This was not necessarily sanctioned (Michelle often truanted) but we saw little evidence of an ability to 'break set' even amongst the good children.

There was least discussion of Mathematics amongst this age range. Work was done silently. Help tended to be practical, with little or no discussion of issues. Vivienne summed up a dilemma expressed by all the poor girls interviewed:

v: When I came to this school I had a Triple 1 which you get in primary school [refers to Band 1 on ILEA's primary school comparability tests, which allocate children to ability Band 1, 2 or 3, before secondary school. This is used to ensure that the secondary school's intake is genuinely mixed-ability. The 'Triple' refers to the areas tested: Mathematics, English and verbal reasoning].

i: Did you enjoy Maths in your primary school?

v: Absolutely detested it.

i: What happened once you got here, then?

v: I don't know, at some point I thought, ugh, I'm no good at Maths and I didn't really try, I suppose . . . now I'm trying to work again. But also I get easily distracted by people . . . who're good at Maths, anyway, so they can distract us and get back on with their work again.

It would, however, be unfair to suggest that the girls accepted unequivocally the teacher's definitions of their ability. Those in our sample resisted the teacher in various ways. Yong, for example, insisted, despite the teacher's misgivings, on attending a group doing work specifically aimed at the O level syllabus. Often, resistance meant refusing to accept the teacher's definitions of what was considered appropriate behaviour and knowledge and thus refusing to ask him for help, or truanting (Hayward, 1983).

The videotapes of the boys in the sample show more interaction between them and the teacher about Mathematics: the teacher corrected work and discussed problems and answers with them in more depth, monitoring their work rates more closely: 'Trevor, you're not doing as much as usual. Mark's obviously a bad influence.' It is the good boys — as chosen by the teacher — who seem to have most contact with him about work, yet only one child from our sample was entered for the O level course in the fifth form and that was a girl who insisted on this against the teacher's wishes. We were unable to explore this because it took place after our fieldwork. The boys, like the girls, discussed their lives outside lessons during Mathematics. Since they were all children doing different mathematical things there was little common ground, although most would have covered most of the areas at some time.

The teacher was understood to be a facilitator and was not often approached for help, although he carefully monitored the class and tried to see every child as often as possible. Yet he too was caught in a double-bind. He worked to facilitate the children's learning by providing the resources and a suitable environment. Out of respect for their feelings, and aware of the fears Mathematics can generate, he tried not to push or to be authoritarian. This, in turn, left the quieter girls struggling, feeling that they could not do the work and that the teacher was unapproachable: the very opposite of what he wanted to convey.

Our strategy for generating the fourth-year secondary sample was different. The first-year sample had been labelled good or poor by their primary teachers, and their progress through the educational system was followed. In looking at the fourth year we had to revert to our original tactic: asking their Mathematics teacher — who, because of school policy, had also been their form tutor since their first year — to select boys and girls whom he considered good and poor at the subject. Eight children were chosen: four girls, two good at Mathematics and two poor, and four boys similarly divided. One of the poor boys had to go into hospital in the middle of the fieldwork and was therefore excluded. Time constraints meant that only one fourth-year class had been observed, so we decided to make up the rest of the sample from other children who were considered significant. This was determined by the amount of time each teacher spent with them, the number of times they were mentioned by other children when interviewed, and their appearance on the videotapes. Five other children were chosen who, in fact, turned out to be considered poor by the teacher — three girls and two boys.

In total, 12 children (7 girls, 5 boys) were interviewed: all did Mathematics together and most did English together. Again we supplied the constructs for the repertory grids after careful observation and after reading comments written by the tutor sets for their tutor on their thoughts about their lesson. By the fourth year optional subjects had been chosen, so that not all the pupils did the same timetable. We therefore decided that the only academic constructs would be in the three 'core' subjects: Mathematics, English and social education. All these were compulsory and we could be sure everyone would have experienced them. The other four constructs — 'personal' ones to do with the traits considered important by the class — were 'helpful', 'hard-working', 'boring' and 'like best'/'like least'.

Comparisons between consensus grids (see Chapter 8) show that by the fourth year there is very little common ground between the sexes. The correlation between boys' and girls' grids is very low (0.47). The construct with the lowest correlation between the groups is that for Mathematics, and the highest correlation is for helpfulness. The girls rate Mathematics more highly than do the boys.

Turning to the interviews, and the choices made of ideal and negative self, all girls chose a classmate as their ideal, except one who chose her mother. No girl chose a male ideal and no two girls chose the same ideal, suggesting that as differentiation in school subjects increases as the children get older, so too does any consensus about admired figures. Maybe the importance of role models diminishes with age and experience, and with the emphasis on individual choice. Choices of ideal self were mainly on grounds of academic prowess, except for one girl who chose someone who was better-looking ('That's the only thing I really worry about'). All the others mentioned the fact that their ideals were clever: 'She knows everything'; 'She's good at Maths'. Two of the girls were more specific:

> She's really clever, she can really get down to work, whereas, if I had to be top of the class, I'd have to be really pushed . . . and I'd have to work really hard. In this school it's quite hard 'cos everyone's always mucking around and there's so much talk, but she can just work in any atmosphere and just get on.

(Of course it was also the school's view that everyone should be *self*-disciplined and motivated.) As another said about a girl she chose as her ideal: 'She's just a really nice person and she's clever. Everything. She's got everything.'

All the boys' ideal selves were male: three were friends with whom they had lessons, one was a fictional character and one a male teacher. The reasons were similar to the girls' in most cases, and revolved around being helped when in need, and people who were nice and clever: 'He's just a nice guy, really clever and that's it' . . . 'because he's good at Maths' . . . 'good friend, nice, and when you need help he's there.' One boy had a specific reason: 'He possesses some qualities of . . . guts which I don't.' The boys were more likely than the girls to mention the importance of being helped.

As for negative selves, all the girls chose someone with whom they had lessons, but this time three of the seven choices were boys, although not the same ones. The girls found it more difficult to articulate their reasons for disliking the boys: 'He just gets on my nerves' or 'He really makes people's lives a misery . . . he's just so horrible. I'd hate to be horrible like that.' Two chose the same girls as someone they were glad not to be like, but not for the same reasons. One felt that she was lively and interesting but talked too much, which meant she didn't get a lot of work done. The other knew more clearly why she was glad not to be like this girl:

> She's not particularly bright . . . she's not really stupid or anything but she seems to be. I don't like the way she dresses . . . she hasn't got a best friend and she's always, like, hovering around with two or three people or by herself and I'd hate to be like that.

This girl is different, doesn't fit in and is, therefore, an outsider.

One girl was chosen by two people — once as an ideal, once as a negative. The differences reflected the two aspects which have been emerging as important to these girls' choices: the fit, or lack of fit, between being good at work and being a nice sociable person. The choice of this girl as an ideal related to her ability at Mathematics and at helping; her choice as a negative self reflected her personality: 'She's not sociable. She doesn't talk to people — she's too shy.'

Two girls — one good at Mathematics, the other poor — chose each other as ideal and negative selves. Not surprisingly the poor girl wanted to be like the good girl, whom she admired and who helped her, whereas the good one felt much more negative about the poor girl. Despite claiming her as a friend, she was clear about her reasons for not wishing to be like her: 'She's so unlucky. She tries so hard . . . she gets nowhere. She's a very stereotyped person and I really can't change her.'

As for other elements, girls were more likely to choose male elements as people they felt positive about, or who were like them in some way, than the boys were to choose female elements, except for one sister or a mother. This suggests that it is easier for girls to see positive things about males than for boys about females. It also reflects the evidence of the repertory-grid consensus: the separation between the groups of children.

The quality all the children, regardless of sex, chose as most positive was the ability to get on well with others and share common interests. The next which most chose was being a friendly listener. All the girls and a couple of the boys (those not good at Mathematics) chose helpfulness. 'Cleverness' was considered positive by five out of seven girls and three out of five boys — two-thirds of the children. 'Lively' and 'nice' were mentioned, as was the importance of confidence and perseverance in succeeding at school. Being 'interesting' (with no more explanation) was a positive quality mentioned only by boys, and 'hard-working' (as a positive quality) was mentioned only by girls.

Four girls and two boys often mentioned as a negative quality insensitivity in the sense of being unaware of others, not listening or being unsympathetic. Most children disliked showing off and being irritating. Girls were most likely to mention shyness as negative. Generally those characteristics most often mentioned were those that would alienate children from their peers: being unhelpful, talking too much and therefore possibly incurring the teacher's wrath, being unsociable or odd. It is interesting that qualities which might seem to inspire sympathy — shyness, unsociability, looking funny — were perceived as negative, engendering dislike rather than sympathetic understanding. Of other characteristics, 'selfishness' was mentioned only by girls and 'boring' and 'unintelligent' only by boys.

One of the most interesting things about the consensus comparisons of these fourth-year children is the differences between the different groups. In the first year, differences between groups of boys and girls, and children who were good and poor at certain subjects, were still small, but the intervening three years widened the gap. Option choices and opportunities to take either of the public examinations must reinforce the split between those children considered good or able and those not.

When asked specifically about Mathematics, the teacher and the subject, the fourth-years mostly claimed to like neither. Two of the poor boys thought Maths 'boring', their most common complaint, followed by one boy's declaration: 'I'm no good.' Five out of seven girls claimed not to like the subject. Two said they just weren't very good and one claimed to be 'not very mathematical'. It is interesting that this girl was the only one to mention SMILE by name, saying she preferred it: 'Yeah, I prefer to do that, when we're all doing different topics, than when we're all doing the same thing in class. You can go at your own speed.' One girl claimed to dislike Mathematics because of the teacher, but generally the girls and boys who disliked the subject talked in terms of their own inabilities. As one boy said: 'I could never be good at Maths, even if I tried.'

Vivienne, whom we met earlier and who had entered secondary school as a Band 1 child, recognized what had happened to her. Now that she was reaching a crucial stage in her career she was beginning to want to settle to more work, but it was not easy: 'Well, now I'm trying to work again. But also I get easily distracted by people . . . who're good at Maths anyway, so they can distract us and get back on with their work again.' Why did she lose interest? The subject was boring and she thought her teacher could be callous and hurtful to those he did not like and who needed a lot of help. This also reflects the earlier concern about the importance of keeping control so that the classroom atmosphere was conducive to work. Other girls were less clear about their reasons and just thought they were no good and that was it.

Mostly it was those considered poor at Mathematics (except one of the boys) who claimed to dislike it. They often attributed their dislike and lack of success to not being good, but it seemed also that their teachers reinforced this role, forcing them into an unbreakable circle of performance. They read the teacher and the lessons as boring and uninteresting and the teacher, for his part, felt that they were uninterested and irrecoverable. This story of bored and irrecoverable pupils contrasts sharply with the view we get of the same pupils in their English classes. Here, they appear as enthusiastic as they are bored in Maths.

While girls have been judged wanting in Mathematics, the same discourses do not come into play when considering boys' relatively poor performance in arts subjects (Cohen, in preparation). Just as boys constitute a higher percentage of O level Mathematics passes and pursue this field to 'higher academic standards', girls' performance in languages, specifically English, follows a similar pattern.

At the end of the third year in this school, pupils are selected as candidates for public-examination classes in English on the basis of their previous class work and teacher recommendations. The pupils do take an exam, but as their teacher states, 'this wasn't necessarily taken into account and that was only if the English teacher couldn't decide'. The decision is therefore left to the teacher's discretion. The school attempts to enter as many pupils as possible for O level, 'to at least give them a chance', as the teacher put it. The English teacher goes on to suggest that:

> Basically, if they can string two sentences together and actually turn up to their lessons, then you give them a chance and some don't manage it and get the boot

within a term. Others will struggle through, but they won't actually do O level in the end. They may well stay in the class but do CSE.

For this teacher the norm is to enter children for O level, whereas for Mathematics it is the other way round. One girl, Latia, provides an example. Considered equally able in English and Maths, she was nevertheless entered for O level in English and CSE in Maths. Her Maths teacher considers her one of the most able girls in the class. She would certainly be expected to get a Grade 1 CSE in her public examination. In fact, Latia's test result was one of the highest among those pupils selected for 'observation' by the teacher as part of our sample. When commenting on her work, her teacher suggests that she is very conscientious, well motivated and ambitious. Latia wants to do well despite lack of interest in Mathematics for its own sake.

The English teacher considers Latia to be in a group he considers without 'natural talent', who should nevertheless pass their O level. He says of her:

> I suppose one might say staid, but she's thorough, she always does her work. It's always good, always accurate — not particularly inspired, but . . . um . . . I'm not necessarily looking for inspiration.

The teachers' comments on Latia indicate that they both consider her capable of obtaining an O level pass (as a Grade 1 CSE is, in theory, equivalent to an O level Grade C pass, at least). Despite this, she is not being entered for O level in both subjects. When asked to rank her subjects in order of preference, Latia rated Mathematics one place higher than English (Maths ranked sixth and English seventh out of a possible eight subjects), yet she considered herself slightly better at English. When asked about her future plans, she said:

L: I plan to go on to the sixth form.
R: To do A levels?
L: Yeah.
R: Then what?
L: Well, then I'll — depending on the results, I'll probably go to college.
R: To do what?
L: I don't even know.
R: So, when you're choosing your A levels for the sixth form, how are you going to choose them?
L: I'll choose English, because that's a subject I like very, very much [. . .] and also the grades I have from my O levels.

Although Latia ranked English as one of her least favourite subjects, she said she might pursue it to A level. It is unlikely that Latia prefers Mathematics because of the teacher, as she ranked the Maths teacher as her least favourite. This suggests that other factors may contribute to her contradictory plan to take English at A level and, despite her ability in Mathematics, not to consider it a possible A level subject at this point.

This case study indicates that the selection practices of the English and Mathematics departments may affect pupils' attainment. Clearly the English Department allows more pupils to enter for O level, exercising less stringest 'rules'. In contrast, a relatively small proportion of pupils are allowed to sit O level Mathematics. Judging by the additional number of female pupil entries overall, the consequences of such practices are more severe for the girls.

Latia is considered a potential CSE Maths candidate and a 'positive' O level English candidate. Despite her preference for Mathematics, she thinks she is better at English. Her 'easier' access or entry into the more prestigious O level may contribute to this view. If Latia works as consistently in Mathematics as she does in English (her Maths teacher suggests that she does, describing her as 'well motivated', 'conscientious') she is still not considered a positive candidate for O level Mathematics. There is, therefore, no reason why she should not assume that she isn't better at English. Pupils' reading of their mathematical ability may be influential in determining their further pursuit of the subject. Note that Latia does not mention Maths as a possible A level subject. She also remarks that her O level grades will be a determining factor in her choice of A level subjects.

A prominent feature of our analysis of the fourth-year data is the difference of interaction in English and Mathematics lessons. In this school English, unlike Mathematics, lends itself to 'open' classroom discussion, frequently involving the teacher. The pupils can discuss aspects of their personal experience, and still maintain contact with the academic purpose of the lesson. Moreover, what may on occasion be thought of as 'idle chat' does not necessarily imply that pupils are not learning. By comparison, most pupils regarded Maths as a solitary activity.

In the following example, the English teacher is reading an essay by a pupil from another school, submitted for O level the previous year. The exam requires twelve pieces of original work from each candidate, four of them essays. The purpose of the exercise is to tell the pupils how to present such an essay correctly. The teacher begins by explaining the marking system, then discusses the ideal length for an essay. He reads the essay, emphasizing its incorrect spelling and grammar. For this he is criticized by a female pupil who considers his emphasis on these mistakes unfair. A class discussion then ensues:

JULIETTE: Give it an A for being funny.
(T begins to read again.)
CAROL: That was good so far.
WAYNE: See you . . .
T: No, she's corrected this.
(Several pupils shout 'she' and then 'ah ah'.)
T: I used 'she' deliberately to be non-sexist, because it's usually referred to as 'he'.
JULIETTE: Oh, don't lie.
(Juliette challenges T, suggesting he is implying that women write awful things. T begins to read again.)
KAREN: What?
ISABEL: Say it again.
WAYNE: You know he's getting at . . . (several pupils laugh).
(T reads again.)

JULIETTE: That's good.

ISABEL: That's . . . uh . . . very inventive, Sir.

WAYNE: I mean that's just like covering every inch of the . . .

ISABEL: Yeah . . . Good . . .

WAYNE: I think you're very . . .

CAROL: Well, what else could you write, then, apart from blades of grass . . .

(Several pupils shout out.)

WAYNE: . . . every inch of the pitch . . .

(T begins to read again. Juliette asks him how old the essay-writer is. T reads again.)

T: Right, I'll leave it at that.

ISABEL: Go on, Sir.

WAYNE: No, I asked first.

T: Isabel, that's just to prove that I'm not a male chauvinist.

WAYNE: Well, you're sexist then. Racist. (Wayne is black.)

T: Racist . . . I hate people with curly hair.

(One male and two white female pupils shout out 'What about me?')

Shortly after this the teacher presents the class with a theme — the history of violence and entertainment — and relates this to the making of an essay plan:

T: Now, people have always been interested in violence in their entertaining . . .

GILLIAN: Not always.

T: There have been occasions in history where there has been extraordinary violence. The violence you saw was actually real, it wasn't some fantasy with actors on the screen. It was actually . . . people went out and saw people being hung. (He continues to explain how to introduce an essay on violence and entertainment.)

These extracts illustrate the kinds of classroom discussion in English lessons. The pupils are encouraged to relate English to important social issues, such as sexism and violence in relation to entertainment; this never happened in Maths lessons we observed in this school. In the English lesson, girls appear at ease in actively challenging the teacher's authority to know and are allowed to do so; this was not possible in the Maths lessons. We should remember how Maths teachers regularly thwarted girls' attempts to challenge their claim to know. Here Juliette challenges the teacher and insinuates that he is sexist, while Gillian refutes his suggestion that people have always been interested in violence in their entertainment.

At no point in the fourth-year Maths classes do the female pupils actively resist the teacher's authority. Consider the following conversation, one of the few where the Maths teacher joins in a discussion about something other than Maths. Isabel and Caroline are discussing the school sports day. The teacher eventually joins in:

T: Caroline, do you want to do a track event?

C: (flicking through SMP book) No, I'm not doing it. No, because I get too nervous when I have to do track.

T: Is there any chance of getting a relay team together?

C: No, I won't.

T: . . . 100 metres. You can do 14.9, can't you?

C: If I can do . . . ?

T: You said you can do 14.9.

C: No, I don't want to do it.

T: Oh, please.

C: No.

T: Oh, please!

This conversation continues until the end of the lesson.

Caroline is clearly resisting the teacher's request. The topic of conversation is school activities, but it is not mathematical knowledge, nor was the conversation an explicit part of the lesson, as in English. There is a serious absence of social contextualization in mathematical work, and this is due to some extent to the SMILE scheme and its emphasis on self-motivation, and on the model of child development discussed in Chapter 3. We do not wish to suggest that English teaching is the model to which Mathematics should aspire. After all, English teaching has its own history, its own struggles, and the discussion in this classroom may well have been unusual. The point here is not to praise English teaching so much as to ask what makes it possible for the girls to engage with one lesson and not with another, to tell their English teacher he is sexist and yet be silenced when they try to challenge the teacher in Mathematics lessons?

Our work here and elsewhere (Walkerdine, 1988) clearly indicates that 'mathematical' meanings and forms are accomplished only by prising them out of and suppressing the practices of which they once were a part. This suppression leads to the possibility of what is known as mastery and its powerful reduction of the social world to an axiomatic system. Yet clearly the practices themselves are profoundly social and political and their suppression contributes to the oppression of women by transforming and suppressing both women's domestic labour and the social practices in which mathematized information is used in modes of government and, indeed, global domination. Small wonder, then, that not one of the fourth-year girls interviewed suggests Maths as a further area of study, while four out of five boys say they need Maths to pursue their careers.

11 Examining Mathematics Texts

We saw in the last chapter that by the fourth-year girls found Mathematics boring and that the pedagogic practices did not attract them or provide a social space for mathematical and numerical analyses. Our analysis of the Mathematics texts used by the school supports and extends this. Although Maths texts are often seen as stereotyped, we think that a more detailed examination of the way these texts work to position readers, and are therefore part of processes of subjectification, is in order.

First we should make several points about the relationship of our work on texts to the classroom analyses. Our data do not support any simple interpretation that girls are failing in Mathematics, so an analysis of texts which supported the idea that stereotyped images contribute to girls' exclusion and failure would be inappropriate. Yet clearly the texts do present problems. We need to integrate the two kinds of analyses, in order to establish precisely what part texts play. To this end we should examine the theoretical issues around subjectivity which we mentioned in the early chapters. The idea of 'reading' is central to our work: that is, power/knowledge positions provide such readings of femininity and masculinity that girls' and boys' performance vindicate the very evidence which power/knowledge relations themselves make possible. Just as we have demonstrated that texts about teaching and learning are themselves part of those power/knowledge arrangements, so are texts to be read by girls themselves. The way those texts constitute their objects is part and parcel of the processes through which subjectification is produced, but it is not the only one. Indeed, it might either support or contradict other positionings open to girls and boys.

Typical approaches to educational texts in the 1970s drew upon the concepts of bias and stereotype. They suggested that sexist images in texts are unreal, as though the 'real' existed outside the pages of books, and the books themselves had no productive effect. We hope that by now we have shown how powerful texts are. (A further discussion of these issues is to be found in Walkerdine, 1985.)

We might note that Mathematics texts have idiosyncratic properties which they do not share with other texts (see Chapter 3; and Walkerdine, 1988). Mathematical statements using signifiers, such as $2 + 3 = 5$, can refer to anything. Only the internal relations of the syntactic string are visible. All reference to relations of signification along the metaphoric axis have been suppressed. This gives the statements power to refer to anything. However, in the process, the statements suppress easy identification by the reader, since, as Rotman (1979) has pointed out, 'mathematical addressees are impersonal'. 'You' and 'I', which psychoanalysts like Lacan claim to be central to subjectification, are missing. Thus Mathematics textbooks are powerful for their role in producing the fantasy of mastery over the physical world and in their use of this powerful discourse.

One of the only studies of Mathematics texts, by Jean Northam (1983), uses the idea of stereotypes. Through analysis of a series of primary Maths books she draws attention to the sexist views contained within them: these, she argues, socialize children into defining Mathematics as a masculine field. Using content analysis, she compares and contrasts the appearance of female and male images and activities. She notes that as children progress through to secondary school the textbooks become correspondingly devoid of female content, until it is finally omitted altogether as GCE examinations approach. This, Northam argues, is parallel with the decline of girls' involvement within Mathematics.

Northam outlines the following guidelines to behavioural criteria for assessment of developmental progress over the first three years:

1 Helps with activities
2 Keeps *himself* occupied [emphasis added]
3 Puts on own shoes
4 Talks freely with strangers
5 Understands simple instructions quickly
6 Draws writing patterns

This is a picture of a compliant and conforming child, whose behaviour is unproblematic. According to Northam:

> The pattern conforms to a female stereotype ... if it accurately reflects teacher expectations of pupils it seems designed to reinforce the kind of teacher-approved behaviour in girls which is likely to impede the development of self-assertion and initiative.

She claims that junior books have a narrative style and follow a number of characters. Although at first the sex-role differences seem diffused, a closer analysis of vocabulary revealed that whereas girls were equally represented, their roles are in marked contrast to the boys'. Northam used the following instances of behaviour to record the differences in role behaviour:

1 Identification-setting and solving of problems
2 Taught and explained processes to others
3 Made something, displayed a skill
4 Planned, initiated, invented
5 Performed, played tricks, boasted
6 Competed
7 Reflected or elaborated upon a process already learned
8 Cooperated, shared, helped, complied
9 Corrected another's behaviour

Her analysis showed that girls are less likely to be involved with teaching, initiating, identification-setting and solving problems. Instead, they become efficient record-keepers, repeating and practising processes already learned.

In secondary school books life moves away from the family towards the peer group and the outside world of business and technology. The domestic sphere is replaced by the adult world of battlegrounds, spaceships, places devoid of women. All activities displayed are male orientated — football, cricket, and so on — and this maleness is reinforced and compounded by its association with history books expounding the mathematical prowess of Hipparcus, Pythagoras and Pascal.

Northam therefore concludes that Mathematics comes to be defined as a male province. The 'real' or 'social' world, although glimpsed only fragmentarily through illustration, serves as a powerful reinforcement of stereotypical female and male roles. Thus the very starkness of the image revealed becomes a main determinant in forcing Maths textbooks into the world of the masculine. The images are secondary to the text, but become symbolic and immediately vivid because they are extremely fragmentary. Northam concludes that the hidden curriculum, the values and assumptions that form part of our everyday existence, should be brought into sharp focus, thereby providing the basis of intervention. This kind of analysis implies that these books reinforce girls' exclusion from Mathematics and therefore contribute to their failure, but since girls do not fail in any general or simple sense, this cannot be precisely what the books do. How do these texts position males and females? How, in other words, is the reader inscribed here, and what relationship do these practices of inscription have to those we have documented in the classrooms?

Bearing these points in mind, we first applied Northam's methods and categories of content analysis to the books used by the participating schools in our primary–secondary transition study. These were from the *Mathematics for Schools* series (Addison Wesley, 1971/2), Level II, Books 3, 4 and 5, used in the primary schools, and in the Secondary School, *Scottish Mathematics Project* (CUP, 1980) books F and X, *Action Maths Book 3* (Cassell, 1973) and the SMILE cards. Our analyses resembled Northam's apart from one major difference in the primary texts: girls and boys were equally represented in her categories 1 and 2. The rest of the results can be summarized as follows:

1   In the primary texts, the home and immediate outside world become the salient reference point. Girls/women are equally represented for identification and teaching: they hold positions of power within the primary framework. On the other hand, they repeat processes already learnt (21.6 per cent as opposed to boys' 6.6 per cent); this regulates them as passive recipients of knowledge.

2   Girls/women are overwhelmingly depicted in cooperative helpful and kind roles which mirror the importance of domestic tasks as a basis for primary computation: shopping, weighing, measuring. Also, women are generally surrogate mothers; they may be teachers, air hostesses, shop assistants, but their main role is caring for others.

3   At the secondary stage, the world of girls and women virtually disappears from the text in everything but the category of identification, whereas male presence actually increases to 93.2 per cent of the total average. Female representation is only 21.6 per cent for identification and plummets to nil for categories 2, 3, 4, 5 and 9. Furthermore, any references to the role

of women and girls become devalued by unscientific references to non-mathematical problems.

4   Mathematics becomes a masculine province. The expounding of male mathematicians' theories sets readers firmly within a masculine framework. The sparse illustrations and gender references contrast markedly with the jolly mixed groups and active participants of the primary texts.

This particular form of content analysis was relatively easy to collate, but there were problems in interpreting the content of child and adult roles using Northam's categories for recording image and behaviour. Although the graphs clearly show the remarkable disappearance of females from the secondary texts, the nature of this phenomenon is obscure. In fact, the content of the female's role changes visibly — not in what she does, but in how she is presented. Thus her comfortable but relatively high status in the primary stage is eroded in the secondary stage, where exclusion and dismissive reference to the female transform yesterday's competent child into today's invisible woman. Then the images in the textbooks are susceptible to ambiguity. Take, for example, category 6: competing. The graphs invariably plummet to 0 at this point or to a very low percentage, but a re-examination of the texts revealed a recurring, constant undercurrent of competition.

The content-analysis approach was useful in actualizing the notion of diminishing representations, but because the categories are ambiguous the results are misleading where text and illustrations fail to correspond. The relation of image to text, and the contradictions inherent in a textual production of the 'unitary and rational subject' — together with images referring to other practices in which subject positions are created — provides an important source of tension and difficulty. Both image and text collude to display increasing mastery in boys and a fictional marginalization and exclusion of girls. The issue, however, is not whether these are 'true' so much as how they produce enterable positions and therefore ensnare their readers within the practices of subject production. In our view these and other texts do not bias or distort reality functioning but, as we have argued, produce places where 'the material' is made to signify. No easy materiality exists outside the practices through which it is read. We have constantly stressed that the process of reading, from statistical evidence through to teachers' judgments and comments on pupils, cannot be separated from the power/knowledge relations forming modern practices of government and subjectification. How then are girls' and boys', male and female accomplishment constituted in these texts, and how does this contribute to the processes of subjectification we have been discussing?

The visual images of the primary school texts reveal at first sight an equal sharing of tasks and activities, a seemingly equal gender representation. On closer analysis the children's positions, which originally appeared diffuse, begin to display subtle and interesting differentiation. In an example illustrating calculation (Book 3, p. 13), the girl uses an abacus while the boy uses arithmetical calculation in tens and units. The underlying meaning here is that girls' mathematical abilities are better aided by external means, whilst boys' mathematical prowess is part of their inherent mental superiority.

There are various examples of subtle techniques in which both sexes are involved in the activity, but only one is in the illustration. Take, for example, the experiential (pp. 16–18): all the shoppers are portrayed as women, apart from a boy child holding his mum's hand and one man made obvious by his tie at the back of the queue. The cashiers are also women. However, the text involves the use of a bar chart, which includes male shoppers. So while the images present shopping practices as female, the text includes only the instance of 'theoretical' males, who are not demeaned by involvement in the actual shopping process.

There is another example of this form of categorial practice and ambiguity in a set of problems constructed around the scores on a pinball machine. Although both sexes are supposed to be playing, the girls are depicted watching — one leaning over the machine, another sucking a lollipop and a third queuing with a boy for change from a smiling female cashier. A further erosion of the girls' participation is that although they occasionally win, the boys consistently score higher averages. Hence 'both-sex' activity has been taken over by boys. This is compounded by the evidence that in the very first example a masculine framework for identification has been established by David, whose pinball wizardry has beaten Shirley by 223 points.

That example is one of several which effectively operate to position girls in a particular way, although both sexes are equally represented. Negation was the major problem when it came to categorization, for the narrative contradicted the implicit meaning of the statement. For example: Q. 'Tom has an apple which he shares equally between Peter and Jane' (Book 4, p. 43). Thus Tom is the subject of identification. He also initiates, performs and helps others, through equal sharing. However, the text continues: 'Mary has a bar of chocolate. To how many of her friends can she give a quarter of the bar?' The illustration shows six of Mary's friends, four boys and two girls. She gives a piece to each boy . . . and the girls don't get any!

Mary, although involved in the same mathematical process as Tom, is positioned in a different way. She is subordinate, although her task is more complicated. She does not just repeat the process already learnt, but needs the help of the reader to do so: a double negation, for although she is totally selfless in giving all her chocolate away, this is devalued because first she needs help, which indicates incompetence; secondly she disregards her two girl friends and gives it to four boys. So she's positioned as selfless and, indeed, as giving more to males than females.

A slightly different form of negation involves a bicycle ride: 'Lucy goes for a ride on her bicycle . . . she records the distance. [Lucy has ridden through a number of villages to arrive at her destination.] However, Alan is in a hurry . . . he studies the map . . . and records the distance.' Certain key words here indicate the urgency and the implied importance, knowledge and skill. Alan is in a *hurry*; he *studies* the map. This signifies that he needs to get somewhere quickly. So it must be important. Unlike Lucy, he obviously has no time for leisurely rides through numerous villages. To compound the sense of male urgency, Tom displays a skill — map-reading — to work out the shortest route from A to B. Lucy's behaviour is characterized quite differently from Alan's. She is 'scatty and leisurely', whereas Alan's behaviour is planned and efficient. Categorization of this effect proved difficult. Although cycling is a 'both-sex' activity, it is problematic and misleading to say that one sex takes the lead over the other, because in fact they are doing different things.

The secondary texts contrast immediately with the primary ones. Smiling affability disappears, to be replaced by line drawings, graphs, charts and diagrams. There are significantly more male gender pronouns, propelling the focus upon a male subject for identification. On the first page of SMP 'F', a puzzle is set: an army is on the move and needs to cross a crocodile-infested river. There is only one small boat, belonging to two boys. How does the army get across to the right bank? Page 4 poses the question: 'Are you a boy? If "yes" turn to the next page. If no, read on . . .' (The flow diagram is comprised of a *knitting* pattern as a basis for problem-solving!!) Page 3 asks: 'Are you a girl? If "yes" turn to the next page. If no, read on.' The flow diagram then constructs a concrete-mixing problem as a basis for problem-solving.

In this text, crossing the gender divide is clearly as prohibited as crossing a crocodile-infested river. This strict division recurs intermittently throughout the book. In one example man becomes the *logos*, his mastery complete: 'Simon the Human Computer', where the narrative issues instructions on playing a computer game. The class has to divide itself into roles: storekeeper, calculator controller, machine operator:

> This accomplished . . . the first three *people* must arrange themselves as shown . . . with the controller seated at one desk, the storekeeper on *his* right and the arithmetic unit on *his* left . . .

The text continues to refer to he/his, producing an unequivocally gendered practice.

The recurrent underlying theme in the secondary books is again the negation of female participation, now in a more acute form. In the instances of identification the girls' frameworks display no competence or skill in Mathematics. Again, an example illustrates this more clearly:

> 24% of the 25 girls in a fourth year came to school with dresses that were the *wrong* length. Two-thirds of the number altered them the same evening. How many girls *failed* to do so? (SMP 'F', emphasis added)

Thus are girls used for identification purposes. They have behaved badly not only by having dresses the wrong length but because a certain number fail to alter them. Not only have they sinned, they have failed to comply with the rules. The reader has to calculate the quantity of the girls' failure — and in a domestic activity, at that.

> Sally has six identical pairs of socks, except that three pairs are white and three pairs are beige. The twelve socks are all loose in a drawer and Sally picks them out one at a time without looking. How many must she pick out to be sure of getting a pair? (SMP 'F', p. 15)

No human computers here, only a poor drudge who gets her socks in a mess and fails once more at a simple domestic task. Girls are presented as incompetent even in the sphere designated theirs. While boys are striving to master the domain of technology, girls are stuck at home failing.

The one example of male failure in *any* of the books is actually presented as no failure at all. A section on angles between lines and planes is projected symbolically into a masculine framework, with the use of phallic signifiers: semi-erect and erect poles. It begins: 'Basil Brayne said . . . Figure 15a shows an upright pole.'

Was he right? Think about it before you read on . . . Basil Brayne was wrong!!

Basil Brayne was used as a focal point after pages of abstract examples . . . he was male and he 'got it wrong'. However, the very name *Basil Brayne* provokes an image of the absent-minded professor who stumbles through experiments making mistakes, but will one day receive the ultimate accolade for a brilliant discovery. Basil Brayne's error, therefore, is not outrageous or silly: just mistaken, part of an experiment; he had *tried* and failed, so that his 'failure' becomes a positive trait. After all, he clearly possesses 'brains' in keeping with teacher judgments and unlike the girls, who are failing to master not only Mathematics — but also simple domestic tasks!

Male sports again become the focal point for identification-setting and problem-solving. Rugby matches, sports commentators, darts players, footballers, canoeists, all centre on traditional male social practices consonant with the repertory-grid analysis of boys' activities presented in Chapter 8. Moreover, repeated referrals to Pythagoras, Venn, Anstrom act further to reinforce the subject's masculinity.

The section entitled 'Computing Project' becomes the pièce de résistance. The photograph used to set the scene depicts a male operator in a stark, square, gleaming, highly functional room reminiscent of the 'white-hot age of technology'. There is no softness, there are no chairs, nothing superfluous to disturb the machine's efficiency. In this way the subject of identification becomes male (the operator), as does the *object* of identification (the computer and computing itself). Within the next narrative, the mysteries of computer technology unfold:

In order to make a computer work for *us* we must be able to communicate with it . . . When the data has been processed, the computer must output information in a form intelligible to *man* or in a form which can be used again as input material. (p. 185, emphasis added)

So the relationship between *man* and machine is finally launched. The generalized pronouns 'us' and 'we' can now be determined as male, as this mode of identification continues throughout the project. Thus *men* make machines and control the input medium, which the computer must decipher and organize, to be understood by *male* programmers. With the further use of black-and-white photographs of male operators and a VDU room in Houston, Texas, filled only with men and machines, the story becomes firmly rooted in male technological supremacy.

Moreover, the use of photographs rather than sketches or line drawings forces the pupil into construing this as a representation of the real world, the adult world, in which men are not only thought to be, but actually are, in control.

How do words, mathematical signifiers and images work together to construct sites for subjectification? And how do these relate to the subject positions produced in other aspects of classroom practice? We argued in the last chapter that fourth-year English lessons provided social topics for discussion, which more easily engaged the pupils. Clearly these texts do attempt to provide sites for identification, but the subject positions they produce consistently present the feminine as marginal, passive, domestic and failing even at the most trivial activities — totally incompetent. By contrast, the masculine is presented as serious and clever; mastery over the physical and scientific world is assured. Where 'feminine' activities are presented they do not allow a social engagement with serious issues. They are trivializing and key into the other designations of females — hard-working, rule-following, not brilliant — that have been apparent in all aspects of classroom practices and in the truths produced about gendered attainment. Thus texts, while producing these views on their own, supplement and extend existing subject positions. They create a fiction of female failure and lack of male success and mastery, against which the girls struggle. Such analysis reinforces the analysis of classroom practices developed in earlier chapters, and provides a disheartening picture. In our final chapter we suggest some ways out of this sorry state.

12 No Charge: Political Arithmetic for Women

The history of numeracy in the early nineteenth century illuminates the new American division of the sex-roles: not only were men everywhere sent into the market-place while women were isolated within a sentimentalised home, but quantification became masculinised, while its supposed opposite, vague intuition, which resists pinning things down, came to be perceived as a desirable, natural and exclusive attribute of woman. (Cline-Cohen, 1982, p. 149)

'Dear Jane,
Are you still loving a man that you know? —'
Is there still no charge? — . . . This nauseating yet riveting ballad, in which the adult's detailing of precisely what motherhood has cost her belies the overt message that 'the full cost of my love/is No Charge', obviously transfixed the imagination of Carla. 'No Charge' reflected an economic and affective relationship she understood very well: 'if you never had no children, you'd be well off, wouldn't you. You'd have plenty of money.' (Steedman, C., 1985, pp. 47, 128)

'Political arithmetic' was one tool for regulating the population through calculating and calibrating attributes, capacities and so forth. We want to make some suggestions for further practical work by deliberately playing on this term. We have so often met with accounts which see women as lacking. Just as frequently we have witnessed the ceaseless hours of regulation and calculation which make up so many women's day. Women's work at home involves mountains of unpaid labour and management of the domestic economy, as our analysis of the work of mothering clearly reveals. In addition, many occupations traditionally open to women, from nursing to secretarial work, involve considerable calculation. However, such aspects of women's labour have not been clearly reflected in the approaches either to Mathematics for girls or to adult numeracy.

Such approaches tend to focus, explicitly or implicitly, on the problems for girls and the lack — whether in terms of lack of early construction experience (Kelly, 1981), lack of confidence and anxiety, or plain incompetence at the higher-order work (see Chapter 2), the effect is to pathologize girls and normalize masculinity. Moreover, adult numeracy schemes for women tend to patronize. Titles like *Sums for Mums* (Graham and Roberts, 1982), intended to make Maths seem less threatening, have pejorative connotations. The more liberal approach stresses how much Maths women do already, using examples like knitting patterns, but the philosophy is still one of 'equal but different': 'Look, ladies, see, you can do it really.' In our view the research discussed throughout this book does not lead to an equal-but-different conclusion at all, but to one of gross inequality: an oppression produced out of a complex mixture of fact, fiction and fantasy. How, then, might we put forward some suggestions for possible new interventions with girls and women?

We shall draw together all the theoretical points and add a summary of the empirical evidence. At this point we are often asked what all this means for anti-sexist work in school, as though there were some easy relation between research and practice. We often feel guilty because we cannot simply produce the magic formula — say 'do this' and all the problems will be solved. In many ways, however, our guilt is misplaced. We have argued throughout that there have been too many easy interventions. This does not mean that we should do nothing. Our work has many implications for the classroom, but none of them would solve the problem of women's oppression overnight. We are talking about a political struggle, which takes time and strategy. We make interventions where we can as part of that struggle, but we do not see any of them as unproblematically the answer. We are envisaging the start of something new. To achieve this we must talk and argue, discuss and plan and try out. We say what kinds of things our work seems to imply. Women mathematicians and scientists, artists and teachers, women calculating and the objects of calculation, must get together and begin to formulate new ways and new strategies.

When we began our work, there was little apparent interest in the topic in Britain. As we have demonstrated, the issue was thought of in terms of a general explanation for a specific problem: the failure of sufficient numbers of girls to enter careers requiring Mathematics. This explanation sought to account for the phenomenon by arguing in a variety of ways that there was something wrong with girls, something effectively that they lacked. Both nativist and environmentalist arguments were mounted, and all found something that needed rectification. Even the 'discovery' that girls were, generally speaking, not doing poorly in primary schools and had a higher educational attainment overall than boys in secondary schools did not deter researchers and theorists, who tended to argue that although girls did well in the early years there was something wrong with their success, or that their putative failure, which showed up only in later years, was actually caused by something in early socialization. For example, adolescent girls' poorer performance on visuo-spatial tests might be caused by their stereotyped socialization experience which prohibited activities such as play with construction toys. We have attempted to demonstrate the difficulties with those approaches and to take apart the assumptions upon which they rest. It is worth restating clearly that we found no inferior performance by girls relative to boys in primary school, nor did we find a falling-off up to the fourth year of secondary school. However, we do suggest that there are massive problems for girls and we do not want our work to be interpreted as implying that there are not.

Let us then summarize the major points we have made about girls and women through all the evidence we studied. Mothers are regulated as the sensitive prop to the playful child. Their domestic labour is transformed into love and nurturance and their capacity to be sensitive is overtly regulated. Those who fail in this task are accused of failing to produce children who will grow to be autonomous and succeed at school. Our analysis suggests that notwithstanding the oppression of women entailed in these arguments, an attempt to provide equal opportunities does not work. The working-class girls whose mothers were most sensitive had the worst problems at 10, while those with the least sensitive mothers were doing best. However, there were massive differences in performance between working- and middle-class schools; this again suggests that the ideal of equal opportunities is not realized.

Mothers, however, are led to regulate their daughters in ways which are supposed to turn conflict into reason. They also help to produce, in their domestic regulation, so-called mathematical meanings which embody anxiety and pain as well as pleasure. They deal with wealth and poverty, with scarce resources, with the terrors for their daughters of growing up into big girls and all that this may mean: physical self-reliance verses intellectual control. Mothers, transformed into the environment which facilitates development, are left with their only site of power: their positioning in domestic regulation and the naturalization of their loving nurturance. They do not, in any simple sense, stereotype their daughters or condition them into passivity; nor do they make them play only with 'feminine toys', and so forth; nor do they produce helplessness as a learned reaction. Some girls want to stay babies but this is, contradictorily, a powerful position. The complexities of the struggle to grow up are, in our view, inadequately dealt with by most current work on socialization, which uses the notions of agent, role and stereotype to blame women further.

The nursery school is not a simple female environment in which girls can do well because the Mathematics is domestic. It is the location of a complex gendered struggle for power, where female teachers can be positioned as powerless by boys and made to feel responsible for the production of sexism as natural. In addition, girls are often thrown back to the domestic as the only place where they can be powerful. There is little evidence to support a 'passive wimp' theory of femininity, but this does not mean that it is easy for girls and women to be strong. Although our work documented some play differences between the sexes, it is simply not true that girls cannot and do not engage in construction play. Moreover, the evidence that this is important to later mathematical performance is ambiguous, to say the least. Here, however, non-school practices begin to be transformed into Mathematics. The transformation takes place and the move is made towards a written discourse which can apply to anything.

In infant school, teachers are positioned as substitute mothers who will produce free and autonomous children. This seems to engender a desperate desire to make children happy and a projection of teachers' own unhappiness, which is masked by the skills necessary to look after others. Teachers are already distinguishing between girls' pathologized hard work and rule-following and boys' flair and potential. Here, most girls, especially working-class white girls and petty-bourgeois black girls, wanted to join the caring professions. Some took up a powerful position in the classroom as sub-teachers; others struggled between being big girls and babies, between niceness and aggression. The one middle-class girl who was doing well was not a sub-teacher, but she was the most anxious about her performance, while being assured that she 'knew'.

This is echoed in the data on girls at 10. Parents of these children struggled and believed in their daughters' education, often wanting them to have a better chance. The extent of working-class parents' self-sacrifice for their daughters counter-points their pathologization in some liberal anti-sexist discourses. Yet how often do black and white working-class mothers get together with middle-class teachers to discuss these calculations? How easy it is to blame working-class women for being more sexist without hearing their stories, without working together! Yet most parents are invited into a school to discuss Maths only to be told about the latest methods, not so that teachers can really listen to and build upon what they have to say. The time has come to work with other women, not to alienate them or to assume that we have all the answers.

Teachers categorize the 10-year-old children in ways which build upon their positions at 6. Boys possess some real but invisible potential. Their poor performance is both excused and turned into a good quality, and their naughtiness and violence are part and parcel of the active child. The discursive positions accorded to boys and girls are sedimented. Girls are seen as hard-working, though this is a more positive category in working-class schools, where there are more sub-teachers. In middle-class schools girls tend to perform well but are constantly told, and feel, that they are not good enough. Their anxiety is strong but underplayed. The test performance of middle-class schools, especially fee-paying ones, is so much better than the working-class ones that it makes a mockery of equal opportunities. Here, gender and class differences are naturalized.

Although not all girls displayed those characteristics seen as feminine, one cannot simply assert that they should be more active. Any behaviour more usually associated with boys was understood completely differently and gender-specifically — rendered pathological. Positioning did not mean that all girls turned out the same, but the barriers of gender and class difference meant that they did not leave home for some easy autonomy in school. Here, their attempts to get power were thwarted by the categorizations which rendered them pathological as soon as they were made. Girls had a difficult struggle asserting their power in the face of this threat and the tightrope they walked between normality and pathology, good and poor performance.

In the fourth year of junior school, girls' and boys' positions are further sedimented. Girls, at the nexus of contradictory relationships between gender and intellectuality, struggle to achieve the femininity which is the target of teachers' pejorative evaluation. They often try to be nice, kind, helpful and attractive: precisely the characteristics that teachers publicly hold up as good — asking all children to work quietly or neatly, for example, while privately accusing the girls of doing precisely these things. Thus they are put in social and psychic double-binds. Few girls achieve both intellectual prowess and femininity.

By the first year of secondary school girls were still succeeding, relative to boys, in their test and classroom performance, but remained the object of pejorative evaluations. Moreover, mastery of Mathematics had been transformed from simple activity in boys, and naughtiness with potential, to the idea that they should challenge the rules of the mathematical discourse itself, but not those of the classroom. The idea of 'flair' and 'brilliance' became attached to a certain way of challenging the teacher's power to know. Boys who did this were accorded the accolade 'brilliant'. However, it was not a simple matter of girls behaving more like boys. Girls' challenges were thwarted. Teachers systematically extended boys' utterances and curtailed those of girls, as though girls' challenges were more threatening.

In the fourth year of secondary school girls were still performing better than boys overall but were often felt to be unconfident and put in the double-bind of not being pushed or helped and often not entered for more prestigious examinations. Performance data indicate that more boys than girls achieve higher-grade O level passes. Nevertheless, it seems that not only are girls entered for such exams in lower proportions, but the classroom processes and psychic struggles we have documented make it difficult for them to push for success. In English, by comparison, they were far more able to join in discussions and the subject was made more socially relevant. We shall suggest why a certain sociality has been excluded from Mathematics and what it might mean to rethink this. There seems no good reason why lessons themselves might not include the kinds of calculations we have been discussing.

On the basis of our work we want to argue that a different kind of intervention into practice is necessary. There needs to be a move away from accounts which blame girls and women. These have led to interventions intended either to shore up a lack or to counter stereotyping. Below we suggest some initial moves.

We have countered arguments which assume that girls' early socialization produces some lack or failure. We have also argued against the theory that Mathematics is a masculine domain which excludes girls because it does not value feminine, intuitive and emotional knowledge and ways of thinking and being. Against socialization arguments we say that there is no simple failure to explain, and that socialization accounts depend on socialization working. Such concepts as stereotype, role and conditioning suggest that girls are moulded by mothers and teachers. They are oppressively woman-blaming and do not account for the positioning of the women themselves. We prefer to see femininity as a site of struggle, where socialization does not easily work and where abnormality is always breaking through. Our empirical work from the early years demonstrates how much girls and women struggle. Mothers struggle in working and regulating their daughters; to manage a domestic economy on often scarce resources; against their own powerlessness. Their daughters struggle to grow up, to leave home or to remain powerful babies who can realize the fantasy of being waited on by their mothers. Little girls in the nursery constantly struggle to have power in their play and can often get it only by enacting a powerful female in a domestic drama. Their female teachers struggle to allow children to be natural and against their own incredible guilt and powerful sexism.

Against the idea of socialization we have attempted to advance another view, derived in part from arguments within Post-Structuralism. We seek to locate the story about girls' failure within a set of scientific strategies for producing the modern order and the idea of the rational, unitary subject: the individual. That girls seem to lack and not to measure up to this individual tells us less about girls and more about the form of government itself. In other words, we are attempting to locate the problem within an account of the social and psychological oppression of women. We do not agree that either patriarchy or capitalism is a monolithic force which imposes socialization on girls. Rather, we are interested in the processes through which the modern order, patriarchal and capitalist as it is, produces the positions for subjects to enter. This is not the same as roles. We have argued that modern government works through apparatuses like schools, hospitals, law courts, social work offices, which depend upon what Foucault has described as techno-logies of the social: scientific knowledges, encoded in practices which define the population to be managed — not through simple and overt coercion, but by techni-ques which naturalize the desired state in the bourgeois order: a rational citizen who rationally and freely accepts that order and obeys through 'his own free will', as it were. Those knowledges, apparatuses, practices, seek constantly to define and map the processes which will naturally produce this subject. They constantly define girls and women as pathological, deviating from the norm and lacking, but they also define them as necessary to the procreation and rearing of democratic citizens.

We claim that knowledges and apparatuses define femininity as a perpetual exclusion from the qualities necessary to produce the rational subject, the rational man, and that beneath this lies a terror; that these strategies are founded not upon a certainty but on a necessity to produce order against a constant threat of rebellion. There is a long history of the oppression of those knowledges in which women had powerful positions, and of the poor, the exploited and the oppressed attempt-ing to rise up against an order which proclaimed a freedom for which they were the price.

The bourgeois order was founded upon a necessary fiction of freedom and equality. The success of girls and women presents a constant threat to that order and to the fears embedded in it. The theories about girls with which we are pres-ented embody the fears and threat on which they are based. It must be constantly reasserted that girls are lacking, because to accept anything else would blow the whole charade apart. It is the threat of the other, of uprising, which necessitates this strategy of government, just as the threat of feminism perpetrated liberal equal-opportunities policies. This is why we dwell on the relationship between fact, fiction and fantasy and have explored so carefully the idea that 'mastery' is a fiction based on shaky foundations and not on the easy certainty that theories of development would sug-gest (Walkerdine, 1988).

We do not want simply to counterpose a Gilliganesque (Gilligan, 1982) sense of the importance of feminine attributes against masculine reason precisely because we think that gender differences are fictions with no firm basis in reality. To reas-sert femininity is to play up to these fictions and their dualism, instead of ques-tioning the very strategy and its role in countering the threat of female power and thereby participating in the oppression of women. We are not saying, either, that a false science obscures women's real attainments and possibilities, or that this is an ideological process amenable to improvement by a true and perceptive feminist science. This position fails to allow for the powerful effects of scientific statements in the regulation of practices: they claim to be true, about reality. They thus have truth effects in positioning subjects within their orbit. Foucault's power/knowledge couple attempts to break down the distinction between science and ideology precisely in order to examine the part played by the sciences in the rational strategies of government we have outlined. They are not false statements that can easily be swept away to tell the truth about women: rather they claim that truth for themselves. We can, however, take that truth apart and present it for the fiction it is.

Where, then, does this leave feminist science? We are claiming that practices create subjectivities. So that no real human subject exists prior to the social practices within which she is subjected. However, those practices read materiality in a particular way; they tell particular stories which are profoundly oppressive. By taking those stories apart and seeing how we are caught up in them, we can begin to tell our own. For example, by analysing how women's domestic labour is transformed into a prop for play and the nurturance of the rational unitary subject, we can examine the painful and oppressive work that goes into this; or we can show that rational discourse is produced not out of certainty but out of a terror of losing control. In other words, we can turn conventional stories on their heads and tell those which the current truths actively suppress. This may look like a feminist science, but it cannot claim to tell the essential story of all women. It could be a point for creation, not for description.

We do not want to assert an essentially female Maths, though we do think some aspects of Mathematics could be changed. Nor do we think that the cause is best served by positing our closeness to nature, which is exactly where we have already been located. That does not stop us subverting that position and using it as a point of resistance. We do think that interventions can be made into school Mathematics. After all, it seems that Mathematics texts and examples focus on science and engineering and that when so-called feminine examples are inserted these involve pastimes like knitting or household tasks such as filling baths or tiling rooms. Yet the cost of women's labour is glaringly absent from such approaches. As we have already said, women are held responsible for all kinds of calculation as well as being the object of it, but all most Mathematics educators can say about calculation is that it is 'low-level'. We know, of course, that higher status is accorded to calculations which require the production of the rational and logico-mathematical discourse in which statements have power because they can refer to anything. Here Mathematics becomes invested in reason's dream of a calculable universe: the control over time and space.

Such a mathematized universe allows strategies of global domination based on cross-national information flows. If this very system is an elaborate fiction which functions in truth, it has real and oppressive effects precisely because it obscures, suppresses and excludes the relations and sources of signification, which are then realigned to produce new and normalizing practices. Such mathematical truths tell definitive stories which preclude others. We argued, therefore, that it is not simply a question of giving examples of knitting patterns in Maths texts, but of examining the powerful effectiveness of reason's dream, in its calculating universe. To subvert this we must re-tell the suppressed stories of women's oppression, to demonstrate how we have been the object of calculation and made also to calculate. We are talking ultimately about a transformation in mathematical discourses themselves, to produce a discursive practice which would not separate rationalization from affect and from the social. This would not be a feminist or female Mathematics, precisely because it would not be a Mathematics as we understand it today. Its limit conditions and bases would be differently drawn.

We can reclaim aspects of what has been accorded women and demonstrate that complex investments are made in keeping things as they are, for women's power and success are intensely threatening. This is not the same as suggesting that the problem lies in teachers' attributions of female performance. The problem is not teachers, for, as we have demonstrated, they are ensnared too. The problem has a complex and multiple causality, within which we have come to understand ourselves and to act in terms of the very discursive practices which define us. Blaming teachers is like blaming mothers for failing to make the fiction of social democracy work. We claim that the mastery of mathematical discourse is not a certain control over the properties of physical objects, but rather a discursive shift which makes statements about the generalizable properties of those objects in order to have power over any thing.

This leads to the fantasy of a calculable universe where everything operates according to quantifiable laws and subjectivity is suppressed. This fiction is central to the calculating project of bourgeois democracy and the strategies of global domination. It transforms oppression into profit as positive and negative integers on a computer screen in a worldwide network of information, or produces complex calculations about the effects of a nuclear strike. These strategies produce as their object the fiction of the Post-Modern subject, inscribed in a fictional world of pleasure and plenty.

Disrupting this dream held out for us is at least as important as the apparent issue of getting more girls to take higher-level Mathematics, which itself feeds into the cosy fiction of liberal equal opportunities, though we are talking about the possibility of women's power and of powerful women. What would it mean, for example, if we were to begin to discuss some of the examples raised in this book? How could such discussions proceed with girls in school, with teachers, with women at home with small children or in adult numeracy classes? How might the relations be made between the discussions and their attendant pain and anger, and the possibility of making the hidden calculations? Paulo Freire argued long ago that literacy was linked to a change in consciousness. What would happen if girls were led to calculate the quantity of their exclusion from interaction in lessons or the number of times they were rewarded for neatness? What would happen if, in an adult numeracy class, women started to calculate the cost of their unpaid labour? What would happen if the emotional and social costs were introduced to the possibility of their mathematized calculation? Might the smooth running of the patriarchal and bourgeois order not be damaged by a myriad tiny indentations of anger?

The fantasy of the rational and autonomous subject is not something to which we are desperate to aspire. It is not the same as the possibility of the power and liberation of women. It is a fiction of a freedom produced in a political order which disguises the oppression required to produce the subject who imagines 'himself' free to act as 'he' chooses. Our accomplishment in Mathematics is a threat which has to be consistently questioned and thwarted, so that we can be seen to possess the characteristics of the nurturant other necessary to uphold the possibility of autonomy. To take apart that fantasy and the fears upon which it rests is a powerful and subversive act, difficult and challenging, but one that we cannot begin too soon.

Afterword

When the Girls and Mathematics Unit was first founded in 1976 there was a dearth of research on girls and mathematics. Such research as there was clearly indicated that girls had some absence or lack as I am at pains to point out in the body of the book. The then prime minister, James Callaghan's speech at Ruskin College in 1976 (p. 19) had highlighted the relation of the impact of second wave feminism upon the importance of the advance of technology and thereby the necessity of producing more graduates, including women, in mathematics and the sciences. However, 21 years later, the situation has changed dramatically. The manufacturing base has declined drastically and so there is no longer any 'white heat of technology'. In relation to this, men are rapidly disappearing from the work force and we are witnessing a rise in service and communications industries, as well as the financial sector. The increase in women's employment, albeit often part-time and poorly paid, as well as the sharp rise in the number of women starting businesses and joining the professions, has produced a situation which is quite different in scope and orientation from the picture 21 years ago. Indeed, considerable concern is now being expressed about the relatively poor school performance of boys in relation to girls. What therefore does all of this mean for the relevance of the arguments contained in the book for the situation we find ourselves in today?

There are several things to note. While it may appear that the fact that girls seem to be doing well at school makes arguments about poor performance redundant, it can be noted that actually the arguments about girls' good performance mirror the earlier discourses about their poor performance! Girls' attainment in literacy, English and languages is not celebrated as an index of cleverness, brains or intellectuality. Rather, those very factors that were considered a problem in relation to Mathematics, namely rule-following, rote-learning, neatness, good behaviour and so forth, are presented as the keys to female success, downgrading that success, while suggesting that classrooms are too feminine and that masculinity is downgraded and discouraged. The ideal child it seems is still a boy, a boy indeed with potential, whose success is being thwarted by women and girls, indeed by the very notion of female success. It is instructive therefore to examine the discourses through which this situation is understood and the way in which what at first appears as a problem with and for boys is too easily translated into a female problem: such a translation certainly accords with educational discourses which target mothers, female teachers, and of course, latterly, feminism. The idea of women's power is certainly a phantasmatic site of some potency in the male imaginary! The investment in reasoning masculinity and women as container of the irrational has not slipped at all. Indeed, what is happening now is testimony to the continuing importance of those arguments.

In addition to this, it is important to note that, in any event, not all girls are doing well, nor all boys badly. The situation at present is divided sharply along class lines. What may indeed be happening is that middle-class girls are being allowed and pushed to achieve academically far more than before (note the way in which we report in this volume that girls in private schools were far more likely to take the position accorded to boys in state schools). Their attainment produces marked competition for boys in similar schools. Such boys are not failing in any sense of the word. I do not think that it is going too far to suggest that middle-class boys are barely allowed to fail academically — far too much is invested in the continuity of their middle-class status, which in fact is being made less secure by the changes in the labour market. However, the boys most hit by the labour market changes are those who traditionally left school without qualifications and whose low levels of literacy could be tolerated in various forms of manual work. It is those boys from the working class, who are faced with the demise of the forms of 'masculine' employment which stressed the strength of the body and are having to face the move to an attractive body, whose only exercise is gained in the gym or the sports field, rather than the factory, if they are to avoid the dole or the poorly paid 'mac' jobs. Their female counterparts, it is true, are more likely to find work, but since their levels of attainment are not high, such work is likely to be poorly paid and in the service sector.

It is simply not the case that all girls are succeeding at school. There is and continues to be a huge class divide, with working-class girls still facing a huge gulf in terms of the possibilities for attainment anywhere near matching that of middle-class girls. Such was obvious for the 10-year-olds, as reported in Chapter 7, but has become painfully clear as the same young women reach adulthood. The working-class girls in the study reported were in schools in which the performance was uniformly much worse than the schools attended by the middle-class girls. The divide got bigger as they got older and a small minority of working-class girls struggled to go on to higher education, while all but one of the middle-class girls did so (the missing girl became a 'New Age' traveller) (Walkerdine, Lucey and Melody, forthcoming). Indeed, the girls in one of the case studies in Chapter 7 make the difference crystal clear. At 10, middle-class Julie was not doing well in Mathematics, nor in school generally. This failure was attributed to 'a block', which necessitated her being coaxed. Working-class Patsy's performance on standardized tests was equivalent to Julie's, but her performance was read as caused by stupidity for which there was no cure. It is in some ways not surprising therefore, that Julie, who thought herself 'too big' and that there was nothing nice about her except her feeding the household pets, did indeed struggle with anorexia, became a dancer and gave it up, but went to university, while Patsy left school with no qualifications and has been in and out of low-level employment.

The future may indeed 'be female', but not in a uniform sense or one which can be easily celebrated (Segal, 1989). Girls are still very clearly being 'counted out' and at a number of different levels. In relation specifically to mathematical attainment, there has certainly been a considerable amount of research in the last 21 years. However, sad to say, much of this has been along the lines that I criticized in this volume.

Let it not be thought, however, that simply because the focus of media attention has shifted to boys, the issues raised here no longer hold. Indeed, in a study in one local education authority, we found that middle-class boys were pushed to succeed at the junior level and that girls' performance generally exceeded that of boys in schools with lower performance, most of which was cross-cut by class and ethnicity. Neither the families nor schools of the failing boys were at all prepared for the huge changes in the labour market, signalled above, which were making themselves especially felt in the area, with all the traditional employers of male manual work having closed down (Lucey and Walkerdine, 1997).

Such boys do not represent the bourgeois subject any more than working-class girls. However, it is important to note what happens to (especially middle-class) girls when they do represent the female entry into the professions. In what sense do they become positioned as the bourgeois subject or on what basis does that subject become feminized? While many of the 10-year-old middle-class girls presented here displayed considerable anxiety about their performance, such performance, while uniformly good in general academic terms, was never considered anything other than simply normal. Indeed quite exceptional performance rarely rated praise when these girls in later years performed outstandingly in public examinations (Walkerdine, Lucey and Melody, 1998). However, the consequences for the girls themselves could be difficult. Many of them in later years presented and discussed symptoms of considerable anxiety: anxiety which was never allowed to get in the way of their academic performance. This anxiety often related to the conflicts between feminine sexuality and intellectuality. While on the surface many of these girls appeared to have a Post-Feminist dream of having one's cake and eating it, beneath the surface many suffered from the feeling that they were never good enough no matter how hard they tried and that their femininity could never ever be allowed to get in the way of their success. If these girls were to be the carriers of middle-class status, they too, like their brothers, could not be allowed to fail. These young women were only too well aware that while they could apparently have everything at 21, they were not about to struggle in the way their mothers had done to balance family and career.

There is no doubt then that while things have moved on, a great deal remains to be done to count girls in. To understand how this might be achieved requires us to do some serious and difficult thinking about gender relations in the school and workplace in the new configurations that will shape the twenty-first century. To that end, I hope that this volume might provide some small signposts along the way.

Valerie Walkerdine
October 1997

References

LUCEY, H. and WALKERDINE, V. (1997) Gender differences in literacy at Key State 2, Report for the London Borough of Greenwich.

SEGAL, L. (1989) *Is the Future Female?*, London: Virago.

WALKERDINE, V., LUCEY, H. and MELODY, J. (1998) 'Class, attainment and sexuality in late 20th century Britain', in MAHONY, P. and ZMROCZEK, C. (eds) *International Perspectives on Women and Social Class*, London: Macmillan.

WALKERDINE, V., LUCEY, H. and MELODY, J. (forthcoming) *Growing Up Girl: Gender and Class in the 21st Century* (working title), London: Macmillan.

Bibliography

AIKEN, L. (1970) 'Attitudes towards Mathematics', *Review of Educational Research*, 40, pp. 557–96.

ASSESSMENT OF PERFORMANCE UNIT (1980a) *Primary Survey Report, No. 1*, London: HMSO.

ASSESSMENT OF PERFORMANCE UNIT (1980b) *Secondary Survey Report, No. 1*, London: HMSO.

ASSESSMENT OF PERFORMANCE UNIT (1981a) *Primary Survey Report, No. 2*, London: HMSO.

ASSESSMENT OF PERFORMANCE UNIT (1981b) *Secondary Survey Report, No. 2*, London: HMSO.

ASSESSMENT OF PERFORMANCE UNIT (1982a) *Primary Survey Report, No. 3*, London: HMSO.

ASSESSMENT OF PERFORMANCE UNIT (1982b) *Secondary Survey Report, No. 3*, London: HMSO.

ATKINS, L. and JARRETT, D. (1979) 'The significance of significance', in MILES, I. and EVANS, J. (eds) *Demystifying Social Statistics*, London: Pluto.

BACKHOUSE, J. (1978) 'Understanding school mathematics — A comment', *Mathematics Teaching*, 82.

BADINTER, E. (1981) *The Myth of Motherhood*, London: Souvenir Press.

BARRETT, M. and MACINTOSH, M. (1982) *The Anti-Social Family*, London: Verso.

BAR-TAI, D. (1978) 'Attributional analysis of achievement related behaviour', *Review of Educational Research*, 48.

BECHER, T. (1981) *Policies for Educational Accountability*, London: Heinemann.

BECKER, J. (1976) *What's Happening in Mathematics and Science Classrooms: Student–Teacher Interactions*, San Francisco: AERA.

BENNETT, F. et al. (1980) 'The limits to financial and legal independence: A socialist–feminist perspective on taxation and social security', *Politics and Power*, 1, pp. 185–202.

BEVERIDGE, M. (ed.) *Children Thinking Through Language*, London: Edward Arnold.

BHABHA, H. (1983) 'The other question: The stereotype in colonial discourse', *Screen*, 24, 6, pp. 18–36.

BLAND, L. (1981) 'The domain of the sexual: A response', *Screen Education*, 39.

BOULTON, M.G. (1983) *On Being a Mother: A Study of Women with Pre-School Children*, London: Tavistock.

BRUSH, L. (1978) 'A validation study of the mathematics anxiety rating scale', *Educational and Psychological Measurement*, **38**.

BULLOCK, A.A. (1974) *A Language for Life*, London: HMSO.

BURGIN, V., DONALD, J. and KAPLAN, C. (eds) (1986) *Formations of Fantasy*, London: Methuen.

BURTON, L. (ed.) (1986) *Girls into Maths Can Go*, London: Holt, Rinehart & Winston.

BUXTON, L. (1978) 'Four levels of understanding', *Mathematics in School*, **74**.

BYERS, V. and HERSCOVICS, N. (1977) 'Understanding school mathematics', *Mathematics Teaching*, **81**.

CHETWYND, J. and HARTNETT, D. (1978) *The Sex-Role System*, London: Routledge & Kegan Paul.

CLARKE, K. (1985) in STEEDMAN, C., URWIN, C. and WALKERDINE, V. (eds) (1985) *Language, Gender and Childhood*, London: Routledge & Kegan Paul.

CLIFT, P. (1981) 'Parental involvement in primary schools', *Primary Education Review*, **10**.

CLINE-COHEN, P. (1982) *A Calculating People: The Spread of Numeracy in Early America*, Berkeley, CA: University of California Press.

COHEN, J. (1979) *Statistical Power Analysis in the Behavioural Sciences*, London: Academic Press.

COHEN, M. (1993) 'A Genealogy of Conversation: Gender Subjectivation and Learning French in England', Unpublished PhD Thesis, University of London, Institute of Education.

CONSULTATIVE COMMITTEE OF THE BOARD OF EDUCATION (1933) *Infant and Nursery Schools (The Hadow Report)*, London: HMSO.

COOPER, H. (1979) 'Pygmalion grows up: A model for teacher expectation, communication and performance influences', *Review of Educational Research*, **49**, pp. 389–430.

COWIE, E. (1978) 'Woman as sign', *M/F*, **1**, pp. 49–64.

CRAFT, M. (ed.) (1980) *Linking Home and School*, London: Harper & Row.

DARWIN, C. (1896) *The Descent of Man and Selection in Relation to Sex*, New York: Appleton (original edn, 1871).

DEEM, R. (1980) *Schooling for Women's Work*, London: Routledge & Kegan Paul.

DEPARTMENT OF EDUCATION and SCIENCE (1967) *Children and their Primary Schools (The Plowden Report)*, London: HMSO.

DEPARTMENT OF EDUCATION and SCIENCE (1982) *Mathematics Counts: Report of the Committee of Enquiry into the Teaching of Mathematics in Schools (The Cockcroft Report)*, London: HMSO.

DERRIDA, J. (1972) *Positions*, Paris: Minuit.

DIENER, C. and DWECK, C. (1978) 'An analysis of learned helplessness', *Journal of Personality and Social Psychology*, **25**, pp. 109–16.

DONALDSON, M. (1978) *Children's Minds*, London: Fontana.

DONZELOT, J. (1980) *The Policing of Families*, London: Hutchinson.

DUNN, J. (1984) *Sisters and Brothers*, London: Fontana.

DWECK, C. and REPUCCI, C. (1973) 'Learned helplessness and reinforcement responsibility in children', *Journal of Personality and Social Psychology*, **25**, pp. 109–16.

DWECK, C., DAVIDSON, W., NELSON, S. and ENNA, B. (1978) 'Sex differences in learned helplessness', *Journal of Personality and Social Psychology*, **36**, pp. 457–62.

DYEHOUSE, C. (1981) *Girls Growing Up in Late Victorian and Edwardian England*, London: Routledge & Kegan Paul.

ECCLES, J.E. et al. (1983) 'Expectations, values and academic behaviours', in SPENCE, J.T. (ed.), *Achievement and Achievement Motives*, New York: Freeman.

EICHENBAUM, L. and ORBACH, S. (1982) *Outside in, Inside out*, Harmondsworth: Penguin.

ERIKSON, E. (1965) 'Inner and outer space: Reflections on womanhood', in LIFTON, R. (ed.) *Woman in America*, Westport, CT: Greenwood.

FELTER, W.L. (1906) 'The education of women', *Education Review*, **31**, p. 351.

FENNEMA, E. and SHERMAN, J. (1976) 'Fennema-Sherman Mathematics Attitudes Scales', *Catalogue of Selected Documents in Psychology*, **6**.

FOUCAULT, M. (1979) *Discipline and Punish*, Harmondsworth: Penguin.

FOUCAULT, M. (1980) *The History of Sexuality, Vol. 1*, Harmondsworth: Penguin.

FRENCH, J. (1982) *Gender Marking in Teachers' Assessments*, Manchester: University of Manchester, Department of Sociology.

FREUD, S. (1920) *Beyond the Pleasure Principle* (Standard Edition of the Complete Psychological Works of Sigmund Freud, Vol. 18), London: Hogarth.

GELLMAN, R. and GALLISTEL, R. (1978) *The Child's Understanding of Number*, Cambridge, MA: Harvard University Press.

GIBBONS, R. (1975) 'An account of SMILE', *Mathematics in School*, **4**, 6, pp. 14–16.

GILLIGAN, C. (1982) *In a Different Voice*, Cambridge, MA: Harvard University Press.

GOLDSTEIN, R. (1973) 'Learning to SMILE', *ILEA Contact*, **2**, 21, pp. 17–19.

GORDON, C. (ed.) (1980) *Power/Knowledge*, Brighton: Harvester.

GOTTHEIL, E. (unpublished) 'Girls, Mathematics and Psychoanalysis', *Girls and Mathematics Unit Working Papers*.

GRAHAM, A. and ROBERTS, H. (1982) *Sums for Mums*, Milton Keynes: Open University Press.

GRUBER, H. and VONECHE, J.J. (1977) *The Essential Piaget*, London: Routledge & Kegan Paul.

GUBB, J. (1983) *GAMMA Newsletter*, No. 4.

HALL, S. and JEFFERSON, T. (1976) *Resistance through Rituals*, London: Hutchinson.

HAMILTON, D. (1981) *On Simultaneous Instruction and the Early Evolution of Class Teaching*, University of Glasgow, mimeo.

HARTNETT, O., BODEN, G. and FULLER, M. (1979) *Sex-Role Stereotyping*, London: Tavistock.

HAYWARD, M. (1983) 'Girls, resistance and schooling', Unpublished MA Dissertation, University of London, Institute of Education.

HENRIQUES, J. et al. (1984) *Changing the Subject: Psychology, Social Regulation and Subjectivity*, London: Methuen.

HIRST, P. and WOOLLEY, P. (1982) *Social Relations and Human Attributes*, London: Tavistock.

HOLLAND, J. (1981) Final Report to the SSRC on Adolescents' Views of the Social Division of Labour.

HOLT, J. (1969) *How Children Fail*, Harmondsworth: Penguin.

HORNER, M. (1968) 'Sex differences in achievement motivation', Unpublished Doctoral Dissertation, University of Michigan.

HOWSON, A.G. (1978) 'Changes in mathematical education since the late 1950s', *Educational Studies in Mathematics*, **9**.

HOWSON, G. (1982) 'Review of girls and mathematics: The early years', *Education*, **159**, 11, p. 188.

HUGHES, M. (1986) *Children and Number*, Oxford: Blackwell.

INGLEBY, D. (1980) 'Review of Lock A Action Gesture and Symbol', *European Journal of Social Psychology*, **10**, pp. 319–28.

JOFFE, L. (1983) *GAMMA Newsletter*, No. 4.

JOHNSON, R.C. (1963) 'Similarity of IQ in separated identical twins as related to length of time spent in the same environment', *Child Development*, **34**, pp. 745–9.

JONES, K. and WILLIAMSON, K. (1979) 'The birth of the schoolroom', *Ideology and Consciousness*, **6**, pp. 59–110.

KELLY, A.V. (1978) *Mixed-Ability Grouping: Theory and Practice*, London: Harper & Row.

KELLY, A. (ed.) (1981) *The Missing Half: Girls and Science Education*, Manchester: Manchester University Press.

KELLY, A., WHYTE, J. and SMAIL, B. (1984) Final Report of the Girls into Science and Technology Project.

KENDALL, G. (1989) *The Child as a Reading Subject*, PhD Thesis, University of London.

KING, R. (1978) *All Things Bright and Beautiful*, London: Wiley.

KOHL, H. (1971) *Thirty-six Children*, Harmondsworth: Penguin.

LACAN, J. (1977) *Ecrits*, London: Tavistock.

LEDER, G. (1980) 'Bright girls, mathematics and fear of success', *Educational Studies in Mathematics*, **11**.

LIEVEN, E. (1982) 'Context, process and progress in young children's speech', in BEVERIDGE, M. (ed.) *Children Thinking Through Language*, London: Edward Arnold.

LIFTON, R. (ed.) *Woman in America*, Westport, Greenwood.

McHUGH, H. et al. (1982) 'The effects of sex-linkage of task, ambiguity of feedback and competition on performance expectations of males and females', *AERA*, New York.

MACCOBY, E. and JACKLIN, C. (1974) *The Psychology of Sex Differences*, Stanford, CA: Stanford University Press.

MATHEMATICAL ASSOCIATION (1956) *The Teaching of Mathematics in Primary Schools*, London, MA.

MATTHEWS, G. and MATTHEWS, J. (1978) *Early Mathematical Experiences*, London: Schools Council.

MILES, I. and EVANS, J. (eds) (1978) *Demystifying Social Statistics*, London: Pluto.

MORRISON, D. and HENKEL, R. (eds) (1970) *The Significance Test Controversy*, Chicago, IL: Aldine.

NEWSON, J. and NEWSON, E. (1976) *Seven Years Old in the Home Environment*, London: Allen & Unwin.

NORTHAM, J. (1983) 'Girls and boys in primary maths books', *Education 3–13*, **10**, 1, pp. 11–14.

NUNALLY, J.C. (1960) 'The place of statistics in psychology', *Educational and Psychological Measurement*, **20**, pp. 641–50.

OAKLEY, A. (1984) *Taking it Like a Woman*, London: Cape.

PARKER, I. (1989) *The Crisis in Modern Social Psychology*, London: Routledge.

PARKER, R. and POLLOCK, G. (1981) *Old Mistresses*, London: Routledge.

PARSONS, J. et al. (1976) 'Attributions, learned helplessness and sex differences in achievement-related expectancies', *Journal of Social Issues*, **32**.

PIAGET, J. (1920) 'Psychoanalysis and its relation with child psychology', in GRUBER, H. and VONECHE, J.J. (1977) *The Essential Piaget*, London: Routledge & Kegan Paul.

PINTNER, R. and FADANO, G. (1983) 'The influence of month of birth on intelligence quotients', *Journal of Educational Psychology*, **24**, pp. 561–84.

POTTER, J. et al. (1984) *Discourse and Social Psychology*, London: Wiley.

RILEY, D. (1982) *War in the Nursery*, London: Virago.

ROSE, J. (1983) 'Femininity and its discontents', *Feminist Review*, **14**.

ROSE, N. (1985) *The Psychological Complex*, London: Routledge & Kegan Paul.

ROTMAN, B. (1979) *Mathematics: An Essay in Semiotics*, Bristol: University of Bristol, mimeo.

SALMON, P. (1976) 'Grid measures in child subjects', in SALTER, P. (ed.).

SALTER, P. (ed.) (1976) *The Measurement of Intra-personal Space by Grid Technique*, London: Wiley.

SAYERS, J. (1982) *Biological Politics*, London: Methuen.

SCHOOLS COUNCIL (1965) *Mathematics in Primary Schools*, London: Schools Council.

SCOTT-HODGETTS, R. (1986) 'Girls and mathematics: The negative implications of success', in BURTON, L. (ed.) *Girls into Maths Can Go*, London: Holt, Rinehart & Winston.

SELIGMAN, M. (1978) *Helplessness, Development, Depression and Death*, New York: Freeman.

SHEFFIELD CITY POLYTECHNIC (1983) *Mathematics Education and Girls*.

SHUARD, H. (1981) 'Mathematics and the Ten-Year-Old Child', *Times Educational Supplement*, 27 March.

SHUARD, H. (1982) 'Differences in mathematical performance between girls and boys', in DES (1982a) *Mathematics Counts: Report of the Committee of Enquiry into the Teaching of Mathematics in Schools (The Cockcroft Report)*, London: HMSO.

SKEMP, R. (1976) *The Psychology of Mathematics Learning*, Harmondsworth: Penguin.

SPENCE, J.T. (ed.) (1983) *Achievement and Achievement Motives*, New York: Freeman.

SQUIRE, C. (1989) *Significant Differences: Feminism in Psychology*, London: Routledge.

STEEDMAN, C. (1985) 'Prisonhouses', *Feminist Review*, **20**.

STEEDMAN, C., URWIN, C. and WALKERDINE, V. (eds) (1985) *Language, Gender and Childhood*, London: Routledge & Kegan Paul.

TIZARD, B. and HUGHES, M. (1984) *Young Children Learning*, London: Fontana.

TOBIAS, S. (1980) *Overcoming Math Anxiety*, New York: Norton.

TOBIAS, S. and WEISSBROD, C. (1980) 'Anxiety and mathematics: An update', *Educational Review*, 50.

URWIN, C. (1984) 'Power relations and the emergence of language', in HENRIQUES, J. et al. *Changing the Subject*, London: Methuen.

URWIN, C. (1985) 'Regulating mothering: The persuasion of normal development', in STEEDMAN, C., URWIN, C. and WALKERDINE, V. (eds).

USSHER, J. (1989) *Psychology and the Female Body*, London: Routledge.

WALDEN, R. and WALKERDINE, V. (1982) *Girls and Mathematics: The Early Years*, Bedford Way Papers 8, London: Heinemann.

WALDEN, R. and WALKERDINE, V. (1985) *Girls and Mathematics: From Primary to Secondary Schooling*, Bedford Way Papers 24, London: Heinemann.

WALKERDINE, V. (1981) 'Sex, power and pedagogy', *Screen Education*, **38**.

WALKERDINE, V. (1984) 'Developmental psychology and the child-centred pedagogy: The insertion of Piaget into early education', in HENRIQUES, J. et al. *Changing the Subject*, London: Methuen.

WALKERDINE, V. (1985) 'On the regulation of speaking and silence', in STEEDMAN, C., URWIN, C. and WALKERDINE, V. (eds) *Language, Gender and Childhood*, London: Routledge & Kegan Paul.

WALKERDINE, V. (1986a) 'Progressive pedagogy and political struggle', *Screen*, **24**.

WALKERDINE, V. (1986b) 'Video replay: Families, films and fantasy', in BURGIN, V., DONALD, J. and KAPLAN, C. (eds) *Formations of Fantasy*, London: Methuen.

WALKERDINE, V. (1988) *The Mastery of Reason*, London: Routledge.

WALKERDINE, V. and LUCEY, H. (1989) *Democracy in the Kitchen? Regulating Mothers and Socialising Daughters*, London: Virago.

WALKERDINE, V., WALDEN, R. and OWEN, C. (1982) *Some Methodological Issues in the Interpretation of Data Relating to Girls' Performance in Mathematics*, British Psychological Society Education Conference, University of Durham, reprinted in *Equal Opportunities Commission Research Bulletin*, No. 10 (1987).

WARD, M. (1979) *Mathematics and the Ten-Year-Old*, Schools Council Working Paper 61, London: Evans Brothers/Methuen.

WARNOCK, M. (1982) 'The last work — for now', *The Times Educational Supplement*, 2 July.

WEEKS (1981) *Sex, Politics and Society*, London: Longman.

WEINER, B. (1971) *Perceiving the Causes of Success and Failure*, New York: General Learning Press.

WEINREICH-HASTE, H. (1978) 'Sex-role socialisation', in CHETWYND, J. and HARTNETT, D. (eds) *The Sex-Role System*, London: Routledge & Kegan Paul.

WELLS, G. (1982) 'Language, literacy and educational success', in WELLS, G. (ed.) *Learning through Interaction*, Cambridge: Cambridge University Press.

WIDDOWSON, F. (1983) *Going up to the Next Class: Women in Elementary Teacher Training*, London: WRRC/Hutchinson.

WILLIS, P. (1979) *Learning to Labour*, London: Saxon House.

Index